CHILDREN, POLITICS AND COMMUNICATION

Participation at the margins

Edited by Nigel Thomas

This edition published in Great Britain in 2009 by

The Policy Press
University of Bristol
Fourth Floor
Beacon House
Queen's Road
Bristol BS8 1QU
UK

tel +44 (0)117 331 4054
fax +44 (0)117 331 4093
e-mail tpp-info@bristol.ac.uk
www.policypress.org.uk

North American office:
The Policy Press
c/o International Specialized Books Services
920 NE 58th Avenue, Suite 300
Portland, OR 97213-3786, USA
tel +1 503 287 3093 • fax +1 503 280 8832 • e-mail info@isbs.com

British Library Cataloguing in Publication Data
A catalogue record for this book is available from the British Library.

Library of Congress Cataloging-in-Publication Data
A catalog record for this book has been requested.

ISBN 978 1 84742 183 8 paperback
ISBN 978 1 84742 184 5 hardcover

Cover design by Qube Design Associates, Bristol
Front cover: image kindly supplied by Anne-Marie Smith
Printed and bound in Great Britain by Hobbs the Printers, Southampton

Contents

Acknowledgements

I am grateful to all the contributing authors, and also to all those – some 70 people – who participated in the seminar series and so helped to stimulate the thinking in this book. I am also grateful to the team at The Policy Press, and to Cath Larkins for transcribing Roger Hart's lecture.

Notes on contributors

Amelia Church is Lecturer in Early Childhood in the Melbourne Graduate School of Education at the University of Melbourne, Australia, where her research interests include developmental pragmatics, ethnomethodology in early childhood, and locally constructed learning through talk-in-interaction. She is the author of *Preference Organisation and Peer Disputes: How Young Children Resolve Conflict* (Ashgate, 2009).

Heaven Crawley is Senior Lecturer in the School of the Environment and Society and Director of the Centre for Migration Policy Research at Swansea University, UK. She is the author of *Child First, Migrant Second: Ensuring that Every Child Matters* (ILPA, 2006) and *When is a Child not a Child? Asylum, Age Disputes and the Process of Age Assessment* (ILPA, 2007) and joint author of *No Place for a Child: Children in Immigration Detention in the UK* (Save the Children UK, 2005).

Julia Davies is Senior Lecturer in the School of Education at the University of Sheffield, UK. She is co-director of The Centre for the Study of New Literacies at the University of Sheffield. She directs the MA in New Literacies and the EdD in Literacy and Language. She has written extensively on her research in the area of new and digital literacies and is co-author (with Guy Merchant) of *Web 2.0 for Schools: Learning and Social Participation* (Peter Lang, 2009).

Jason Hart is Senior Research Officer in the Refugee Studies Centre at the University of Oxford, UK, and Director of the MSc in Forced Migration Studies. He is the editor of *Years of Conflict: Adolescence, Political Violence and Displacement* (Berghahn Books, 2008).

Roger Hart is Professor of Psychology and Geography, and Director of the Children's Environments Research Group, at the City University of New York, USA. He is the author of *Children's Participation: From Tokenism to Citizenship* (UNICEF, 1992), *Children's Participation: The Theory and Practice of Involving Young Citizens in Community Development and Environmental Care* (Earthscan, 1997) and many other publications on children's rights and participation, and an editor of the international journal *Children, Youth and Environments*.

Vicky Johnson is co-director of Development Focus Trust, based in Brighton, UK, which undertakes work in community assessment and action, child participation and rights, participatory monitoring and evaluation, and research. She is the leading author of *Listening to Smaller Voices* (ActionAid, 1994), *Stepping Forward: Children and Young People's Participation in the Development Process* (IT Publications, 1998) and *Gaining Respect: The Voices of Children in Conflict with the Law* (Save the Children, 2006). She is currently completing a PhD at the University of Central Lancashire on children's participation in evaluating services.

Ravi Kohli is Head of the Department of Applied Social Studies at the University of Bedfordshire, UK. He is the author of *Social Work with Unaccompanied Asylum Seeking Children* (Palgrave, 2006) and co-editor of *Working with Unaccompanied Asylum Seeking Children: Issues for Policy and Practice* (Palgrave, 2007).

Anne-Marie Smith is Postdoctoral Teaching Fellow in Childhood and Youth Studies at Liverpool Hope University. Since completing her doctoral research in Mexico, she has worked as children's participation coordinator at the Liverpool World Centre, UK. Her research has been published in English in *Children, Youth and Environments* (17:3, 2007) and in Spanish in Corona Caraveo and Linares Pontón (eds) *Participacion Infantil y Juvenil en America Latina* (Universidad Autónoma Metropolitana, Mexico, 2007).

Nigel Thomas is Professor of Childhood and Youth Research at the University of Central Lancashire, UK and co-director of The Centre, which promotes and researches children's and young people's participation, inclusion and empowerment. He is the author of *Children, Family and the State: Decision-Making and Child Participation* (The Policy Press, 2002) and *Social Work with Young People in Care* (Palgrave, 2005), joint editor of *An Introduction to Early Childhood Studies* (Sage Publications, 2004) and *A Handbook of Children's Participation* (Routledge, forthcoming), and co-editor of the journal *Children & Society*.

Li Wei is Professor of Applied Linguistics, **Zhu Hua** is Senior Lecturer in Applied Linguistics and **Chao-Jung Wu** is Research Associate, all at Birkbeck College, University of London, UK. Li Wei is the principal editor of the *International Journal of Bilingualism* and also edits the book series *Child Language and Child Development*. Zhu Hua is the editor of *Interperspectives: Journal of Transcultural Education*.

Foreword

Trisha Maynard

This challenging book had its origins in the seminar series convened by Nigel Thomas when he was a colleague in the Department of Childhood Studies at Swansea University. From its inception the Department, now the Centre for Child Research, has featured a strong shared commitment to interdisciplinary work informed by a discourse of children's rights, and in particular to exploring the potential and meaning of children's 'participation'. Our disciplines include sociology, education, psychology and health sciences, each with its own knowledge base and values, and implicit and explicit ways of thinking, acting and meaning-making. Viewing the child as competent is thus contextualised and interpreted within the frame of particular disciplines. For example, in relation to my own discipline of education, a commitment to children's rights and participation has underpinned our explorations with early years teachers of the significance of the strong, 'rich' child of the Reggio Emilia pre-schools. It is also reflected in our involvement in an exciting study (Waller et al., 2006), inspired by the work of Mary Kellett and led by Nigel Thomas, in which colleagues formed a research team with children from two local primary schools and provided them with research training and support, so enabling them to explore issues which they identified as being important or of concern.

The research seminars organised by Nigel Thomas were especially challenging. First, while the three extended seminars which have led to this book were underpinned by a shared commitment to children as competent social actors, collectively they moved us into unexplored territory, challenging participants to explore the intersections between children's and young people's participation, children and young people as refugees, and children's and young people's use of language. Second, presentations were given by speakers from an even more diverse range of disciplinary backgrounds, and focused on children of different ages in different contexts engaged in ordinary and, as it appeared to many of us, extraordinary activity. Third, the seminar series attracted regular attendance from academics across the University (including colleagues from geography, law and medicine), as well as local practitioners (from headteachers to staff from non-governmental organisations). As a result, the seminars not only led to lively debate but also provided a focus for, and extended, the multidisciplinary work routinely being undertaken within the Department. In short, it encouraged us to become involved in interdisciplinary inquiry.

Interdisciplinary inquiry is neither easy nor comfortable, although it is often exhilarating. It requires us to move out of our disciplinary comfort zones, to use other 'frames' to interrogate our own ways of thinking and vice versa, so gaining greater insight into implicit as well as explicit values, ideas and practices. One of the particular strengths of this book is that this challenge is handed on to the reader; indeed, while it is possible to dip into individual chapters, and certainly each chapter is of importance in its own right, there is much more to be gained from reading the text as a whole, exploring themes and engaging with key ideas. The concept of 'autonomy' is one that I found particularly fascinating to track and consider. Is autonomy interpreted as being independent (doing things oneself) or self-governing (having the right to decide)? How is it achieved, and is independence seen as a worthwhile aim for children and young people in all cultures?

The text is also important for the fascinating evidence and detail it provides of the lives of children living in difficult circumstances – as Nigel Thomas puts it, children at the *margins*, including those who are displaced and dislocated. In this respect, the text provides exceptional insight into the ways in which children manage their lives and relationships, and the strength, resilience and linguistic creativity that children demonstrate as active players within their own contexts and cultures, particularly when not overly – or overtly – controlled by adults.

Finally, as the title makes clear, this text also highlights and explores issues of power and politics; in this respect, also, the book makes a significant and groundbreaking contribution to the field. As Nigel Thomas indicates, there is often a reluctance, even among those who express their commitment to children's rights and participation, to engage with the complexities of adult–child and child–child power relations, and a tendency to view children as apolitical. This book demonstrates through a close examination of children's activities that this is not the case, and explores within different contexts how (and how well) children use language and communication to manage their lives within an adult-dominated world.

Before reading this book I was aware that the term 'participation' has become almost a slogan, and that much of what is currently done in its name in formal settings could be described as artificial, narrow and tokenistic. Collectively the authors reminded me that while children may be excluded from various aspects of social life, they are already, both formally and informally, actively participating in many others. What is needed from us as adults is a willingness to consider why and how children are excluded, to broaden our interpretation of 'participation' and, in our interactions with children, to demonstrate that we recognise and value their contributions. As Nigel Thomas eloquently reminds us, if children are willing to communicate it is important that we listen and take seriously their concerns and ideas – even if we do not always like what we hear!

Reference

Waller, T., Morgan, A., Thomas, N. and Waters, J. (2006) 'Children as researchers: affordances and constraints', Learners' Voices, British Psychological Society annual conference, Open University, November.

Professor Trisha Maynard
Centre for Child Research, Swansea University
January 2009

Introduction: children, politics and communication

Nigel Thomas

This book is about how children and young people communicate about matters of importance or difficulty, how they decide what to tell adults and what not to tell them, how they organise themselves and their lives and how they deal with conflict in their own relationships and in the world around them. It is also about how adults can interact effectively with children and young people, on both an individual and a societal level, in ways that are sensitive to their feelings and empowering and supportive of their attempts to be autonomous. All contributors start with two assumptions: that children are not only developing competence for the future, but are also actors in the world today; and that they have things to teach us, both about their own lives and about society.

The contributors are all social scientists of one kind or another. Between them they bring perspectives from disciplines as diverse as psychology, geography, anthropology, sociology, social work, linguistics, political theory and development studies. They are pursuing research, and in some cases are engaged in policy debates, in three areas that at first sight may appear distinct: children and young people's participation, children and young people as refugees, and children and young people's use of language.

The contributors were originally brought together in a series of three extended seminars, which were explicitly intended to explore the common ground between these areas. This was the result of a perception that there was work going on in the analysis of children and young people's participation, and in the study of migration and displacement, that deserved to be brought together; and further, of what was little more than an intuition, that social research into children's use of language and communication might be relevant to both of these areas. What was remarkable in the experience of the seminars was how strongly the same themes and issues recurred across the series. In particular, all the contributors found themselves reflecting on the ways in which children and young people manage under difficult circumstances, and how they take responsibility for their own present and future lives. The chapters that follow have in the main developed from the work presented in those seminars.

This book is predominantly about children at the *margins*, in one way or another: children in communities in revolt in rural Mexico, children growing up in Chinese families in England, children with ME who are isolated at home, children living under occupation in Palestine, children negotiating their way through the asylum system in the UK. However, it is not about children as victims. Rather, it shows children taking charge of their lives: whether that be running 'kid's clubs' in Nepal, making links with each other on websites, finding ways to manage their disagreements, or defending their national identity.

The contributions to this book question many of the conventional ways in which children are still perceived, even after 20 years of progress in children's rights and of critique and reconstruction of ideas about childhood. Children are still frequently seen as apolitical, and even when they are 'listened to', what they have to say may be (bracketed and) discounted. In contrast, the contributors to this book show how much of what children do can be understood as political – either in terms of the issues with which they engage or in terms of what we may call the *micropolitics* of their interaction with each other and with adults.

Although there has been a growing emphasis on 'participation' in recent years, much of this activity is firmly adult-led. Spaces for children's autonomous activity, especially in a collective form, are severely restricted in all parts of the world. The particular shapes taken by these processes vary in different contexts, and the contributions to this book represent work from every continent.

We hope that the book will be useful and relevant for policy makers and practitioners engaged with children and young people. Understanding childhood better is of limited benefit if it does not affect what happens in the world. Many of the authors have strong links to policy and practice, and are able to point up the implications of their work in their individual chapters. In the concluding chapter I attempt to draw these implications together and develop them further.

Chapter One, by **Roger Hart**, is based directly on a lecture that he gave in Swansea in 2006, and introduces our overarching themes of the spaces for children to self-organise and the ways in which they can or cannot exercise control over their lives. Using a deliberately broad-brush approach, Roger Hart reviews 40 years of 'progress' in children's participation, suggesting that the same period has seen an erosion of children's visibility in public space and of their opportunities to organise for themselves, and a reduction in their interaction with adults. He begins to develop a model for mapping children and young people's participation visually, and argues for a move away from looking simply at 'participation' as currently defined, to focus more broadly on how public and communal life can be revived for *all* generations.

Chapter Two, by **Vicky Johnson**, is also about children and young people's self-organisation. Vicky Johnson uses her own experience of conducting evaluations in the UK and other countries to ask whether adult acceptance of children's organisations may depend on how far adults are involved in the process of initiation – whether, in fact, adults really *want* children to organise autonomously. Examples from community consultation processes in the UK, and from international programmes in Nepal and South Africa, are used to show that understanding how children and young people comprehend their own situations, and identify their own solutions, is an essential starting point for policies and projects that seek to give children and young people space to communicate and organise in a positive way. In turn, this may enable spaces to open for communication across age groups and generations, rather than only inviting children onto adult territory – again, echoing a theme of Roger Hart.

Chapter Three, by **Anne-Marie Smith**, is based on ethnographic research carried out in Oaxaca City, Mexico. It focuses on the lives of the displaced children of Loxicha, in particular their involvement in their community's political struggle, and explores the challenges this involvement presents for existing notions of childhood and of child participation, as framed by the United Nations Convention on the Rights of the Child (UNCRC). The children of Loxicha have played a key role in their community's struggle, going on marches and participating in sit-ins and hunger strikes. At the same time, they also play, work and go to school. Drawing on current debates in childhood studies and children's rights advocacy, Anne-Marie Smith questions the ways in which the childhoods experienced by the Loxicha children are redefined to suit adult notions of 'lost childhood', overlooking the complex and multilayered nature of their daily realities.

In Chapter Four, **Jason Hart** looks at the ways in which displaced children may take part in political violence, including the young people often described as 'child soldiers'. He examines how their activity is often explained away in terms of child immaturity or adult exploitation, and argues instead for a greater respect for such young people's understanding and agency, and for a more rigorous analysis of the conditions in which they live their lives over time. He also asks that research and policy examine the interaction between the lives of children displaced by conflict around the world and the policies of Western governments, which simultaneously feed the conflict and define those displaced as unwanted 'asylum seekers'.

The following two chapters are specifically about asylum, currently one of the dominant, even defining, issues in child rights and welfare. As **Heaven Crawley** points out in Chapter Five, the experiences of separated children who seek asylum in the UK, and their attempts to negotiate the complex array of individuals and institutions with whom they come into contact, are increasingly well documented. Less well considered is the extent to which the success, or otherwise, of these children in securing access to international protection and to appropriate housing, welfare and educational support is determined, not only by the individual experiences and abilities of the children concerned, but also by a particular conceptualisation of childhood that pervades the asylum process. Heaven Crawley's chapter examines how children's experiences of conflict, of human rights abuses and of loss are assessed and interpreted. She draws in particular on the experiences of children whose physical appearance and personal stories lead them to be 'age disputed' and treated as adults. For this group of children, a conceptualisation of childhood that requires them to be apolitical, asexual and passive has concrete and significant implications for their ability to rebuild their lives.

In Chapter Six, **Ravi Kohli** examines how refugee and asylum-seeking children, when they have arrived in industrialised nations, often remain silent, or speak in guarded ways, about their lives and circumstances. Not only their presence, but also their limited talk, can be the occasion of suspicion among citizens of host nations. Ravi Kohli's chapter looks at how silence and limited talk are used as powerful protective shields, when refugee children feel their sense of safety and belonging to be threatened in hostile contexts. The chapter reviews research evidence about ways of establishing trust for refugee children, as a foundation for resettled lives. It proposes that only with the establishment of such trust, combined with an unthreatened future, can such children begin to talk about their lives in depth and detail.

The next three chapters extend the focus on language and communication, using methods from sociolinguistics, conversation analysis and literacy studies to show what we can learn by attending closely to the detail of how children and young people use and adapt linguistic codes, and conversational and textual rules, to achieve their social objectives in real-life interaction.

In Chapter Seven, **Li Wei**, **Zhu Hua** and **Chao-Jung Wu** examine the strategic use of code-switching – the alternation of languages in conversational interaction – as a symbolic and creative resource by

Chinese-English bilingual children in the family and classroom. While code-switching, a uniquely bilingual behaviour, has been studied extensively by linguists and psychologists, it has not been taken seriously as an effective tool for speakers themselves in resisting the dual pressures of traditional values and institutional policies. Using audio-recorded interactional data collected in families and schools, Li Wei and his colleagues demonstrate how bilingual children use code-switching creatively as a symbol of resistance in the face of traditional cultural values and language ideologies.

In Chapter Eight, **Amelia Church** shows how the methods of conversation analysis can help us to understand processes of conflict between young children. Examples of spontaneous arguments between four-year-old children show that, although conflict is not always resolved, one can distinguish three possible outcomes in children's disputes: resolution, abandonment and teacher intervention. Close analysis of these three dispute 'closings' reveals that very specific linguistic resources are used by young children to manage disagreements with peers. The linguistic concept of 'preference' is found to be an organisational property of children's verbal conflict, and the outcome of disputes is determined by the way in which children mitigate each turn at talk. This chapter exemplifies children's competencies in social interaction and demonstrates that close attention to features of talk-in-interaction affords a rich understanding of children's social worlds. In particular, Amelia Church draws attention to some specific ways in which young children develop communicative repertoires and strategies to get noticed, achieve their objectives and manage different situations.

In Chapter Nine, **Julia Davies** reflects on the ways in which many young people are using the internet as a way of keeping in touch with likeminded others, thickening existing social ties with those whom they know from face-to-face contact, and also developing new relationships with others whom they only know 'online'. Her analysis, drawn as it is from the study of literacy as a social practice, uses different methods from the two preceding chapters, but is similar in being centred on close attention to features of actual conversation. Julia Davies shows us how young people use textual devices and affordances as a way of marking out affiliations and shared values, how they often use online arenas to present particular 'online versions' of themselves, and how this can help them to collaborate in constructive ways to deal with problems.

In the Conclusion, I draw together themes from all the preceding contributions in order to ask some questions about child–adult relationships, questions of theoretical interest that are also salient for practitioners and policy makers. Political and social theory are beginning to engage, from different directions, with questions about how communities of meaning and action are constructed when communicative styles and competencies are divergent. In the Conclusion I attempt to explore the nature of this engagement, and point to some future directions, both for research and for social action in communities.

ONE

Charting change in the participatory settings of childhood[1]

Roger Hart

Introduction

Participation has become a word that everyone seems to use today to legitimise their programmes with groups that are considered in some way to be marginalised. This includes a wealth of discussions about the growth of 'children's participation' in society in line with the call of the United Nations Convention on the Rights of the Child (UNCRC). The phrase is used with people working within very different ideologies concerning the appropriate roles of children, but almost all of them write about children's programmed activities. In the UK, most of the emphasis seems to be on children's participation in decision making in formal settings with adults or consultation of children by adults, even though the rationale that is commonly given is the much broader goal of the promotion of citizenship. In this chapter I argue that the emphasis on children's decision making with adults and consultation by adults in formal settings is a much too narrow view of children's social participation for citizenship.[2] We need to address not just children's voices in governance but also children's participation in civil society. I use the term children's social participation in this chapter to refer to all of those instances where children collaborate with other children or with adults, to make decisions or plan activities together from building a play house to organising a football game. If we are to reflect fully on how children are, and could be, involved in the processes of building a more participatory democratic society we need to simultaneously map out the formal changes in governance alongside the dramatic changes that have been taking place in children's everyday social lives with peers and their non-formal relations with adults in their communities. I believe that these have greater importance for the reproduction of a democratic civil society than that brought by any mandated, or formal, participation in the form of children's forums, councils and local government consultations, or from school citizenship curricula.

In this chapter I will begin to sketch out the range of domains of social participation of pre-adolescent children in the UK that I believe have been changing. While valuable research has begun on some of these domains there does not yet seem to be any recognition of the need to map these out comprehensively and in relation to one another. First, we need to carefully chart how children's autonomous activities with peers have changed over just one generation. Children have always learned social skills and participated in the reproduction of their communities through their non-formal activities with other children and the state has often tried to intervene and control these processes.[3] For example, there has recently been much concern by the UK government with youth delinquency in the UK. But there is a larger story that we need to map – of the multiple ways in a range of settings that the state, and national institutions, have chosen to set the stage for the socialisation of citizenship by influencing how children interact with one another – in neighbourhoods, schools, play resources, sports facilities and after-school programmes. In discussions of the development of children as citizens in the UK, the child-to-child dimension seems to have been greatly under-recognised and under-theorised. Even those who promote the UNCRC write of the triad of 'the child, the family and the state', as though other children themselves are not an important part of the processes of social reproduction and transformation. But we also need to systematically assess how children's non-formal participation with adults has changed. I will therefore briefly summarise some of the changes that I believe have been occurring in the nature of children's social participation in the family, in the school, in after-school activities, in membership organisations and religious institutions, in community holiday rituals and, of course, through the internet.

I will be relying partly on reflections from my own childhood in the UK for making a rough sketch of what has changed. I will try to balance these with the observations of a social scientist who cares a great deal about the subject. Using ones own childhood memories as a reference for thinking about change has some serious limitations. Not only are the dangers of nostalgia clear but there is also an inevitable tendency to see one's childhood as some kind of baseline rather than as an arbitrary moment in time. Additionally, and not surprisingly, I find that I am able to reflect much more fully on the social relations of boys than girls. I can only say that I find this strategy useful as a first step, while knowing full well that the result will only be a pencil sketch of a complex story.

Formal opportunities for children's voices to be heard in governmental and institutional settings

There can be no doubt that there are many more opportunities for children to have a voice in the official deliberations of government agencies and services than there were a generation ago. What is meant by the word 'participation', and what its primary benefits are considered to be, varies greatly. I will not review all of these different positions here, but simply say that I believe that the right to have a voice, as called for by the UNCRC, has been an extremely important benchmark in the growth of children's right to protect themselves from abuse or neglect. This has been particularly important for children in some majority world countries, but also in nations like the UK. This has involved the individual empowerment of children as individual defenders of their rights as well as the participation of groups of children. The UNCRC has also led to some progress in giving children a voice regarding governmental provision of resources and services for them. But there does not seem to have been much progress in bringing more participatory engagements between groups of children and adults in institutional settings and programmes, from schools and after-school clubs to sports and recreation programmes.

Most of the progress that has been made in the UK on the social participation of children relates to the fulfilment of those Articles of the UNCRC that are normally thought to refer to participation – Articles 12 and 13 on the rights to have one's views heard, to express oneself and to have access to and share information. But there are a number of other ones that have important implications for children's social participation in their communities. These include the rights to play, to have access to the cultural and artistic life of the community, to form associations and to non-discrimination.

Children's autonomous social participation in play with peers

In many ways, the 1950s in the UK were perhaps a special time for children's non-formal participation with peers in their communities. There was a sense of stability and security in the welfare state and, due to increases in wages for most families, children were commonly no longer relied on to be economic providers – there was pocket money and freedom to play. From all that we know of the dramatic reduction of children's spatial freedom in their communities since the 1960s, it seems likely that the opportunities for free play, independently organised by children with their peers, have also diminished.[4] The reasons are complex and overlapping, but they include:

- the increased percentage of parents who work away from home;
- parental fear and paranoia related to the media coverage of dangers, especially crime;
- the growth of individual competitiveness, particularly through the school system;
- the privatisation of public space;
- the commodification of children's lives through increased channels of marketing; and
- the internet.

In their free play, children learn how to participate with one another. Opie and Opie (1969) described richly the content of the rhymes and games that children passed on and transformed. But children also pass on different ways of relating to one another that range in varying degrees from the authoritarian or bullying to the participatory and considerate as they go about the serious business of picking teams, forming 'gangs', inventing membership rituals, building dens, making rules and so on. We have seen a modest growth of social science research inside child cultures in recent years, but we have much to learn about how children's social relationships are changing and how they variously contribute to the making of culture (Corsaro, 2001; Holloway and Valentine, 2003; Thorne, 2003). Children do not just internalise adult skills and knowledge; they also contribute to the processes of social reproduction by appropriating and reinventing culture (Bruner, 1986). Children do this both through creative communal activity with their peers and by negotiating and creating culture with adults (Corsaro and Miller, 1992; Corsaro, 1997).

In the long hours of freedom from adult constraint, children in the past generation built their own local participatory cultures all over the UK in ways that were very different from today. I do not want to romanticise childhood as some kind of glorious place full of the likes of Tom Sawyer and Becky Thatcher. Children often bullied each other and it was sometimes ugly. For example, in choosing sides for a football team there was usually no sense of democratic process. Typically, two of the most popular, athletic, boys would place themselves as captains to take it in turns to pick the best and the fastest of the bunch and leave the fattest or clumsiest boy lonely at the end of the process. But although many hours were spent free from direct adult supervision, children were not as segregated from unrelated adults in their community as they are today (see also Smith, this volume). They were the dominant actors in public spaces of residential areas – more aware of what was happening in the streets, pavements, parks and playgrounds than were the adults in their lives, but they came into contact with adult neighbours, greengrocers, dog walkers and others in the normal course of being free to explore their community. There is no doubt, however, that this was truer for boys than for girls.

Research tells us that free play, which is play directed by children themselves, has decreased in the UK as it has throughout the countries of the minority world. In addition to all of the restrictive forces described above, parents have been told that unless they programme their children's out-of-school time they will not be able to compete in the newly competitive global economy. I know from my research that many parents in the US struggle to make sense of this given the freedom that they knew as children, and I suspect that this is true of parents in the UK too (Hart, in process). Many of them wonder about the loss of their children's free playtime with peers but the dominant advice they receive is that children's play needs to be guided by adults. There certainly are values to play with adults but not to the exclusion of 'free play' with peers. In free play, children organise their activities and make decisions with one another in a qualitatively different way than when an adult is involved. We know from contemporary developmental theory, building on the work of Vygotsky (1978), that children in groups of mixed ages and abilities learn a great deal from one another by 'scaffolding' their learning on the shoulders of one another (Winegar and Valsiner, 1992). Newson and Newson (1967) described convincingly the different kinds of opportunities for age and social class mixing and the building of community that occurred on the streets of Nottingham before children moved to the housing estates on the edge of the city with their low density, recreation grounds and private gardens for children's play. They also described the awareness that parents had of much of these relations between children as they all lived together in close quarters. We need to think what these kinds of changes have meant for children's participation in their communities, and with their identification with their communities, especially in this era of privatisation of play and recreation.

There has long been a fear by government authorities of children being socialised on the streets, because of both the uncontrolled influences of adults and the unguided and unbridled processes of children learning from children. Many social reformers and politicians presented playgrounds, recreation grounds and centres as the solution for building healthy and responsible citizenship (Goodman, 1979).[5] While this was initially because the reformers were anxious to get the children under their control, the model of isolated playgrounds seems to have later become a norm, largely through bureaucratisation. Funding for play provision has been closely related to the fear of losing control, as with UK funding after the Toxteth riots. This goal of segregating children needs to be seen as part of a larger historical movement since the 19th century in Western countries to segregate children from the adult world, and to stream children into age groups in all aspects of their life (Hareven, 2000). But research in many parts of the world has since shown that children generally prefer not to be isolated away on playgrounds but to be in a closer, interactive relationship with others, including family, friends and neighbours, as described by Jane Jacobs (1961). In her very different vision of civil society, she argued that streets and pavements were appropriate spaces for children because they were able to learn social values and skills from one another and from neighbours. Some policies have occasionally been developed that support Jane Jacobs' vision such as the 'woonerf' concept of the Netherlands, involving the closing off of streets to through traffic, and, more recently, 'home zones' in the UK.[6] But the more common approach continues to be a simpleminded belief in segregating children.

Planning policy has played an important part in the erosion of children's self-generated activities because of the loss of accessible and appropriate space. Spaces available to children in the UK have become increasingly controlled (Hart, 1978[7]). The more space is demarcated for a specific function, the more it comes under the sway of those who define that function. My childhood community, on the edge of Nottingham, has a small river and next to the river there are wild fields of long grass, known to us all as 'Geoff's'. It was an excellent space for free play invented by children. As Lefebvre (1991, p 83) put it, 'the more a space partakes of nature, the less it enters into the social relations of production', or for a child, the wilder a space is the less it is demarcated and the less power it has to demand certain behaviours from that child. Since my childhood, the local authority has expanded the sport field but left some of the long grass. A local planner tells me that he is aware of the value of this wild land for children and dog walkers but the primary reason it survives is that it is a flood plain that cannot be built on (Hart, 1982). As it happens, most parents do not seem to allow their children to go to play in this non-specific place for children anymore.

I knew from an early age that planners did not like wild land. I lived in a council house, my father was a professional gardener and we did not have a wild garden. My father let me commandeer a very small space at the end of the garden but the garden that was most interesting to all of us children who lived in the cul-de-sac was Nigel's. It was wild, with grass sometimes waving above our heads, and we used it to full effect for many adventures until the local authority kicked the family out because of their unkempt garden. Planning policies all over the UK have destroyed small areas of unused land that was in effect 'common land' for children through residential infilling. But we should not see children as passive recipients of these changes. Children themselves participate in changing the nature of social space. As they develop new kinds of activities with one another, many previous uses of the land in their communities decay and disappear. Through their collective actions, children not only alter their surroundings but also the social practices that take place in certain places. In this way, children themselves contribute to the way the landscape affords opportunities for the play and social participation of future cohorts of children.[8]

In addition to space, the materials made available to children have changed. Toys are heavily marketed directly to children through television, the internet and video games and they come with ready-made scripts.[9] Illich (1973) wrote long ago how some materials and technologies lend themselves more than others to 'conviviality'. By this he meant 'the creative intercourse among persons and the intercourse of persons with the environment' (1973, p 11). Many modern toys lend themselves to group play of children just as much as older ones – transformers are no different in that sense from toy soldiers. But palm-held electronic games are different in that they call for closed use by individuals. Along with all of the electronic media that children now play with indoors, they need to be put into the mix of factors that affects the degree of children's conviviality through play.

With fewer opportunities to play with peers and to be spontaneously engaged informally in the lives of adults, we can say that children are less embedded in their communities than they were – at least in 'communities' in the geographic sense. This loss of a sense of community with known adults and peers affects parents' confidence to let their children have freedom outdoors, which in turn further diminishes their spatial freedom. All of these things together mean that community in the spatial sense is less made by children and we may hypothesise that their sense of identity with their surrounding community is also diminished from what it used to be for children. We may expect that children now contribute less to the 'bridging' form of social capital, that is cooperative connections between people from different walks of life, which theorists of community development consider to be more valuable than the 'bonding' type of social capital found between family or closely connected people (Portes, 1998; Putnam, 2000). Whether social capital is an appropriate concept to apply to children's social lives is apparently a point of debate in the UK (Morrow, 1999). But we know from past research that children do play a role in building community social relationships beyond that of family and immediate neighbours and that these are different from those of adults, although today, for pre-adolescent children, these out-of-school friendship networks are more under the influence of adults than they were.[10]

There are many benefits from children being able to play with one another in a self-directed manner: learning the skills of cooperation to achieve their goals; experimenting with different roles, including leadership and power; negotiating rules for their play; resolving conflicts; struggling with fairness or morality; planning and creatively using their resources; and so on. Much of this learning is made possible by the absence of adult authority – leaving children to learn to self-organise. Interactions among peers provide distinct developmental opportunities because unlike adult–child interactions with one-way instruction they are usually characterised by a bi-directional give-and-take. Children actively construct the parameters of their relationships. This greater flexibility allows children to test their understandings and adapt them to the requirements of ongoing interaction. Same-age interactions might seem to provide optimal conditions for such experiences, but there are other benefits that may be derived from mixed-age interactions if there is not too great a difference in ages; adolescents and preschool children will typically result in the same differential of power and knowledge that characterises adult–child interactions.

In my research In New England I have found that a most revealing question to ask is 'Can you tell me about when you get to do things with friends that are not organised by adults?' This question, which no one has ever asked them before, instantly receives an enthusiastic response. Even the most programmed of children describe small cracks between adult-organised events where they eke out some free time with peers such as waiting for an organised sport to get started or time with friends on the school bus. These hidden times, which are so important to children, are important indicators for us if we are interested in knowing how to improve affordances for children's self-initiated activities.

Having argued for the benefits of free play with peers it must be recognised that there are important roles for adults even in the non-formal settings of play outdoors, as role models and sometimes to resolve conflicts or intervene in situations of abuse. So the problem is not one of finding a way of letting children be free but of finding a better balance, to allow 'free play' with adults nearby. Children reveal that they too would not want this extreme vision of a segregated culture of children (Hart et al., 1997).

Finally, in thinking about the extent to which children are involved in self-generated communal activities we need to consider the internet. Some believe that the internet, along with video games, is the primary reason for the loss of children's outdoor activity because it seduces children indoors but research in the UK has revealed that this is an exaggerated view that falsely separates the virtual world out from children's direct social contacts (Holloway and Valentine, 2003). Research with adolescents and youth suggests that to some degree the internet has created a substitute for the loss of free direct contact between peers. However, at the present time at least, pre-adolescents rarely use the internet for social networking and so I will not dwell on it here. But clearly this is a part of the complex charting of children's societal participation that we need to understand.

Participation in the family

Politicians in the UK frequently blame families for what they see as a loss of control and discipline with children and a failure to cultivate responsibility. They typically imply that parents have failed, as though discipline was something entirely delivered from above. Parents have been facing a barrage of societal changes that affect their parenting and are struggling to work out how to address these changes – a task not necessarily made easier by the battalions of child 'experts' like us offering contradictory advice! There is a great deal of research that shows that parents have distinct ideologies of childrearing. Many parents try to establish a climate of self-determination without losing control, and this 'authoritative' style of parenting, in contrast to 'authoritarian' and 'permissive' parenting, is the subject of a considerable body of research (Darling and Steinberg, 1993). Whether or not a child is raised with a participatory style that leads to greater self-determination and cooperative activity would seem likely to have important implications for the degree of participatory orientation to society that they will have and perhaps even their later political orientation.[11]

Much attention is given by the popular press to the decline in family meals as an important indicator of the loss of the family as a socialising unit. But there are other dimensions to consider. For example, how has the family changed as a setting where children participate in the care and management of things, and does this have implications for the more general development of children's participatory competencies? We know that parenting guides still promote the importance of household chores in the primary school years as a way of promoting a sense of responsibility as well as the learning of practical skills. In most families in the UK, children are no longer really needed for the functioning economy of the family, but many parents still seem to believe that chores are important for the development of their children as competent, responsible children. How much are children doing this with a sense of truly contributing in a significant way is an important question (Morrow, 1994).

Most parents are aware of all of these kinds of big changes in the nature of childhood and some of them are so concerned that they try to find ways to resist them. I am finding from my research in a New England town that some parents are concerned about the loss of free play and autonomous activity with peers. They choose homes that they know will maximise their child's freedom – notably those on cul-de-sacs or at the end of a lane – and they seek out other parents who they know recognise the value of free play outdoors and consider this in their choice of 'play date' locations for their children. But for most parents it is enough of a struggle to keep up with the demands of balancing work and parenting and they follow the norms established by other parents around them.[12]

Schools as settings for social participation

Schools seem to have played a central role in the move to a more individualistic orientation to the socialisation of children. British primary schools in the 1960s and 1970s were impressive to the rest of the world because they had pioneered and evolved child-centred learning where children were more in control of their learning and could co-learn with each other in groups. The physical design of schools evolved in ways that afforded group learning, with the teacher as a 'facilitator'. This model was valued not only for its pedagogic merits but also because autonomous learning and cooperative behaviour was seen by some educators, at that period of history, as a valued dimension to develop the society. The progressive 'open classroom' is a much more weakly classified space; that is, the functions of the spaces, the available materials and the rules for their use are not precisely spelled out.[13] The theories behind this more democratic pedagogy were highly progressive and so it should not be too surprising that this model has not continued as the standard of British public primary school learning.

Citizenship education, fostering the active civic engagement of children, has now become a formal part of the school curriculum in the UK.[14] Unfortunately, it is generally not conceptualised sufficiently broadly to incorporate the kinds of everyday opportunities for social participation and cooperation that are the focus of this chapter.

Schools are central settings in children's lives for learning about political power, participation and justice. Even five-year-olds after entering school quickly develop a fairly accurate understanding of the roles of different people in the schools. By the end of their elementary school years they have a very complete understanding of political authority and power.[15] Yet the official position is that rather than working to establish democratic schools as models for the society we want, we teach about democracy. Education on democracy is like education on rights: give people information and they will show indifference, give people power or responsibility and they will pursue knowledge because they see the need for it. It is almost a hundred years since Dewey (1916) wrote about creating democratic microcosms in classrooms but democratic classrooms in public schools today remain the exception. If children are given the opportunity to participate in democratic settings in their everyday lives in school or in clubs and if they are the partners in the making of rules and in maintaining the effectiveness of their group's functioning, then they each can become the democratic educators of one another. Research on progressive schools has shown that children come to represent social systems differently when they discover that one can have authoritative systems that are not necessarily authoritarian ones and that one can achieve social consensus through discussion and negotiation (Hart et al., 1997; Rogoff et al., 2003). From such schools we can expect children to learn about personal obligation, mutual responsibility and the importance of self-restraint – qualities that the government has been so concerned about in its contemporary criticisms of the social and moral behaviour of children. Unfortunately, the emphasis in training today is not to have teachers seeing their roles as setting up the social ecology of the classroom to maximise children's abilities to learn from one another in this way.

In Colombia, officials at the highest level of government, as well as in non-governmental organisations, have been developing participatory approaches to working with children as a way of breaking the culture of violence in their country. But the Colombians not only recognise the importance of the kind of active citizenship work that is most frequently discussed in relation to the UK school system: children researching neighbourhood quality and organising campaigns on issues beyond the school walls. They also give great emphasis to building '*convivencia*' – the values and skills of mutual living – within the school. This philosophy has been operating the longest in the '*escuelas nuevas*' or 'new schools'. Rather than one-shot conflict resolution programmes to reduce bullying or the introduction of some other social programme, they provide a sustained attempt to change the norms of social relationships by how programmes and schools are run. In the best of these schools there are so many committees for a very broad range of dimensions of school management that all children are involved, not just the select few popular children. But they also have child-centred individual and group learning as a core philosophy, adopted from the English primary schools of three decades ago (Escuela Nueva Foundation, 2007). So effective are these schools that a recent comparative study found that the democratic behaviours fostered in the *escuelas nuevas* reach the surrounding community of adults via the children: the Escuela Nueva Foundation found statistically significant higher levels of social capital in the communities that had an *escuelas nueva*. This is a very important result in a nation that is struggling to escape its violent history but it is also important data for any nation that cares about building a more civil society and participatory democracy.[16] The recently developed 'rights respecting schools' in the UK now seem to be offering a valuable experiment in this direction.[17]

We are still living with an age segregation in schools that was invented at the time of the Industrial Revolution, even though many educators now know of the multiple benefits of age mixing in learning. Furthermore, the degree of age segregation has probably become worse now that children are spending less time in non-formal settings outdoors. Children's after-school programmes are typically segregated, just like school. Building on Vygotsky's (1978) ideas of co-learning between children, we now have a theoretical basis for understanding why so many small, mixed-age, village schools were good. Also, many years ago, ecological psychologists had a fascinating counterintuitive finding about children's participation in schools but unfortunately the research findings did not reach the school planners. They found that even though larger schools offered more resources, children in small schools participated in a greater range of activities (Barker and Gump, 1964). This was because even a small school wants a diversity of activities such as a football team and a theatre programme but with far fewer children there is greater opportunity for each child to participate in a range of these alternative experiences.

The classroom is inevitably a more vertically organised behaviour setting than the school playground. But lunchrooms are a kind of space that lies somewhere between the free play of the school playground and the directed learning of the classroom, and for that reason they deserve attention in this chapter. In many primary schools of the 1960s in the UK, lunchrooms were in many cases important spaces for informally promoting sharing and caring, both in their design and in the rules for setting up tables and serving. In the best of schools, children were encouraged to take over responsibilities for organising the meal experience, with some freedom, with children inventing what happened at their table, decorating it, choosing who was going to carry out different tasks and so on. Somehow the collective values of this kind of participatory learning experience were forgotten in the rush to privatise and to offer total freedom of choice to individual children.

Participation in after-school programmes

In response to the forces described at the start of this chapter, organised after-school activities have grown dramatically in one generation in the UK. Today it is commonly seen as bad parenting to allow children to play unsupervised in the streets, and when the children become adolescents they tend to be seen as minor criminals. The children of better-off families send their children to a cornucopia of private after-school opportunities for all kinds of extended learning. For the children of less wealthy families, the children's clubs of the UK, like the after-school programmes of the US, are frequently programmed by adults as more schooling; they are typically not about free play or child-designed activities in a safe space (Smith and Barker, 2000). Furthermore, these clubs are commonly held in a school building, bringing with it all of the affordances and symbolism of the school. The clubs that self-consciously try to be democratic in allowing children to choose their activities are the exception. As a result, the clubs seem to offer considerably less opportunity for autonomous peer group activity than did the children's membership organisations that were once used by a large proportion of the nation's children.

Participatory opportunities in membership organisations

Children's membership organisations have decreased dramatically over the past few decades. Boy Scout and Girl Guide troops were ubiquitous. They had a heavy emphasis on social and moral development but they were not organised in ways that maximise children's democratic participation. They were loosely structured on a military hierarchic model of leadership. They nevertheless offered many young people a relatively high degree of autonomous activity, including time away from home where children organised activities with their peers. We do not seem to know enough about the reasons for the decline in popularity of these organisations and whether there are other forms that might work. Was the hierarchic and programmed nature of these organisations a factor and, if so, could highly participatory membership organisations be more successful?[18] Given the existence of children's groups with high levels of self-management in other countries, the issue is clearly not one of children's limited capacities (Rajbhandari et al., 2001; Hart and Rajbhandari, 2003; see also Johnson, this volume).

The decline of children's membership organisations may well be just the result of too many other attractions in a media-saturated hyper-commercialised society but the problem may also be that the UK has not experimented sufficiently with opportunities and supports for children to come together to self-organise. Perhaps the failure to experiment is related to a fear of children and youth. Whatever the reason, we need to ask what the 21st-century version of the Scouts and the Guides would look like. We need to think of new kinds of sustained opportunities for children as democratic citizens. Contrary to the popular public image, adolescents in the US have revealed from recent research that they would like to have opportunities to be involved in membership organisations if they were able to take some control in the management of these settings, with caring supportive adults alongside rather than directing them (Hart et al., 1997).

In all cultures, the idea of supporting children and youth to form their own groups is new and has many challenges. Even though other nations have some valuable lessons to teach us about participatory organisation with children, all of the talented youth workers that I have met overseas are quick to insist that they have a lot to learn on this theme. For example, they commonly support very dynamic participatory groups of children for a few years but these groups tend to mature and die, as older children do not want younger children to join the group (Hart, 1992). In rare cases, I found that an organisation has some form of 'shadowing' or apprenticeship by younger children as a self-generative strategy. We need to enable children and young people to experiment with many such alternative strategies for sustaining groups. Knowing how to animate children to feel free to initiate their own activities and then to remain available on the sidelines rather than directing them is a very different training from that given to most educators.

Children's central participation in festivals and holiday celebrations

There are few instances where children play a central role in reproducing traditional events in the UK. Even in the 1950s, the preparation for Bonfire Night was one of those rare instances in our culture of how children pass on a festival tradition largely through child-to-child communication. Primary school-aged children commonly organised this event with their peers. Guy Fawkes was stuffed with our fathers' clothes, and dropped onto soapbox carts made by us. We dragged these wagons around our neighbourhood, collecting funds from adults with plaintive cries of 'Penny for the guy'. From the proceeds we bought fireworks and carefully, admiringly, placed them into boxes and took them out again, and again, to look at them or sometimes to 'test' them out with our friends. There was danger in this of course, and some families did take it upon themselves to try to graduate exposure to this risk. But the weeks of preparation for Bonfire Night were an entirely child-organised process involving high levels of cooperation between children and a great deal of negotiated participation with adults. It is now a largely adult-programmed affair.

The night before Bonfire Night was known as Mischievous Night. Such pranks as knocking on front doors by tying of front-door knockers with string were so ubiquitous that the folklore was that it was legal, or at least semi-legitimate, and that the local copper would not arrest us. Again, this particular ritual was truly a child-to-child organised affair. There were repercussions with individual adults but they were generally not seen as negative for the community. I remember one night when we exchanged gates between houses all over the community. I can still see in my mind dozens of adults wandering around on a sunny morning trying to find the correct owners for one another's gates and generally having a good laugh about it. I understand that rather than seeing children as having a degree of licence to play pranks, this kind of activity is now seen as serious anti-social behaviour. But for most children in the UK, Mischievous Night has been replaced by Halloween, imported from the US through the media and all of the pumpkin regalia sold in supermarkets. It is a family affair rather than a children's event and is a much more tame event commonly involving accompaniment by adults to neighbours' houses to collect sweets – 'treats' without the 'tricks'. Other countries have similar traditions such as St. Martins Day on 11 November in The Netherlands where children go from house to house singing songs, like many English children once did alone with Christmas carol singing. The tradition continues in The Netherlands but again it is with adult supervision.[19] These changes are undoubtedly largely related to reductions in children's freedom within their communities and changing ideas of risk-taking and the control of children (Gill, 2007).

It is worth noting that it is still common in many countries of the majority world for children to have very central roles in reproducing community rituals. In contrast, in the UK, these kinds of traditions seem to have retreated entirely into the privacy of the home, such as putting up the Christmas tree and decorating it, or they have become commercial events. In neither case do they have the same significance for the reproduction of community.

Social participation in organised sports

School sports and organised games for children have always had the double goal of fostering both individual skills and group cooperation in the form of competition with others (Goodman, 1979; Cavallo, 1981). But organised games have become a much more adult-programmed domain than in the past generation of children. Informal games organised spontaneously by children have become a relatively rare phenomenon. This is partly due to the loss of children's spatial freedom. It is also related to the planning and recreation policies described previously that create more spaces that dictate their function for specific activities rather than allowing children to appropriate spaces to create their own organised games and sports (See Lefebvre, 1991; Harvey, 2000). We will need to include these changes in our overall assessment of how we enable children to develop their cooperative capacities and to participate in the building of community.

Social participation through work activities

It is easy for us to forget that many children, especially in the past, learned a great many skills of social participation through work. Newspaper rounds, a rather romanticised work of children in the past in the UK, was an activity offering high degrees of autonomy to children and the jobs and the training were typically passed on between children. But many other jobs involved children apprenticing themselves informally to adults – typically people known to the family. The ease with which children were able to work with adults in non-formal ways in their communities in the past is captured by 'Bob-a-job' work, which involved tens of thousands of Cub Scouts earning money for their troup by finding work in homes all over their communities for one week in the summer. Children's engagements with work vary greatly with social class of course and the knowledge and skills gained through participation in work reproduces class differences (Bourdieu and Passeron, 1977). But this work also introduces many children to meaningful participation through collaborative work with adults and how this story has changed should be a part of our survey.

Some ways forward

I have argued that the nature of children's non-formal social participation in their communities should be thought of as central to the making of civil society and should be investigated by social scientists with a similar vigour to the study of children's formal participation. We have choices about the kind of society we make for, and with, children. We are already beginning to see some fascinating signs of change in Europe and North America related to public concern over the spaces that we make available for children. The transatlantic concern with children's obesity is largely a top-down movement but there is also a groundswell of parent concern over the loss of children's contact with nature and a concern over the loss of free-play activity. There does not yet seem to be any broad concern by parents or policy makers in the UK or any nation over the erosion of children's opportunities for non-formal social participation as a fundamental part of the reproduction of democratic civil society but some good research on this theme might make a difference.

A major area for improving opportunities for children's social participation is in after-school programmes. The UK government currently has an emphasis on social exclusion and sees children's participation as a strategy for bringing excluded children into the mainstream as responsible citizens. But the programmes do not typically seem to be trying to replace the kinds of losses I have described in this chapter, that is, high levels of autonomy in children's after-school programmes with caring adults working alongside. A recent review of participation programmes in the UK concluded that only a minority of participatory programmes involve working relatively intensively with small numbers of children over sustained periods and involving children directly in the management of projects (Evans and Spicer, 2008).

We need to help many adults see their professional roles with children less as planners and managers and more as role models, stagehands, and sometimes arbitrators and emergency aides. The 'play work' profession has evolved these qualities since its emergence after the Second World War. Adventure playgrounds were developed to provide a microcosm of physical opportunities and challenge for city children but now, in a changed era, many play workers have been pulled into more programmed settings and even privatised ones. In reaction to this, play workers have become strong advocates for the promotion of free-play opportunities.[20] Good play workers are models of the kinds of professionals we need in large numbers to support children. They are experts at observing and listening to children in order to know how to support them rather than directing them in play (Benjamin, 1974). Unfortunately, play work remains a relatively under-recognised and understaffed profession given the changing needs of society.

Finally, I would like to return in a full circle to the issue of children's formal participation. I join many of my British colleagues in criticising the kinds of participation strategies that are typically used – one-shot consultations or children's forums (Hallett and Prout, 2003). In contrast, I propose that if we wish to involve children in community governance it should be at the very local level, it should involve all children, not representative children, and it should equally involve adult residents. Intergenerational community planning events where parents and grandparents share what they valued as children alongside children's own evaluations of their communities today have particular potential. When adults truly speak from memories of their own childhoods they seem to engage with children in more horizontal ways than is typically the case in adult–child exchanges. Whether or not this particular strategy is developed, we need to go beyond simple strategies for listening to children's voices if we are to build more democratic communities. We need to consider how children and adults come together, and could come together, in meaningful dialogue.

Notes

[1] This chapter is based on a lecture given at University of Wales Swansea in November 2006, which was recorded on video and later transcribed by Cath Larkins.

[2] Attempts by government agencies to involve children have become common in the UK, but these are commonly criticised as being largely limited to

'consultation', and are often token in scale and sustainability. In recent decades, government agencies and NGOs have come to deliver their priorities for children through participatory programmes such as 'Agenda 21' for sustainable development, HIV prevention and violence prevention. These are not open agenda opportunities for children, but settings for delivering messages in deeper ways than the teaching and information strategies of the past. They are often disguised as being participatory when in fact they are highly programmed affairs. The rationale that is given is the UNCRC, but the UNCRC clearly calls for children to have a voice on all matters of concern to *children*.

[3] In addition to calling for children's voices to be heard, the UNCRC more generally recognises the value of self-determination in children's development and also articulates children's right to gather with their peers.

[4] Many of the articles in the journal *Children's Geographies*, and even the emergence of the journal itself, support this observation in the UK. In my own longitudinal and cross-sectional study of the changing geography of childhood in a small town in New England, I am documenting the same dramatic erosion of children's self-directed play with peers and how parents are dealing with this (Hart, in process).

[5] Goodman (1979) describes the ideological struggle behind the attempts of the reformers who tried to fish children off the crowded streets of Manhattan and into playgrounds in the early part of the 20th century.

[6] Home Zones: www.homezones.org/links.html; for the UK Children's Play Council: www.ncb.org.uk/cpc/publications

[7] These programme notes to the BBC film Play and Place include an account of the importance of opportunities for children to have free, undemarcated space. The second half of the film focuses on children living on the edge of Coalville, Leicestershire. Their favourite play places were dens, located in fields that were being rapidly covered by housing while the film was being shot.

[8] In a valuable effort to contribute to the evaluation of children's participation in communities, Chawla and Heft (2002) have drawn on concepts from ecological psychology to consider qualities of environments that are likely to afford children opportunities to develop a sense of competence. In addition to a child's own sense of self-efficacy from taking action, they recognise Bandura's (1997) evidence that observing someone like themselves accomplishing something they would like to do, also fosters a sense of self-efficacy.

[9] The integrated selling of toys with television scripts of how to use them appears to have influenced the degree to which children make their own play scripts versus play that is pre-scripted by the things that they are seduced into buying. Some play theorists argue, however, that this kind of thinking under-recognises the remarkable transformative power of play and that children will always modify the scripts they are given (Sutton-Smith, 2001).

[10] In my current research in a New England town, one of the greatest challenges to parents is to offer 'play dates' that successfully balance children's preferences with their own concerns for children's socialisation (Hart, in process).

[11] Unfortunately, research on the political socialisation of children within families has generally looked naively at the relationship between the political party orientations of parents in relation to those of their children rather than at family politics and the everyday way in which power is exercised as a factor influencing children's ideological orientation to participation (see Jankowski, 1992).

[12] These conclusions come from my current research in a New England town but I suspect they have some relevance to the UK too.

[13] Bernstein (1973) describes how this model involved an 'invisible pedagogy' where a child has a large diverse space in which to operate in contrast to the 'visible pedagogy' of the traditional classroom with its blackboard, chair and book as its clearly displayed key features. Bernstein points out, however, the irony that in this kind of space the child's learning activities are made highly visible, enabling strategic intervention by a teacher.

[14] www.teachingcitizenship.org.uk/

[15] Before adolescence, children tend to think that societal decisions emanate from the free will of individuals; they do not recognise the formal impersonal component of role relations (Hart et al., 1997).

[16] A recent comparative study of 25 schools in two of the more violent areas in Colombia found that the 15 schools using the escuela nueva methodology had a direct and significant impact on the participation and democratic behaviour of its graduates within the community and on the parents (Forero and Rodríguez, 2002).

[17] Rights Respecting Schools, UNICEF-UK: http://rrsa.unicef.org.uk/

[18] Even the more progressive organisation, Woodcraft Folk, seems to have only a limited commitment to building children's participatory skills and capacities to self-organise.

[19] Personal communication with Lia Karsten.

[20] www.freeplaynetwork.org.uk; www.playwales.org.uk; www.playengland. org.uk

References

Bandura, A. (1997) *Self-Efficacy*, New York, NY: W.H. Freeman.

Barker, R. and Gump, P. (1964) *Big School, Small School: High School Size and Student Behavior*, Stanford, CA: Stanford University Press.

Benjamin, J. (1974) *Grounds for Play*, London: Bedford Square Press.

Bernstein, B. (1973) *Class Codes and Control: Volume 3*, London: Routledge.

Bourdieu, P. and Passeron, J.C. (1990) *Reproduction in Education, Society and Culture*, London: Sage Publications.

Bruner, J. (1986) *Actual Minds, Possible Worlds*, London: Harvard University Press.

Cavallo, D. (1981) *Muscles and Morals: Organized Playgrounds and Urban Reform, 1880-1920*, Philadelphia, PA: University of Pennsylvania Press.

Chawla, L. and Heft, H. (2002) 'Children's competence and the ecology of communities: a functional approach to the evaluation of participation', *Journal of Environmental Psychology*, 22(1-2), pp 201-16.

Corsaro, W.A. (1997) *The Sociology of Childhood*, London: Pine Forge Press.

Corsaro, W.A. (2001) *We're Friends Right? Inside Kids Culture*, Washington, DC: Joseph Henry.

Corsaro, W.A. and Miller, P.J. (eds) (1992) *Interpretive Approaches to Children's Socialization*, New Directions for Child Development, No 58, San Fransisco, CA: Jossey-Bass.

Darling, N. and Steinberg, N. (1993) 'Parenting style as context: an integrative model', *Psychological Bulletin*, 113(3), pp 487-96.

Dewey, J. (1916) *Democracy and Education*, New York, NY: Macmillan.

Escuela Nueva Foundation (2007) Escuela Nueva: Learning to Learn and Coexist Peacefully, www.fao.org/sd/erp/documents2007/ VCOLBERTEscuelaNueva2-2007.pps

Evans, R. and Spicer, N. (2008) 'Is participation prevention? A blurring of discourses in children's preventative initiatives in the UK', *Childhood*, 15, p 50.

Forero, C. and Rodríguez, D. (2002) 'School system and democratic behavior of Colombian children', Paper presented to the Sixth Annual Conference of the International Society for New Institutional Economics.

Gill, T. (2007) *No Fear: Growing Up in a Risk-Averse Society*, London: Calouste Gulbenkian Foundation.

Goodman, C. (1979) *Choosing Sides: Playground and Street Life on the Lower East Side*, New York, NY: Schocken Books.

Hallett, C. and Prout, A. (2003) *Hearing the Voices of Children: Social Policy for a New Century*, London: Routledge.

Hareven, T. (2000) *Families, History and Social Change: Life Course and Cross-Cultural Change*, Oxford: Westview Press.

Hart, R.A. (1978) *Play and Place: Transforming Environments*, London: BBC/Open University (programme notes for the film from www. cerg1.org).

Hart, R.A. (1982) Wildlands for children: a consideration of the values of natural environments in landscape planning', *Landschaft und Stadt*, 14(1), pp 33–40; also published in the *Bulletin of Environmental Education*, 1983, no 141.

Hart, R.A. (1992) *Children's Participation: From Tokenism to Citizenship*, Florence, Italy: Innocenti Research Centre.

Hart, R.A. and Rajbhandari, J. (2003) 'The children's clubs of Nepal: evaluation of a democratic experiment', in K. Sabo Flores (ed) *Youth Participatory Evaluation: A Field in the Making*, San Fransisco, CA: Jossey–Bass.

Hart, R.A., Daiute, C., Iltus, S., Kritt, D., Rome, M. and Sabo, K. (1997) 'Developmental theory and children's participation in community organizations', *Social Justice*, 24(3), pp 33–63.

Harvey, D. (2000) *Spaces of Hope*, Berkeley, CA: University of California Press.

Holloway, S. and Valentine, G. (2003) *Cyberkids: Children in the Information Age*, London: Routledge/Farmer.

Illich, I. (1973) *Tools for Conviviality*, New York: Harper and Row.

Jacobs, J. (1961) 'Streets and sidewalks: assimilating children', in *The Death and Life of Great American Cities*, New York, NY: Random House.

Jankowski, M.S. (1992) 'Ethnic identity and political consciousness in different social orders', *New Directions for Child Development*, 56, pp 79–91.

Lefebvre, H. (1991) *The Production of Space*, Oxford: Oxford University Press.

Moore, R. (1986) *Childhood's Domain*, Berkeley, CA: MIG communications

Morrow, V. (1994) 'Responsible children? Aspects of children's work and employment outside school in contemporary UK', in B. Mayall (ed) *Children's Childhoods: Observed and Experienced*, London: Falmer Press.

Morrow, V. (1999) 'Conceptualising social capital in relation to the well being of children and young people: a critical review', *Sociological Review*, 47(4), pp 744-65.

Newson, J. and Newson, E. (1967) *Seven Years Old in the Urban Environment*, Harmondsworth: Penguin Books.

Opie, I. and Opie, P. (1969) *Children's Games in Street and Playground*, London: Oxford University Press.

Portes, A. (1998) 'Social capital: its origins and applications in modern sociology', *Annual Review of Sociology*, 24(1), pp 1-24.

Putnam, R.D. (2000) *Bowling Alone: The Collapse and Revival of American Community*, New York: Simon and Schuster.

Rajbhandari, J., Hart, R.A. and Khatiwada, C. (2001) *The Children's Clubs of Nepal: Evaluation of a Democratic Experiment*, Kathmandu, Nepal: Save the Children Alliance (and the associated methodological video 'Mirrors of Ourselves: Tools of Democratic Self Reflection for Groups of Children and Youth', New York, NY: Children's Environments Research Group, www.cerg1.org).

Rogoff, B., Turkanis, C.G. and Bartlett, L. (ed) (2003) *Learning Together: Children and Adults in a School Community*, Oxford: Oxford University Press.

Smith, F. and Barker, J. (2000) 'Contested spaces: children's out of school care', *Childhood*, 7(3), pp 315-33.

Sutton-Smith, B. (2001) *The Ambiguity of Play*, Cambridge, MA: Harvard University Press.

Thorne, B. (2003) *Gender Play*, New Brunswick, NJ: Rutgers University Press.

Vygotsky, L.S. (1978) *Mind and Society: The Development of Higher Mental Processes*, Cambridge, MA: Harvard University Press.

Winegar, L.T. and Valsiner, J. (1992) *Children's Development Within Social Contexts*, Hillsdale, NJ: Lawrence Erlbaum Associates.

TWO

Children's autonomous organisation: reflections from the ground

Vicky Johnson

Introduction

This chapter draws primarily on research in community settings in the UK, but also on international examples, to explore some of the tensions around children and young people's autonomous organisation in everyday life. Taking 'autonomous' to mean self-governing and independent, I look at how organisation and communication initiated by children and young people can be either facilitated or blocked by adults, sometimes being seen as 'anti-social behaviour'. Attitudes that exclude children and young people from decision making, and policies that restrict the safe spaces where they can meet and communicate with each other, are contrasted with ways in which adults can encourage and support children's own ideas and initiatives, and promote more open communication.

Activities that are initiated by adults to engage children in formal decision-making processes, such as school councils and youth forums, can undoubtedly be led and controlled by children to a greater or lesser extent. However, here the focus is on situations where children and young people themselves reflect on their everyday lives and initiate their own organisation. Examples abound that show how young people, when given the chance, can provide positive solutions, often in the face of dismissive and negative attitudes towards them that can prevail in local communities.

The chapter first gives a background to the participatory challenge in the UK and internationally and then seeks to show, using examples from the UK and the developing world, what needs to be done to promote children and young people's autonomous organisation:

- Recognise the often negative social attitudes towards young people.
- Appreciate the need for safe spaces where young people can meet, and listen to what they say.
- Interact with young people in their own domains.
- Understand the power relationships in different social and cultural settings, and the local and national policies that affect young people.
- Understand the positives and negatives of autonomy, and monitor the impact of initiatives on different children's lives.
- Be prepared to negotiate and support children and young people's autonomy.

The challenge of participation

Many of the examples used in this chapter come from work in England and Wales, where children and young people's participation has become part of the rhetoric of many government policies under New Labour. Initiatives such as New Deal for Communities, Neighbourhood Renewal, Children's Funds and Children's Trusts have participation as integral, as does the Every Child Matters policy framework. The Children's Commissioner for England, appointed in 2005 following similar appointments in Wales, Northern Ireland and Scotland, is also intended to give children a voice in national policy.

There is, however, a wide variety of ways in which people and organisations can interpret children and young people's participation and child rights. The working context of different attitudes and organisational starting points has to be taken into account when interventions are considered. (There is no point in asking people, either adults or children, about their perspectives if nobody is really listening and willing to act on their views.) There are also wide-ranging perspectives among different community members, young and old, and no single solution fits all. Participation in community development, and supporting children and young people's participation in community solutions, requires partnership, dedication and inspiration.

In the wider world, participation has been very much at the forefront of international development assistance since the late 1990s, with emphasis moving from a needs-based to a rights-based approach to development. Many international non-governmental organisations (NGOs) and donors have advocated this approach to local partners. In research on child rights and evaluation carried out in Nepal and South Africa (Johnson et al., 2001a), a survey of organisations was conducted to explore how children were involved in different programmes and what pressure was placed on local organisations by international NGOs and donors to follow a rights-based approach incorporating a participatory ethos. There was again a wide variation in how the concept of children's participation was implemented, ranging from 'ticking the boxes' to detailed and innovative work that really responded to children's agendas. While there has been a strong movement in children's rights among many organisations working specifically with children as their target group, many organisations working to facilitate broader community development have not fully taken on board more participatory work with children. Often children's clubs and education programmes are seen as being relevant to children, whereas income generation, forestry and water programmes, for example, are not, despite the evidence that exists showing that children spend much of their time collecting water and fuel in rural areas and are often critically important to the household economy. It is therefore important to a rights-based approach to establish how a broader range of projects, services and policies respond to or determine their direction from the expressed needs of children. Central to this is respecting children and young people as important and active members of the community, as well as developing indicators that are child-sensitive and developed with children, to help to establish how children's lives are affected by change (Chawla and Johnson, 2004).

Negative social attitudes towards young people

Recognising that children and young people are often faced with negative social attitudes is critical to finding ways to improve their lives, including supporting their autonomy. Percy-Smith (1998) identifies negative social attitudes as a key barrier to why young people remain largely excluded from local democratic processes.

The following examples, taken from action research with Development Focus in three neighbourhood renewal areas in Brighton and Hove, carried out using an approach called Community Assessment and Action (CAA),[1] show that many adults from communities in disadvantaged areas of the UK are worried by young people even gathering on the streets or in outdoor spaces to meet up with each other: young people are seen as *problems* in their communities. Many adults over 30 associate young people with anti-social behaviour and increased fear of crime. The young people 'labelled' as problems are often 16- to 25-year-olds, but may include much younger children. Common complaints include young people 'hanging around' on the streets, as well as more specific accusations of graffiti and riding motorbikes. However, in many of these same communities, it has been children and young people who have come up with solutions: youth clubs and cafés, skate parks, counselling support and access to different sports and computer facilities.

In Hollingdean, the key issues prioritised by residents were those relating to children and young people.[2] Older residents frequently identified problems with regard to younger people, yet rarely identified solutions; however, many younger people spoke of changes that they would like to see and solutions to issues raised by others in the community. At the same time, young people felt that they were victimised and not listened to. Some of the concerns expressed by adults aged 25 and over, and particularly strongly expressed by residents aged 60 and over, related to vandalism, drugs and alcohol, and pavements being used for cycling and skateboards. Both young people and adults referred to a 'generation gap' in understanding, which had to be solved by talking and listening to each other rather than making assumptions. Solutions from young people included recreational facilities and making the community centre more welcoming for young people.

In Queens Park and Craven Vale, concerns were also expressed about the lack of facilities for young people and their poor relationship to the police.[3] Residents directly related the lack of facilities for teenagers with the high level anti-social behaviour in the area. Adults blamed young people for many of the problems in the area, while young people said that they were themselves victims of crime, that more facilities were needed as young people get bored and that youth workers can help to improve their relationships with the police. There was also an acknowledgement that it is not just young people who produce 'anti-social' behaviour, and that drug dealing and drunken behaviour by adults are a major cause for concern (Brighton and Hove City Council, 2003).

In Brunswick and Regency, young people felt as insecure on the streets as any other groups. They wanted more youth centres with longer opening hours and more affordable activities, especially in the winter so that they could meet friends in a safe environment.[4]

Safe spaces for young people and listening to young people

There needs to be more appreciation that what children and young people really want is a safe space where they can meet and socialise, as Roger Hart notes (this volume). Since the 1970s and 1980s, advocates have campaigned for *physical* space for young people in cities, and also recognised that children and young people need *social* space, so that they can be part of city life (Ward, 1978, 1990). Examples of how children can participate in helping to understand and plan interventions in cities include the 'Growing up in Cities' project (Chawla and Johnson, 2004). Hart (1997, p 193) emphasises the importance of 'fostering a sense of place and an affection for the local environment and community in childhood'.

In Langley Green in Crawley[5] a high priority among young people was 'a place to chill' with no imposed agenda, a place 'to hang out without having to learn anything'. They also suggested that young people could help to manage such a space. Young people thought that there was more in the area for younger children, and pointed to a lack of facilities for teenagers and young adults. Different ethnic groups had different perspectives: for example, some white young men felt that provision was targeted towards Asian youth and that new youth provision should cater for them as well (Crawley Primary Care Trust, 2004).

'Children's autonomous activities and use of space often cause anxiety and alarm in senior generations. Their worries may reflect protective concern about children's welfare, but can also result from feelings that adult values, comfort and safety are under threat' (Hill and Tisdall, 1997, p 110). Hill and Tisdall suggest that this is accentuated when young people have subcultures that contrast with the prevailing norms. They discuss the different meanings and functions of play, and how children's own cultures enable them to pursue autonomous interests that disregard adults, but that children's use of their environment is influenced by physical factors and distance from family and friends, but also by 'their perceptions, preferences and fears, and negotiations with parents, peers and significant others' (1997, p 107). They point out that teenage activities developed among peers can meet with parental disapproval, but also that peer support and communication play a vital role in learning about the world and forming a social and personal identity.

Interacting with children in their own domains

White and Choudhury (2007) challenge practitioners to go out of their offices to where poor children are, in order to find ways to support them in their struggles, build on their resources and foster strategic alliances. They recognise the influence of adults in helping to shape the agency of children and advocate mobilisation rather than some of the models of participation that mean that children are on display at international events and meetings. As O'Kane states (2006, p 164), 'we need to maintain and strategically work towards our vision where children are recognised as competent and valued actors in decision-making processes on all issues concerning them'.

In the CAA approach, Development Focus trained teams of residents and workers as researchers to work in schools and local groups, and on the streets. To inform the streetwork, an exercise is carried out to create an 'access map' where local residents are asked to identify where people gather or 'hang out' so that the team can go and speak to them. For example, in Crawley[6] a local team of researchers found that the best time to talk to young people in the age group 16-24 was around the shops in the evenings, and in Croydon[7] young people of this age were spoken to at colleges, bus and tram stops, outside the local bowling alley and fast-food outlets. In the latter research the youth service also offered to arrange meetings with a local youth group, although it was also important to access young people who were not already involved in organised groups and activities. In work carried out in neighbourhood renewal areas the local detached youth workers are often key informants in research with marginalised young people.[8]

Different tools and techniques can be used to engage with young people in a way that is fun and at the same time rigorous. In much of the research presented in this chapter, participatory appraisal visuals are used as a way of engaging with children and young people on the streets and in small group work, for example using diagramming, mapping, ranking and drawing to explore their issues. Another technique is to use role play to understand the lives of young people. For example, when working with an organisation in Bosnia and Herzegovina[9] this approach helped to explore how they had come into conflict with different law-making and enforcement agencies (Johnson and Nurick, 2006).

Local power relationships and local and national policies

While there is a clear case for listening to children and young people's own solutions and understanding their everyday lives and realities, there is also a need for more analysis of power in decision making and to explore the perceptions of different adults in communities towards young people, in different cultural and socioeconomic contexts. Boyden (1996) shows how much there is to be learned about what it means to be a child in different social contexts and the impact of everyday attitudes and practices in different cultures and societies. She points to the need to 'understand the status and circumstances of children in different cultures and especially to highlight the problems and needs of those children who, because of their social status, are marginalised socially, economically and politically by national society' (1996, pp 21-2). Morrow (2006) challenges adults not just to listen, but also to act on what they hear. She reinforces the view that participation needs to be understood within particular contexts, taking into account the different characteristics of children in terms of gender, social class, dis/ability, ethnicity, religion and previous experiences of participation. Barriers to their meaningful participation need to be fully recognised in order to have more effective engagement of the younger generation.

Involving local reference groups[10] formed of service providers and policy makers can be an important aspect of research processes to encourage commitment in response to the views of people in the community. Without involvement of those people who hold the power in relation to resource allocation and service provision in the community, the views of residents including young people can be lost. The following examples demonstrate how service providers have been able to respond to young people's suggestions for improving their communities.

In Bewbush and Langley Green in Crawley, members of local reference groups of service providers agreed that the issues raised by young people were important and should be acted upon. In Bewbush, a new voluntary organisation was set up to follow up on action suggested by residents and young people. Taking forward solutions suggested by young people in the community depends on local service providers taking their views seriously with accountability for taking action and responding to consultative processes. An important aspect of this is to assess whether projects and services are informed by the expressed needs of children, through monitoring and evaluation processes that include indicators that are child-sensitive and developed with children and young people (Johnson, in press). It is only in this way that evaluation shows how projects and services are changing children and young people's lives.

Waiton (2001, p 9) recognises the 'steady erosion of their [young people's] rights to a safe environment beyond the home ... children are not criminals for whom "no-go areas are appropriate"'. There needs to be more analysis of national and local policies that affect children and young people's lives in terms of their freedom of movement and their right to associate freely, and also how these policies are being applied on the ground. As Mayall (1996, pp 161-3) says, 'In practice, children do not live lives separate to those of adults', but the domains of school and home and 'many of the times and spaces between are constructed by adults' and children often lack the opportunity to participate in them.

Although participation has moved further up the political agenda, there are still policies that run counter to this, as demonstrated in an evaluation of children's services in Croydon.[11] Some young people felt that they were not allowed to be out on the street because of a few young people who might behave badly. For example, there was an increasing number of Anti-Social Behaviour Orders (ASBOs) whereby behaviour was criminalised that was not previously seen as criminal, and Dispersal Orders whereby young people were not allowed to gather in certain places at particular times. In effect, outdoor spaces where young people might previously have been able to socialise had been restricted. Staff and volunteers working on a community bus travelling to disadvantaged areas to provide a mobile youth centre said that on some occasions they had not been able to work in areas where there were Dispersal Orders (Johnson, 2003; Johnson and Nurick, 2007).

When children in the Croydon evaluation were asked about problems in their lives, many issues arose relating to feeling safe in and outside the home. A few children expressed fear of gangs of young people on the street and aggression from other children including siblings, but some also talked about their fear of adults and the fear they felt inside their homes. Children, especially in schools that provided counselling services and drop-ins, talked about the help that they needed in the form of opportunities to talk to others about their lives. Teachers in schools where the research was carried out addressed many of these issues in Personal and Social Education (PSE) lessons. So while there is much media attention given to aggression and anti-social behaviour by young people, and many adults expressing fear of young people, there is a need to balance this with a fuller understanding of children and young people's realities. Many of them are just as worried about anti-social behaviour as anyone else. To them it hardly seems fair to put blanket restrictions on their use of outside space and restrict their opportunities to socialise with each other, because of a relatively few troublemakers (Johnson and Nurick, 2007).

Natalie Bolzan's (2005) research in Australia suggests that the adult community's views of young people are characterised by, on the one hand, very negative perceptions that appear to have their roots in the media discourse of young people as problematic, and on the other hand, strongly positive perceptions that are largely based on personal experience.

The positives and negatives of autonomy and monitoring impact

With a culture of youth gangs in the UK and in other countries around the world there is an increasingly vocal concern, highlighted by media attention, about the negative effect of young people's autonomous organisation. There are, however, many situations where, especially in times of conflict and oppression, children and young people have been at the forefront of positive political lobbying and reform. In South Africa, children have been part of the struggle against apartheid for many years. Feinstein et al. (in press), using examples from Bosnia, Guatemala, Nepal and Uganda show how child-led organisations and children's capacities can be strengthened to enhance children's role as agents of peace. O'Kane (2006) points to the achievements of many children's organisations in South and Central Asia where young people have been enabled to form their own associations or organisations so that they can work collectively on issues that affect them. Judith Ennew has consistently talked of the resourcefulness of children in street and working situations in forming their own support groups and having their own coping strategies to help each other in adverse situations (Ennew 1994).

Research for the Save the Children Alliance submission to the United Nations on violence demonstrates the positive and negative aspects of children's autonomous organisation (Johnson and Nurick, 2006).[12] The findings showed that children on the margins of society really wanted to link with each other and talk to others in similar situations; children and young people who had been in conflict with the law wanted space and time to communicate with each other. Young men in Bosnia-Herzegovina identified the benefits of linking with others to try to get out of trouble, while acknowledging that peer pressure may have initially led them into the same difficult situations. In Tajikistan, street children got together in groups to support and protect each other, but in the same groups some children experienced sexual abuse and fear of other children. In Honduras, gangs were involved in drug trafficking, but much of the criminal behaviour in these gangs was driven by drug addiction (Johnson and Nurick, 2006).

Looking at development processes in general, people tend to focus on education and children's clubs as projects relevant to children, but in fact many interventions across different sectors impact on children's lives. When children in Nepal[13] looked at the Himalayan Community Development Forum's (HICODEF's) community development programme overall they preferred the forestry and water project.

Their involvement in these projects was minimal – they participated in the labour but not in the planning, so that, for example, a tap put into the school was too high for the children to reach. However, what these projects did was to give children more time, enabling them to go to school and to play (Johnson et al., 2001b, p 2). Children became very animated when showing researchers the different types of games that they now had time to play. Income generation projects in Nepal have also sometimes meant that children are involved, for example, in looking after goats, and therefore have less time to go to school and play (Johnson et al., 2001a, p 1). In South Africa, examples of where interventions have inadvertently affected children's time, space and social relations in the community include tourism projects and land reform policies that change children's roles and social networks (Ewing et al., 2001). We have to gain a better understanding of how policies and projects affect the everyday lives of children, especially in terms of time, space and social networks, which in turn have an impact on their degree of autonomy in their everyday lives.

Negotiating and supporting autonomy

The trust and relationships that develop between different parties – between adults and authorities, between different groups of adults, between adults and children, within groups of children – will vary in different situations and therefore the way in which children and young people's autonomy is negotiated and accepted will differ depending on context. Punch (2004) refers to negotiated autonomy, and discusses how the ways in which children respond to adult control over their lives varies with context.

In research on children's participation in evaluation carried out with the HICODEF in rural Nawalparassi in Nepal, boys and girls expressed their views on how they felt within their roles in the household and in their community (Johnson et al., 2001b, p 2). Visual methods of evaluation were then developed with children to evaluate the community development programme facilitated by HICODEF. Before this project the staff of HICODEF felt that children's groups that they had helped to establish were the only ways in which children and young people could really participate in the programme. Indeed, when children's groups were evaluated, both boys and girls discussed how they experienced an increased sense of confidence. How well the children's groups worked depended mainly on whether they had effective child leaders, so despite being initiated and facilitated by HICODEF staff, their success depended on whether children decided to take leadership roles. Where the groups were successful they also engendered greater respect between ethnic groups and between girls and boys. There was, however, a varied response from adults about how they accepted such changing roles for children in their cultural context – some feeling that children should continue in their more traditional roles and some seeing the benefits of change.

In the HICODEF community development programmes in Nepal (above), staff acted as facilitators. Where previously they may not have included children in the planning of broader development programmes, for them the relevance of children's participation across the programme was highlighted through gaining more insight on the impact of programmes on the lives of children. The facilitators worked with a range of different children, both in children's clubs, and with children in different community settings. Sharing participatory skills gained through this type of process needs to be supported and funded. In South Africa, where there is a strong historical context of children's involvement in rights in the context of apartheid, many staff from a range of organisations in the voluntary and statutory sectors expressed a need for support in implementing rights-based approaches on the ground through more training in participatory methodologies (Johnson et al., 2001a, p 1).

In an evaluation of a scheme run by Save the Children UK to support peer-led projects around the UK,[14] some of the young people felt that their ideas were too hard to get off the ground, however mentors took on a key role in supporting and encouraging young people to plan and implement their projects. When some young people identified that they were under stress in trying to cope with running their project, the mentors could work out the type of additional support they needed to run and manage the group. This type of mentoring support for young people implementing their own ideas can be invaluable and many of the projects evaluated were shown to have a positive influence on the young people themselves, their peers and, to varying extents, broader policies and services. Mentoring can encourage and support children to negotiate more autonomy to take their ideas forward, however it does require a commitment of time and resources (Johnson and Nurick, 2001).

With regard to research in disadvantaged communities in the UK, I have already raised in this chapter the solutions put forward by children and young people in terms of adults needing to listen and take their views seriously and finding different ways for young people and adults to start communicating with each other (see sections on 'Negative social attitudes towards young people' and 'Safe spaces for young people and listening to young people' in this chapter). Discussing children in care, Thomas (2002, p 191) points to how formal decision-making processes 'lack ... connection with the everyday texture of children's lives'. He suggests that processes need to be flexible and responsive to the ways in which different children communicate and the ways in which they resolve problems with adults and in families, recognising that the degree of autonomy of a child in having a say depends on many factors including the values and skills of adults in the family. These concepts can be applied across the spectrum of different children and young people in society, while still recognising their individual differences.

To provide effective support for children and young people's autonomous organisation, several key questions need to be addressed:

- How do children and young people perceive their role in their local communities, and how does this relate to adult perceptions?
- Does support for children and young people's autonomy take full account of the cultural context – young people's own subcultures, local power dynamics with adults and other children in the family and the community?
- Are children and young people central to decision making, or merely consulted for policy purposes?
- Which children and young people are being involved?
- Do monitoring and evaluation use child-sensitive indicators, and monitor the impact of initiatives on different children's lives?

Conclusions

A key message from this chapter is that researchers and practitioners need to continue to listen to children's own solutions and understand their realities in different environmental, cultural and political contexts. This involves interacting with children in their own domains, recognising power differentials in everyday life and analysing power and relationships within and between different people in communities – between different groups of adults, between adults and children and between children. This will also allow us to understand how children and young people can be supported to make their ideas a reality and to negotiate a greater level of autonomy. This also requires institutional or organisational analysis and an appreciation of how attitudes of staff and spaces for participation can change within organisations and communities. Barriers to communication and trust have to be identified and solutions to overcoming them explored.

The key message from the ground is that children and young people value time and space to socialise together, and also that they have ideas for interventions in their local communities that can give them safe spaces to communicate with each other. Children and young people's scope for self-initiated or autonomous activities is limited by the effective closing down to them of spaces outside and on the streets. If a rights-based approach is being advocated, then perhaps more attention should be paid to Article 15 of the United Nations Convention on the Rights of the Child (UNCRC), which refers to children having the right to meet with others and to join or set up associations, unless the fact of doing so violates the rights of others.

In order to review the kind of support needed to work in more positive participatory ways with children and young people, adult and children's perspectives, relationships and forms of communication, and their ideas on innovation and autonomy need to be understood, while recognising that there can be positive and negative outcomes for the different children involved. For example, children's autonomous organisation can be both the reason why children and young people get into crime, but also part of the solution, highlighting the importance of understanding change and context in children's lives. Thus, changes for the different children and young people need to be monitored throughout any process of intervention, rather than assuming greater children and young people's autonomy to be necessarily beneficial to all children involved.

Providing a focal point or person that children can turn to if they want to or need to, for example having mentors – who can be adults or other children and young people – can be one form of support. This, however, requires adequate capacity in child rights and participatory approaches, physical and organisational space, and resources. Encouraging more dialogue and communication between adults and children is a solution suggested by young people, as well as having more spaces and places for them to meet and communicate with each other. Organisations need to support dialogue so that differences can be worked through and solutions explored and prioritised by different people in communities including children and young people. The positive stories of change need to dominate the media and academic airways to counteract the negative press given to children and young people in society.

Notes

[1] The methodology is rooted in action research and teams of residents and workers are trained using the CAA approach to develop local needs assessments,

action plans and evaluations. It employs many visual participatory appraisal approaches and methods.

[2] In Hollingdean, three hundred people in the community were interviewed using the CAA, representing over 10% of the population (Brighton and Hove City Council, 2000).

[3] In Queens Park and Craven Vale, 391 adults and children were interviewed, representing over 10% of the population (Brighton and Hove City Council, 2003).

[4] In the Brunswick and Regency area, 808 residents were consulted (SEA, 2004)

[5] One hundred and twenty-seven young people, aged 16-24, were asked about their issues and solutions relating to health.

[6] In the South of England during research for the Primary Care Trust.

[7] Also in the South of England during research for the Extended Schools Programme.

[8] For example in Queens Park and Craven Vale in Brighton and Hove.

[9] An organisation, Chukka, supported by Save the Children UK that supports young boys and young men to rehabilitate and rebuild their lives after they have been in conflict with the law.

[10] In the CAA process it is important to engage with different stakeholders and often a local 'reference group' of service providers and policy makers is formed or an existing forum invited to be involved throughout the period of the research.

[11] Different barriers to achieving positive impact on children and young people's lives were explored as part of the evaluation of the Croydon Children's Fund for Croydon Voluntary Action (Johnson, 2003).

[12] Development Focus Trust worked with Save the Children country programmes in Bosnia-Herzegovina, Ethiopia, Honduras and Uganda, also drawing on examples from other Save the Children country projects, and the study was commissioned by Save the Children UK (Johnson and Nurick, 2006).

[13] Research funded by the Department for International Development (DFID) carried out by Development Focus with partners in Nepal and South Africa. Research in Nepal was carried out with the Himalayan Community Development Forum (HICODEF).

[14] This evaluation of the Saying Power Scheme carried out by Development Focus for Save the Children UK involved research with young people running projects and their peers to develop indicators to determine impact. Many of the projects run as support groups, drop-ins and peer education and the issues covered are identified by the young award holders (16-20 years) who apply for funding and include working with children who are Travellers, carers, disabled, self-harming, young single parents, asylum seekers, facing drug addiction, lesbian, bisexual, gay and transsexuals (LBGT).

References

Bolzan, N. (2005) '"To know them is to love them", but instead fear and loathing: community perceptions of young people', in J. Mason and T. Fattore (eds) *Children Taken Seriously in Theory, Policy and Practice*, London: Jessica Kingsley Publishers.

Boyden, J. (1996) 'Social and cultural meanings of childhood', *Development*, 39(1), pp 18-22.

Brighton and Hove City Council (2000) *Hollingdean: Mapping for the Future*, Brighton: Brighton and Hove City Council with Development Focus, Health Promotion East Sussex, Brighton and Hove, Sustain.

Brighton and Hove City Council (2003) *Queens Park and Craven Vale Neighbourhood Action Plan 2003-2006*, Brighton: Development Focus and Brighton and Hove City Council.

Chawla, L. and Johnson, V. (2004) 'Not for children only: lessons learnt from young people's participation', *PLA Notes*, p 50.

Crawley Primary Care Trust (2004) *H.I.P. Langley Green – Health Improvement Project: A Report of Information and Ideas from Local People on how to Improve their Health*, Crawley: Crawley Primary Care Trust and Development Focus Trust with West Sussex Sure Start and Early Years and Childcare Services and West Sussex Voluntary Organisation Liaison Group.

Ennew, J. (1994) *Street and Working Children: A Guide to Planning*, SCF Development Manual No 4, London: Save the Children.

Ewing, D., Apelgren, E. and Mathe, M. (2001) 'A land reform case study in Cremin, Kwazulu Natal, South Africa', in V. Johnson, E. Ivan-Smith and R. Nurick (eds) *Rights through Evaluation: Putting Child Rights into Practice in South Africa and Nepal*, London: Development Focus (Study also available from Immediate Development Communications, Durban, South Africa).

Feinstein, C., Giertsen, A. and O'Kane, C. (forthcoming) 'Children's participation in armed conflict, post conflict and peace building', in B. Percy-Smith and N. Thomas (eds) *A Handbook of Children's Participation*, London: Routledge.

Hart, R. (1997) *Children's Participation: Involving Young Citizens in Community Development and Environmental Care*, London and New York: Earthscan Publications/UNICEF.

Hill, M. and Tisdall, K. (1997) *Children and Society*, London and New York: Longman.

Johnson, V. (2003) *The Croydon Children's Fund: First Year Evaluation Report*, Croydon: Croydon Voluntary Action.

Johnson, V. (forthcoming) 'Rights through evaluation and understanding children's realities', in B. Percy-Smith and N. Thomas (eds) *A Handbook of Children's Participation*, London: Routledge.

Johnson, V. and Nurick, R. (2001) *Young Voices Heard: Reflection and Review of the Saying Power Awards*, Birmingham: Save the Children UK.

Johnson, V. and Nurick, R. (2006) *Gaining Respect: The Voices of Children in Conflict with the Law*, London: Save the Children UK.

Johnson, V. and Nurick, R. (2007) *The Legacy: The Croydon Children's Fund*, Croydon: Croydon Voluntary Action.

Johnson, V., Ivan-Smith, E. and Nurick, R. (2001a) *Rights through Evaluation: Putting Child Rights into Practice in South Africa and Nepal*, Brighton: Development Focus.

Johnson, V., Sapkota, P., Sthapit, S., Ghimire, K.P. and Mahato, M. (2001b) 'Rights through evaluation: Nepal case study', in V. Johnson, E. Ivan-Smith and R. Nurick (eds) *Rights through Evaluation: Putting Child Rights into Practice in South Africa and Nepal*, Brighton: Development Focus (also available from HICODEF, Nawalparassi and ActionAid Nepal, Kathmandu).

Mayall, B. (1996) *Children, Health and the Social Order*, Buckingham: Open University Press.

Morrow, V. (2006) 'Social capital: a flawed concept', in Van Beers, H., Invernizzi, A. and Milne, B. (eds) *Beyond Article 12: Essential Readings in Children's Participation*, Bangkok: Black on White Publications: Knowing Children.

O'Kane, C. (2006) 'Key reflections and learnings from children's participation and children's organisations in South and Central Asia: moving towards partnerships with adults', in H. Van Beers, A. Invernizzi and B. Milne (eds) *Beyond Article 12: Essential Readings in Children's Participation*, Bangkok: Black on White Publications: Knowing Children.

Percy-Smith, B. (1998) 'Children's participation in local decision-making: the challenge for local governance', in V. Johnson, E. Ivan-Smith, G. Gordon, P. Pridmore and P. Scott (eds) *Stepping Forward: Children and Young People's Participation in the Development Process*, London: IT Publications, pp 225-9.

Punch, S. (2004) 'Negotiating autonomy: children's use of time and space in rural Bolivia', in V. Lewis, M. Kellett, C. Robinson, S. Fraser, and S. Ding (eds) *The Reality of Research with Children and Young People*, London: Sage Publications, pp 94-119.

SEA (Share, Engage, Act) (2004) *Brunswick and Regency Neighbourhood Action Plan 2004-2006*, Brighton: Development Focus and Brighton and Hove City Council.

Thomas, N. (2002) *Children, Family and the State: Decision-Making and Child Participation*, Bristol: The Policy Press.

Waiton, S. (2001) *Scared of the Kids*, Sheffield: Sheffield Hallam University.

Ward, C. (1978, 1990) *The Child in the City*, London: Bedford Square Press.

White, S.C. and Choudhury, S.A. (2007) 'The Politics of child participation in international development: the dilemma of agency', *European Journal of Development Research*, 19(4), pp 529-50.

THREE

The children of Loxicha: participation beyond the UNCRC rhetoric?

Anne-Marie Smith

Introduction

I met the displaced 'children of Loxicha' while carrying out my doctoral fieldwork in Oaxaca City, Mexico, between 2001 and 2002. In Oaxaca City they were simply referred to (by journalists, residents and local non-governmental organisations [NGOs]) as 'los Loxicha'. Their real home is San Agustín Loxicha, located in the southern region of the state of Oaxaca, as detailed below, but this chapter is based on their time living in a protest camp and a shelter in the city of Oaxaca.

At the time of this research the group was made up of approximately 15 children ranging from age three to fifteen who had been living in the protest camp in the city's central square for four and a half years, where their day-to-day lives included a participatory role in their community's political protest.

Via an exploration of the elements surrounding their day-to-day lives, and the ways in which they are portrayed and viewed by the local media and residents, this chapter seeks to generate debate about how we have come to 'box' participation into very clear spaces – spaces that have largely been devised by adults. In particular, the discussion here explores the idea of child participation in relation to its political possibilities, raising such questions as: Who sets the child participation agenda? Which 'types' or degrees of child participation are pleasing to adults (and therefore applauded and promoted) and which are disregarded either for their ambiguity or because they represent a threat to the status quo?

The sociopolitical context in Oaxaca from the late 1990s to 2002 provides a volatile backdrop to the lives of the Loxicha children, and is described in the next section.

Oaxaca: political violence and displacement

> The primary targets of [the] strategies of militarization are indigenous communities in Chiapas and Oaxaca. The fundamental result is ... the self-censorship and fear that has become part of people's lives. And then there are the hard-core human rights abuses including assassinations, kidnappings, torture, rape, and illegal detentions. (Stephen, 2003, p 391)

The region of Oaxaca that is subject to the militarisation described by Stephen above is in the mountainous region between the Sierra Madre del Sur and the Pacific Coast (see Figure 3.1), and includes the Loxicha children's rural home, the community of San Agustín Loxicha. Poverty and marginalisation have driven many families to migrate from rural areas to the urban centre, Oaxaca City, where many adults and children work in the informal sector as street or market vendors.

Oaxaca is home to 25% of all Mexicans living in extreme poverty (INEGI, 2001). The conditions of poverty and social exclusion experienced by the majority of the rural and indigenous population in the state of Oaxaca are, according to the World Bank, at the core of the armed conflicts and violence in the region (World Bank, 2003, p 3). According to Amnesty International, Oaxaca, together with Guerrero and Chiapas, has the most rights violations of any Mexican state. While former President, Vicente Fox, pledged to 'end the impunity that characterized much of the previous 70-year rule of the PRI' and to 'fully uphold human rights and the rule of law' (Amnesty International,

Figure 3.1: Map of Mexico showing Oaxaca

2002, p 5), disappearances and human rights violations are not yet a thing of the past in Mexico.

After a first appearance in the 1970s, the guerrilla movement EPR (Ejército Popular Revolucionario – Popular Revolutionary Army) re-emerged in 1996 in Oaxaca where they carried out several coordinated armed attacks against the Mexican Army and public security forces in those states as well as in Tabasco and Mexico City (see Stephen, 2003).

Shortly after the EPR's first attack in Oaxaca, 'police and military units swept through the area of Loxicha, arresting groups of men and piling them into pickup trucks' (Lawyers Committee for Human Rights and Miguel Agustín ProJuárez Human Rights Centre, 2001, p 5). According to a group of Mexican NGOs and a defence lawyer handling the Oaxaca cases, 'officials arbitrarily detained 127 people – torturing 100 of them – and carried out 32 illegal searches and five executions' (Human Rights Watch, 1999, p 79).

Following the EPR uprisings and the consequent arrests, on 10 July 1997 the women and children of Loxicha set up camp in the central Zócalo (city square) in front of the municipal government buildings in Oaxaca City where they lived, as displaced people, for four and a half years until December 2001 (see Plate 3.1).

The women and children and other relatives of the prisoners formally joined to form the Familiares de los Presos Políticos de Loxicha

Plate 3.1: Loxicha children in the Zócalo, Oaxaca City

Source: Author

(Relatives of the Political Prisoners of Loxicha) under the organisational name of the Organización de Pueblos Indígenas Zapotecas (OPIZ – Organisation of Zapotec Indigenous Peoples).

By October 2001, the women in the Zócalo were known as las permanentes (the permanent ones), because their husbands or male relatives made up the 20 remaining prisoners still held despite the federal amnesty earlier that year.[1] The camp in the Zócalo became the focal point of the Loxicha struggle, and was also their home, as described by an OPIZ spokesperson:

> The camp became our home, and the arrival place for each compañera looking for a relative: husband, son, father, brother. This camp became a space for the collective effort of civil society forces committed to the difficult task of demanding justice. (Sumano, 2001, p 7A)

On Christmas Eve 2001, the women and children moved out of the Zócalo and into a shelter, following an agreement with the municipal government. After four and a half years of sleeping on the ground and living in an exposed public space, they now had warm beds, running water, private showers and toilets, and a safe area in which the children could play. On the day of the move, however, some of the children were a bit forlorn, asking: 'What are we going to do there? Here there is always a lot to do'. As Ayala Ortíz, a representative from the Oaxaca branch of the LIMEDDH (*Liga Mexicana para los Derechos Humanos* – Mexican League for Human Rights) put it, 'Certainly there are mixed emotions, because this has been home for most of these children who were practically born here and grew up here and know no other home than this one' (Sumano, 2001).

Indeed, the appearance of being 'at home' in their public home belied the day-to-day hardships that the children and their mothers had to endure. However, it also revealed the complex and multifaceted nature of their childhoods. As discussed later in the chapter this complexity was overlooked in local press articles of 'los Loxicha', which portrayed the children as victims of a political situation and always as unhappy. This reflects the predominance of fixed notions of childhood, of assumptions as to what children ought to be doing, and of the boundaries perceived to delineate children's activities.

Boundaries of childhood and parameters of participation

> 'I want to be 18, to be an adult once and for all.' (Isidro, 10 years old)

This generational and linear perspective on childhood, expressed in Isidro's wish to get through the stages of childhood, echoes the predominance of views that consider children as one thing or another, as oppositional dichotomies (Prout, 2005). Children are thus viewed as dependent or independent, innocent or deviant, working or at play, 'little children' or 'little grown-ups' and so on.

In a similar way, the United Nations Convention on the Rights of the Child (UNCRC) frames childhood as one predetermined state, one that is 'other' to the adult phase of life, and one that develops in a linear fashion: a child is a person under the age of 18 (Article 1, UNCRC) and on the way to being an adult. Articles 12 to 15 of the UNCRC (pertaining to the child's right to express their views, freedom of expression, association, thought and peaceful assembly) perhaps did not envisage children's participation in political activity. If the rhetoric about children as active citizens and participants in society is to have any real meaning, it must incorporate children's informal and often non-definable roles within community struggles such as that of the Loxicha people. This involves a necessary move away from viewing children as 'mini-adults' in groups that are carbon copies of adult structures, set up to include an 'executive board', a 'chairperson', a 'treasurer' and so on, such as school councils or 'parliaments' that mirror adult structures rather than begin from a terminology or organisation established by the children themselves. The key issue here is power, defined by John (2003) as the 'fourth P' (after the three P's that make up the UNCRC: protection, provision and participation). Forums such as children's parliaments adopt political structures and hierarchies and provide spaces for young people to debate and voice their views and opinions on local, national and international issues that concern them. However, as long as boundaries are in place, and as long as those working alongside young people hold on to a narrow concept of childhood, then the power of children's participation is inherently limited.

In a discussion about children's rights and the culture of childhood, John (1995, p 106) asks whether the UNCRC 'acknowledge[s] the power of children other than in adult-bestowed terms?'. These 'adult-bestowed' terms define the boundaries of children's participation. While there are many examples of children and young people's participation in decision making, from community projects (Hart, 1992) to municipal budgets (Guerra, 2002), examples and acknowledgement of children's active political participation has received less attention. This may be due to the perceived threat to society's 'norm' of political processes, or because this is simply not taken seriously. A few notable exceptions are, for example, Peterson and Read's (2002) study of children and their portrayal in Central American wars, and Corona and Pérez Zavala's (2000) study of children's political participation in Tepoztlán, Mexico. Corona and Pérez Zavala crucially point out the need for a critical review of the discourse of children's participation, which, while opening valid space for children to express views and opinions, risks overlooking 'real' experiences of child participation in, for example, popular resistance movements.

Coles (1986) was one of the first researchers to argue for the recognition of children's engagement in and understanding of political processes. The fact that children do not have a vote, he argued, does not mean that they are secluded from political life and neither are they shielded against the fall-out from political processes. The children of Loxicha, as beings under the age of 18 in Mexico, do not have a vote; their status as indigenous, displaced and poor children adds to their marginalised position in Oaxacan society. Nobody would contest that they are exercising their right, as per Article 15 of the UNCRC, to 'the freedom of association'; however, while the adults who walk alongside them in political protest marches continue to receive violent threats and harassment by police (even though they too hold the rights to assemble and associate freely), the children are invisible and non-threatening participants in the same event. This is not in any way to suggest that the children ought to be harassed by police, but rather to highlight their invisibility in this political struggle.

Their participation is thus not only subsumed in the adults' activities, but fails to fit into an acceptable form of 'children's participation'. Although politics and popular resistance have largely defined their childhood, the children's presence within the Loxicha struggle is viewed as something to be pitied. A year's participant observation and the development of close relationships with the Loxicha children and their families reveal a portrait that contrasts considerably with such a view: the combined elements of resilience, agency, happiness, freedom and flexibility, which characterise the children's lives, present a challenge to prevailing notions of childhood, a challenge that requires close attention if we are truly to take children and what they do seriously.

Political childhoods

> For many the very essence of childhood, at least in contemporary western terms, prohibits political participation such that the 'political child' is seen as the 'unchild,' a counter-stereotypical image of children that does not fit with the way we commonly view childhood. (Stainton-Rogers and Stainton-Rogers, 1992, pp 32-3, cited in Wyness et al., 2004, p 82)

The notion of unnaturalness in the 'political child' cited above echoes Ennew's (2002) definition of street children as existing 'outside childhood', with both ideas reflecting the dominance of fixed views of how, what and where children 'should' be. The traditional perception of childhood as a time of innocence and play does not accommodate the possibility, for example, of a child's participation in war or guerrilla activity, which would be considered a destruction of childhood and an affront to such innocence. The possibility of children's political agency is not – or very rarely – affirmed by NGOs or academics, as observed by Peterson and Read (2002, p 226) in a study of children's participation in war in Central America: 'Most NGOs and scholars issue unqualified condemnations of children's participation in political movements. Their critiques are based – explicitly or implicitly – on an assumption that children can only be victims, never victimizers; only acted upon, never actors'.

This suggests that children can only become 'truly' active in a political sense when they reach the age of 18; this is a perception that underwrites the UNCRC's definition of a child and is evident, for example, in Citizenship curricula in schools, which aim to prepare children for adult life. This reflects a linear view of childhood, tracing a chronological progression from child, to young person and finally to adult where 'each stage brings with it a progressively more developed sense of rights, duties and obligations' (Wyness et al., 2004, p 81). But beyond the arena of voting and participating in social and political debate, what of children whose childhoods are political due to the circumstances into which they are born, such as the children who are the focus of this chapter? This question applies to thousands of children across the world, born into situations of conflict such as those in Afghanistan, Bosnia, Iraq or Rwanda. These children challenge the assumption that children 'do not ordinarily inhabit the civic or political spheres' or that they 'cannot tell us anything interesting about the political world' (Wyness et al., 2004, p 81).

The Loxicha children are perhaps not politically active in the same way as child combatants or guerrillas, but they are nonetheless playing a part in a political struggle. It would appear that children's political participation is officially recognised only when it occurs within the definable contexts referred to earlier. In the absence of such clear agendas and definitions, children's presence within a movement or process evidently loses its impact within the participation debate. The children of Loxicha are not part of a children's group set up to empower them or to promote their participation, they do not attend strategy meetings, do not have 'agendas', do not plan protest actions, have not been given titles or roles by the adults around them (for example, 'group leader' or 'young Member of Parliament') and they have not been politicised in a specified or agency-led format. They have grown up within a politically charged environment, where protests, marches, sit-ins, press photo calls and hunger strikes are all part of their childhoods. I contend that this constitutes a form of political participation, and as such merits recognition.

Small political activists?

Throughout the course of a normal day in the lives of Eyasha[2] (10 years old) or her sister Lupe (five years old), they would go to work, take part in a march or a sit-in outside the government buildings, go to school, barter for a good price with the orange seller, play on the swings, do homework and look after their baby brother. This is the multifaceted, fluid reality that defies definition, perhaps pointing to a need to abandon the quest for a classification or 'boxing' of these experiences of childhood.

'Everyone, big and small, forms part of the struggle' – this observation was made to me by the vice-president of the OPIZ in casual conversation, and was later made to the press (*Noticias de Oaxaca* newspaper, 27 December 2001) in relation to the time spent living in the Zócalo: 'the families, women, boys and girls did not leave the struggle because to give it up meant leaving the prisoners on their own'. The children took part in protest marches organised in Oaxaca City, marched to Mexico City alongside the adults, and even joined a seven-day hunger strike – including children as young as nine and ten. Apart from the obvious health dangers, this also took the children out of school for some time, causing considerable disruption to their progress. The children of Loxicha have thus spent a great part of their young years walking alongside the adults in protest marches, carrying banners and shouting for the freedom of the prisoners (Plate 3.2).

Plate 3.2: Small political activists

Source: Author

When I first saw the children marching, I was struck at their ease in this role of what I initially termed 'small political activists'. Such a definition, however, defines them directly in relation to adult (that is, 'big') political activists; is this the only way we – adults – can make sense of the sight of a child marching in protest against injustice and political violence? If we are to take children seriously, as advocated in the children's rights discourse across the globe, then the parameters that confine children's participation to what adults consider safe or 'child-friendly' environments must be lifted. More importantly, ignoring the kind of participation practised by children like those from Loxicha is to ignore their voices; in effect it is to deny them their right as per Article 12 of the UNCRC ('the right to express those views freely in all matters affecting the child'). They simply want their fathers released from prison, and together with their mothers they are voicing their protest and demands. They are players in a political struggle that by all appearances is an adult one, but one that is obviously the children's too. The image of small children marching with adults in political protest naturally confuses and disturbs the adult onlooker who adheres to clear generational boundaries between what children should or should not be doing (Plate 3.3). The Loxicha children seemed to accept it all as part of their lives rather than any kind of hindrance or hardship, and as such their activism blurs all perceived boundaries.

Plate 3.3: Alma and Alina on a march, Oaxaca City

Source: Author

One morning, while the children were busy drawing some pictures under a tree in a yard, one of the boys started softly chanting:

> *El pueblo unido, jamás sera vencido....*
> [The people united shall never be defeated....][3]

Nobody looked up except me, and a few of the other children joined in, until all of them – still concentrating on their colouring tasks – were singing this old revolutionary chant as if it were a nursery rhyme. This sense of ease in what I perceived as a political childhood permeated their day-to-day existence, and being participants in a political struggle came naturally to these children. That evening I recorded this incident in my fieldwork diary as follows (12 May 2002):

> If these children could have things their own way, they would still be in the green, walking two hours to school through the mountains. They would still be tending their goats and cows. They would still be living in the ignorant bliss of the city. They would have no idea where the governor of their state lives. And if they had it their way, these children would be humming a nursery rhyme while they draw, and not a political freedom song.

But would they? In hindsight, my assumption that they would otherwise be singing 'normal' children's songs is one that is based on a fixed and limited idea of what childhood should look like – and a certain nostalgia for a 'lost childhood'. The politically charged environment surrounding the daily lives of the Loxicha children cannot be ignored, nor can it be lamented as something that is taking away their childhood. Nor should it necessarily be perceived as being entirely novel or shocking: it is simply part of their reality. The political context does not completely define who they are as children – they also spend a great deal of time playing marbles and hide and seek, doing homework and household chores. The following anecdote goes some way to illustrate this multifaceted aspect of the Loxicha children's lives.

While living in the Zócalo, the children had developed a friendly relationship with the guards at the municipal offices. One day I was playing ball with Alma and Alina, two sisters, when Alma stopped playing for a minute, and poked her head through the bars of the locked gate and shouted at the guard sitting on the other side:

> *Libertad! Libertad! Libertad para los presos de Loxicha!*
> [Freedom! Freedom! Freedom for the prisoners of Loxicha!]

She then grinned at me like any seven-year-old and carried on playing ball. This scene reflected the double-sided nature of this girl's childhood: political activist one minute, sweet-faced seven-year-old the next. To me, the outsider, it was extraordinary to observe these two seemingly opposed facets of childhood: this, again, had more to do with my Northern notions of childhood, and reflects society's tendency to view childhood in dichotomous terms, defining children as one thing or the other. For Alma, playing ball and being part of the *lucha* were normal elements of her childhood, and she moved between them seamlessly. The police guard laughed and just waved at Alma; he and the other guards had become used to the presence of the Loxicha families, and did not consider the girl's behaviour to be threatening in any way. Whether this was because she was a seven-year-old child or because the guard was so used to this kind of thing is an interesting question. Had an adult shouted these words at the guard, it is doubtful that they would have been laughed off as easily.

Perceptions of childhood gone wrong: 'poor, innocent, victims'

An important element to emerge from my research with the Loxicha children was the way they were represented in the local media in Oaxaca, and how Oaxaca City residents perceived them. The frequent marches by supporters, hunger strikes by the prisoners and the ongoing strife in the Loxicha region were covered in both the local and the national press and always with reference to the women and children living in Oaxaca City. Echoing a similar tendency in reporting and research that homogenises street children into a single category (on this see Glauser, 1997; Hecht, 1998; Ennew, 2000), local press stories often wrote about the Loxicha children under the umbrella definitions of 'poor children' or 'street children' and solely from the perspective of them as victims of the political situation.

One day I came across a local press article about child poverty in Oaxaca, with an overview of NGOs working with the area's marginalised children; the accompanying photograph, taken in Zócalo, was of two of the Loxicha children, Eyasha and her brother Isidro (*Noticias de Oaxaca*, 17 March 2002). No doubt since they were wandering around the Zócalo selling chewing gum and collecting money for the Loxicha cause, they presented the right image of 'poor children' to fit the story. Their identity was not acknowledged in this article, neither by the author nor by the photographer. I showed the picture to Eyasha, who was shown holding a Loxicha collection tin, and she asked if she could keep it for her album. She expressed no concern that her picture, together with her brother's, had been printed in the newspaper, nor did she enquire what the article was about. On the one hand, her reaction highlights how being in the public eye, particularly while living in the Zócalo, had become normal for these children; on the other hand, it is also a succinct illustration of the disparity between my perceptions, as adult and outsider, and Eyasha's view of her reality – what I perceived to be a breach of her privacy and identity, she regarded as a day-to-day and regular occurrence.

The caption underneath the photograph read:'for those who have less – at least 20 civil organisations [are] working for them [these children]'; less – by the author's prerogative less – in effect defined Eyasha's and Isidro's childhood as a single 'type' that entirely disregards the complex and multifaceted aspects of their lives. Furthermore, it implied that the children in the picture were included in the care of these 20 NGOs referred to in the article, a fact evidently not corroborated by the journalist. It is clear that the journalist had placed the Loxicha children into the categories of 'poor' and 'children of the streets', and presumably the photograph of them 'begging' was intended to rouse pity and concern.

Children who live in exceptionally difficult circumstances to a large extent live 'outside childhood and outside society', to once again use Ennew's (2002) definition. They also exist beyond the ideals and childhood parameters set by the UNCRC. Particularly while they were living in the Zócalo, the Loxicha children seemed to live a distinct childhood; it only becomes 'distinct,' however, when placed in juxtaposition to other perceived 'normal' childhoods (if there is such a thing). Their daily lives, as explored above, make up *their* normal childhood. They have moved from a rural existence of tending animals and fields alongside school and chores, to one of begging, selling chewing gum and participating in political marches.

A further illustration of how the press sought to portray the Loxicha children as simply pitiful victims is evident in Plate 3.4. Humberto is five years old and cannot read or write Spanish yet. When the men in jail began their fourth hunger strike in December 2001, Humberto and his mother and sisters were taken to visit their father. This photograph shows Humberto holding up a banner that reads:

> *Exijo al presidente Vicente Fox la libertad de mi padre y de mas paisanos presos injustamente.*
> [I demand from President Vicente Fox the release of my father and other prisoners, unjustly imprisoned.]

An adult wrote the banner Humberto is holding up, and Humberto was obviously asked to 'pose' for this picture, a small boy asking for

Plate 3.4: Humberto at the prisoner's hunger strike

Source: *Noticias de Oaxaca*, 7 December 2001

his father's freedom. This was good press, and the use of an image of a vulnerable-looking five-year-old child to elicit sympathy for a cause mirrors similar devices used by development agencies in appeal campaigns.

This emphasis on the helplessness and victimisation of children is obvious in another article published in a local Oaxaca newspaper around Christmas, an ideal time for tugging at the public's heartstrings. The article, which included a photograph of one of the younger Loxicha children asleep on the ground, was entitled 'The Loxicha children ask for the release of their fathers as a Christmas present' (*Noticias de Oaxaca*, 24 December 2001). This article talked about one of the children, Alma, in the following terms: '[Alma], who has neither a voice nor any dreams and will not have a Christmas....'. This description contrasts drastically to the Alma I knew, the same vivacious girl who shouted at municipal guards as described in an earlier anecdote, and who joined political protest marches with vigour. As for not having a Christmas, the children in fact enjoyed two parties held especially for them over the holiday season that year. From my privileged position of having almost daily contact with the Loxicha children and families, I was able to see the extent to which this particular newspaper article was misrepresenting these children, in simplistic and superficial terms that – given the festive season – would appeal to readers.

This media construction of Alma's childhood creates an unrealistic portrayal of the person she really is, presenting only an image of an unhappy child. As Patricia Holland (1992, p 148) observes in a study of British media pictures of children, 'without the image of the unhappy child, our contemporary concept of childhood would be incomplete'.

The reality that has been imposed on the adults in the Loxicha context has to a great degree undermined the 'innocence' of their children, and these adults have not been able to protect them from the harsh consequences of that reality. On the other hand, the idea that their childhood would otherwise be a 'carefree and happy' time is an imported idea of childhood. Had these children never been involved in this political struggle, they would nevertheless have had the difficult childhood of poor, rural, marginalised and indigenous children.

Young veterans of political activism

Despite the disruption and the change to their lives, the children have integrated happily into city life, perhaps because they have the routine of school in addition to the other elements that make up their daily realities. They have learned to move between worlds: theirs is a fluid existence between their Zapotec identity and language, and the urban and Spanish-speaking world of school; between the political world of the Loxicha struggle and the 'normal' day-to-day childhood world of games, homework and chores. While the political context has been the principal preoccupation of their parents, it is only one – albeit important – aspect of the children's lives. The way they have been represented in the local press, however, does not do justice to these diverse elements of the children's lives, reflecting a need among adults to hold on to what Buckingham terms 'a kind of sentimentality' about children that 'fails to acknowledge the diversity of the lived experience of childhood' (2000, cited in Prout, 2005, p 15).

I have maintained close contact with one of the families, and visited them again in January 2006. It struck me that the sisters Olivia and Eyasha (now 16 and 14) were already 'veterans' of their *lucha*, now facing – and more concerned with – different challenges: their mother's threatening 'boyfriends', the pressures of school, and problems with boys. The girls no longer visit the jail; they told me their father has a 'new woman' and that they have no time to go. Their father has thus become a distant figure, and the Loxicha case is no longer a big news item as most prisoners have been released. When I asked Eyasha if she and her sister still went on marches, she laughed and replied: 'Oh no! I have lots of homework!'. Her older sister Olivia has learned how to use the internet and sends me regular emails. As a researcher and an 'outsider' it is my feeling that participation in the *lucha* was an element of their childhoods that I was privileged to observe at a specific moment in time; politics, hunger strikes and protest marches do not define who they are now, although it continues to define who their fathers are, and to a large extent, their mothers. In other words, the context of their childhoods has changed; hence the focus of future research among the young people of Loxicha (at least those who remain in the shelter in Oaxaca City)[4] will undoubtedly follow a significantly different path.

Conclusion

The global discourse of children's rights has promoted the notion of children as competent participants in society, and while this idea is supported by sociological research and practice, in day-to-day life children continue to be seen as smaller people in need of adult protection and guidance and who remain without any recognisable status or power until they reach the age of 18.

The mismatch between the Loxicha children's lived realities in Oaxaca and the persistence of normative notions of childhood within local programmes, press portrayals and adults' perceptions stands in the way of an effective translation of the children's rights discourse. However, the necessary shift in perceptions may be regarded by many as an imposition on if not a threat to 'traditional' concepts and also to the status quo. Despite the advocacy and rhetoric around notions of children's agency, self-determination and participation, it may be useful to ask how many adults truly support such prospects.

That they work and contribute to the family income, are responsible for feeding and looking after younger siblings or go on political marches, are not at any point identified by the Loxicha children as exceptional elements of their lives. Nor do they recognise that such roles illustrate a movement between the established worlds of childhood and adulthood. This may be simply due to the fact that children do not question the ins and outs of their childhood to the extent that adults do. Another explanation is that these are only 'exceptional' activities if they are viewed from a normative, fixed and adultist standpoint. Therein also lies a crucial issue at the core of the debates: it is adults who lead discussions about 'who' children are, 'what' childhood is and 'how' they should participate in society.

The political aspect of the lives of the Loxicha children presents a vision of childhood that is perhaps understudied because of its ambiguity. The Loxicha children do not fit into a neat research category such as 'street child' or 'working child'. They move between worlds – they are indigenous children from a rural home who now move in an urban environment, they are displaced as the result of a situation of political violence, they are involved in a day-to-day struggle for the recognition of the rights of their Zapotec community, they go to school, they feed and care for younger siblings and they sometimes work. They do not fit into most local NGOs' criteria for inclusion in their programmes. Indeed, a local NGO that initiated a support programme with this group and their mothers, withdrew after a couple of months claiming that the 'unstable and errant' nature of their lives meant that it was difficult to keep records of the families. The organisation's street programme coordinator explained that since the children had moved to a shelter they no longer fitted the label of 'street child' in need of their support. She concluded, somewhat disturbingly, 'these children will probably end up working on the street, so we'll be able to pick them up then'.[4]

While some adults may argue that the Loxicha children's participation in marches and sit-ins does not constitute political activism, the fact that these activities are difficult to categorise does not mean that they do not count. The ways in which the Loxicha children have taken part in their community's political *lucha* are perhaps discounted because they are unpalatable to the pundits of 'nice' participation, in particular those working within the boundaries of NGO agendas. Furthermore, the fact that the Loxicha children participate in a community struggle, that is, as one mixed group of adults and children, blurs those boundaries that often define and demarcate children's participation in other forums such as parliaments or children's committees. In this sense they are participating 'outside the box' or norms.

In Oaxaca, the Loxicha children are regarded with pity by local residents and portrayed as victims in local press articles. There is no question that hardship, violence, poverty and the effects of displacement and political repression have marked their lives. What, however, is the alternative to these locally held perceptions of the Loxicha children? To disregard the whole picture of their childhood is to ignore the realities of their daily lives. Yet, a recognition and celebration of their agency and political participation in their community's struggle, their freedom of movement between roles and their responsibilities within their family and community structures would undoubtedly disturb the status quo and normative views of childhood vulnerability.

Furthermore, and perhaps more significantly, this recognition would entail an acknowledgement of the children's awareness of the volatile nature of the Loxicha struggle, where there exists evidence of human rights abuses against many of the children's fathers (see Human Rights Watch, 1999). This scenario is speculative, but nevertheless presents a possibly threatening option for adults, as it is one that potentially opens a real political space for children.

The lives of the Loxicha children in Oaxaca clearly present a type of children's participation not envisaged by the UNCRC and its ideals. An acknowledgment of the roles children can play in political activity has not been forthcoming in the advocacy for children's rights, in particular within debates around their participation rights. Their voices are being listened to and their views incorporated into many areas of decision making, facts that would have been inconceivable at the beginning of the 20th century. It is perhaps time, however, for notions of children's participation to move beyond the present vision, which, while having opened hitherto unexplored territory for many young people, remains nonetheless carefully contained by clear – and adult-imposed – conceptual and linguistic parameters.

Acknowledgements

Acknowledgement is due to the online journal *Children, Youth and Environments*, where a more extended version of this chapter appears (Smith, 2007). I am grateful to the Economic and Social Research Council (ESRC) for funding this research (2000-05) at the Institute of Latin American Studies, University of Liverpool, UK.

Notes

[1] The Loxicha situation has changed considerably since my research and last visit in 2006. Through regular correspondence with people involved with the Loxicha families, and recently with Olivia via email, I have kept abreast of developments, and have updated my information as far as possible. A detailed history of sociopolitical developments in Loxicha can be found at www.mx.geocities.com/opiz_lox/. At the time of writing, most of the men had been released from jail; these do not, however, include the fathers of Olivia and Eyasha referred to in this chapter. In July/August 2007, the EPR was behind another spate of violent activity, calling for the release of remaining prisoners. The names of children and adults have been changed to protect their identity.

[2] This has been the chant of anti-authoritarian protests across Latin America since the late 1960s.

[3] There are now just two families living in the shelter, where one ex-prisoner has also set up a mechanic's garage (February 2008).

[4] Interview with street educators programme coordinator, 21 May 2001, Oaxaca City.

References

Amnesty International (2002) 'Ochoa's memory merits a full investigation into her death', Press Release, Mexico: Digna, available at www.amnesty.org/ai.nsf

Coles, R. (1986) *The Political Life of Children*, Boston, MA: Atlantic Monthly Press.

Corona, C.Y. and Pérez Zavala, C. (2000) 'Infancia y resistencia culturales: la participación de los niños en los movimientos de resistencia comunitarios', in N. del Río (ed) *La Infancia Vulnerable de México en un Mundo Globalizado*, Mexico: UAM-UNICEF, pp 127-45.

Ennew, J. (2000) *Street and Working Children: A Guide to Planning* (2nd edition), London: Save the Children.

Ennew, J. (2002) 'Outside childhood: street children's rights', in B. Franklin (ed) *The New Handbook of Children's Rights: Comparative Policy and Practice*, London and New York: Routledge, pp 388-403.

Glauser, B. (1997) 'Street children: deconstructing a construct', in A. James and A. Prout (eds) *Constructing and Reconstructing Childhood: Contemporary Issues in the Sociological Study of Childhood* (2nd edition), London and Philadelphia, PA: Routledge Falmer, pp 145-64.

Guerra, E. (2002) 'Citizenship knows no age: children's participation in the governance and municipal budget of Barra Mansa, Brazil', *Environment and Urbanization*, 14(2), pp 71-84.

Hart, R. (1992) *Children's Participation: From Tokenism to Citizenship*, Innocenti Essays No 4. Florence: UNICEF International Child Development Centre.

Hecht, T. (1998) *At Home in the Street: Street Children of Northeast Brazil*, Cambridge: Cambridge University Press.

Holland, P. (1992) *What is a Child?: Popular Images of Childhood*, London: Virago.

Human Rights Watch (1999) *Systemic Injustice: Torture, 'Disappearance' and Extrajudicial Execution in Mexico*, New York: Human Rights Watch.

INEGI (Instituto Nacional de Estadística y Geografía) (2001) *Síntesis de Resultados – XII Censo General de Población y Vivienda 2000*, Estados Unidos Mexicanos, Aguascalientes: Instituto Nacional de Estadística, Geografía e Informática.

John, M. (1995) 'Children's rights in a free-market culture', in Stephens, S. (ed) *Children and the Politics of Culture*, Princeton, NJ: Princeton University Press, pp 105-37.

John, M. (2003) *Children's Rights and Power: Charging Up for a New Century*, Children in Charge, Series No 9, London and New York: Jessica Kingsley Publishers.

Lawyers Committee for Human Rights and Miguel Agustín ProJuárez Human Rights Centre (2001) *Legalized Injustice: Mexican Criminal Procedure and Human Rights*, New York and Mexico City: Lawyers Committee for Human Rights and Miguel Agustín ProJuárez Human Rights Centre, available at www.humanrightsfirst.org/index.aspx

Noticias de Oaxaca newspaper, Oaxaca: www.noticias.com.

Peterson, A.L. and Read, K.A. (2002) 'Victims, heroes, enemies: children in Central American wars', in T. Hecht (ed) *Minor Omissions: Children in Latin American History and Society*, Wisconsin and London: University of Wisconsin Press, pp 215-31.

Prout, A. (2005) *The Future of Childhood*, The Future of Childhood Series, London and New York: Routledge and Falmer.

Smith, A.-M. (2007) 'The children of Loxicha, Mexico: exploring ideas of childhood and the rules of participation', *Children, Youth and Environments*, 17(2), pp 33-55.

Stephen, L. (2003) 'The construction of indigenous suspects: militarization and the gendered and ethnic dynamics of human rights abuses in Southern Mexico', in M. Gutmann, F. Rodriguez, L. Stephen and P. Zavella (eds) *Perspectives on Las Américas: A Reader in Culture, History and Representation*, Oxford: Blackwell, pp 383-403.

Sumano, A.G. (2001) 'Y cuatro anos, seis meses y 14 días después…', *Noticias de Oaxaca* newspaper, 25 December, p 7A.

World Bank (2003) *Mexico Must Combat Poverty in the South to Consolidate Economic Prosperity*, Bank Study, Mexico City, World Bank, www.worldbank.org

Wyness, M., Harrison, L. and Buchanan, I. (2004) 'Childhood, politics and ambiguity: towards an agenda for children's political inclusion', *Sociology*, 38(1), pp 81-99.

FOUR

Displaced children's participation in political violence: towards greater understanding of mobilisation[1]

Jason Hart

I am telling the stories of my country. I can't help it if those stories are steeped in politics. That's the reality I've been living in. That's the reality that these people have been living under. The lands are filled with mines. The markets are filled with ammunition and weapons. All you have to do is look at the children and you'd see the politics that have gone into shaping their lives. That's just the reality of life here. Ghobadi (2004)

In his film *Turtles Can Fly*, Bahman Ghobadi presents a stark picture of Iraqi Kurdish children and their struggles to survive around the time of the US-led invasion of 2003. Towards the end of the film a group of boys head off to the nearby town to obtain guns and then set these up on the roof of their school as defence against a possible military attack. This is not recruitment in the conventional sense but the self-mobilisation of a group of children under the leadership of a 13-year-old. Ghobadi's film also shows us the rape by Iraqi soldiers of a young girl and her subsequent suicide, the wretched living conditions in a makeshift displacement camp, and large numbers of children engaged in the manual defusing of landmines for meagre pennies. Amid these horrors, the children's efforts to arm themselves are hardly shocking. Indeed, given the dangers and deprivation, such action appears tragically reasonable: an expression of young people's determination to survive against considerable odds in a setting where adults have failed in their duty to protect.

Often absent from the burgeoning literature and debate on children's involvement in military action and political violence is careful attention to the processes through which mobilisation occurs. The appalling cases where children are abducted and compelled to take part in acts of brutality are well known. Yet not all rebel groups and government forces operate in the same manner in pursuing the recruitment of underage personnel. It would be misleading to consider the actions of a group such as the Lord's Resistance Army in northern Uganda – notorious for its abduction and brutal initiation of children – as typical. From Sri Lanka to Colombia and Nepal to Sierra Leone, it is apparent that in many, if not most, locations where children are associated with military groups, recruitment cannot be explained *solely* in terms of physical coercion and intimidation. Furthermore, as Ghobadi's film illustrates, organised groups may not be necessary for children to mobilise and take up arms. Therefore, in the effort to prevent children from engaging directly in political violence we are bound to consider in careful detail their motivations.

Undoubtedly, the reasons and processes that lead young people to such activity are complex and multifaceted. Different theories abound, embracing issues of sociocultural environment, biogenetics, libido and cognition, as well as personal experience (Boyden, 2007, p 274). This chapter is a modest contribution towards an understanding of mobilisation. It takes as its focus displacement camps, considering the specific dynamics within such settings that may contribute to the involvement of young people with military groups or in some form of ad hoc political violence. As I shall argue, there is a pressing need to reinvigorate discussion about young people's engagement with appreciation for both the sociohistorical dimensions of displacement *and* the potential of displaced teenagers to engage in political violence in an informed and purposive manner. In developing this argument, I shall draw particularly on my own research with Palestinian refugee children, mindful that, as with discussion of any specific population group or context, the observations offered may have more or less applicability elsewhere.

Agency

Within both the contemporary discourse of children's rights and the emerging discipline of childhood studies, much attention has been given to the notion of agency. Earlier assumptions about the inherent passivity of children have been challenged head-on and largely replaced by a vision of the child as 'a subject of rights who is able to form and express opinions, to participate in decision-making processes and influence solutions, to intervene as a partner in the process of social change and the building up of democracy' (Santos Pais, 2000, p 4).

Article 12 of the United Nations Convention on the Rights of the Child (UNCRC), which speaks of the right of children to 'express ... views freely in all matters affecting (them)', is the common starting point for activists and development practitioners who seek to enlarge the space for children's participation and the exercise of agency. The stated right to 'express ... views' has been interpreted as encouragement for children's engagement – verbally and through action – across an array of settings and processes (Ackermann et al., 2003).

In practice, however, the promotion of participation within a rights-based framework has not been a one-way street heading towards the greater involvement of children in all arenas and forms of public life. While the young have been recognised as legitimate actors and facilitated in certain activities and processes, other settings are placed off-limits ever more emphatically. Children's involvement in military-type activities, perhaps more than any other, has come to be seen purely in terms of violation rather than as an instance of participation or the exercise of agency. Suggestion that the young may engage in the support or practice of political violence by their own volition is commonly countered by statements such as the following, taken from the 'Machel Report' on the impact of armed conflict on children: 'rather than exercising free choice, these children are responding more often to a variety of pressures – economic, cultural, social and political' (Machel, 2001, p 11). 'Free choice' is a complex concept, for adults as well as the young. Moreover, we may wonder how many of the world's children – especially in the global South – enjoy lives and choices unconstrained by material forces. How should we understand freedom of choice for the estimated 674 million of the world's children who live in absolute poverty, or the 376 million who lack access to the most basic of human necessities – a clean supply of water? (Gordon et al., 2003). In relation to the particular focus of this chapter, we may ask about the ways that, and extent to which, children living in displacement camps – often through compulsion – are free to make meaningful choices about their lives. Instead, I shall suggest, it is necessary to consider carefully how context and experience – whatever that may be – inform action. In this case, how is it that residence in a displacement camp is implicated in the mobilisation of young people?

Competence

The evidence strongly suggests that children who participate in military-type activities are predominantly in their teenage years. From the American Civil War (Murphy, 1990; Keesee, 2001) to the British

Army in the First World War (Van Emden, 2005), and more recent conflicts in countries such as El Salvador (Read, 2001) and Sierra Leone (Peters and Richards, 1998; Rosen, 2005), it is young people from the age of roughly 14 or 15 upwards who have principally been involved as combatants. Younger children's participation has commonly been confined to ancillary roles, with varying degrees of risk. Thus, while there are certainly important exceptions, mobilisation is primarily a teenage issue, tending to involve males more than females.

Age/maturity in relation to children's participation in military-type activities has not received much attention in the literature on recruitment, particularly from authors writing from an advocacy or security perspective. The so-called 'Straight 18 position', according to which recruitment of anyone below the age of 18 should be seen as a rights violation, tends to foreclose consideration of difference in experience, competence and circumstances among all those conceptualised within the category of 'children'. Moreover, there is a tendency to infantilise older children – considering them through the prism of ideas about early childhood (Rosen, 2005, p 135).[2] Yet teenagers are likely to differ from young children in numerous ways that significantly mediate the experience and impact of political violence.

Conceptualisation of the differences in intellectual competence between younger and older children requires particularly careful consideration. The reliability of chronological age alone as a marker of competence is a point of keen debate. On the one hand, Jean Piaget and his followers, notably Lawrence Kohlberg (1976), have offered a view of child cognitive development as occurring in a universal series of stages, suggesting a 'natural' connection between chronological age and human cognitive ability. Thus, the capacity to make proper sense of issues within particular domains of social existence is considered to unfold in a preordained manner linked closely to physical maturation. Understanding of the profound and complex moral issues involved in political-military activity has come to be seen as beyond the ken of all those deemed 'children'. As Jo Boyden (2007, p 273) has observed:

> By arguing that children enter into advanced thought comparatively late in childhood, the suggestion seems to be that children have only a tenuous grasp on moral judgement. Hence, children are presumably regarded as not having fully internalised the regulations governing accepted behaviour and thereby are more liable to take part in 'mindless' atrocities.

In opposition to the Piagetians, a view of the environment as critical in cognitive development has gained increasing support. Taking a lead from Lev Vygotsky (1978), numerous researchers have illustrated that specific competencies are built through a child's engagement within the settings of everyday life (for example, Rogoff, 1981; Lave, 1990; Cole, 1996). Thus, it is likely that a child who grows up in a politically fragile environment requiring her or him to negotiate serious threats on a daily basis will develop the competence to grasp issues around the use of military power, the morality of such usage and its consequences at a younger age than a child in a more stable sociopolitical setting.

The individuated, abstracted approach of the Piagetians finds expression within the literature on children's military-type activities in a tendency to focus on the immaturity of individuals. For example, according to Singer (2005, p 67), 'In the end, children may join such (military) groups simply because they are kids, and the slightest of whims or appeals may suffice to impel them to enter war'.

The Vygotskyian approach, by contrast, encourages us to explore the development of cognitive competence as an inter-subjective process without making hasty assumptions regarding disposition or ability. Attention should be focused on the ways in which children construct meaning and pursue action through sociality: their ideas, motivations and aspirations evolving in relation to the changing social, political, moral and economic environment. In this way we are moved from a static, deterministic account of children's mobilisation to one that is dynamic and multifaceted, demanding examination of each different setting within which such mobilisation occurs. Nevertheless, there are bound to be certain differences between older and younger children, in general. This is due partly to the extent (as well as content) of individual experience and partly to a function of biological processes that inevitably, to paraphrase Alan Prout (2005, p 111), are 'translated into culture'.

My intention in offering this brief discussion of agency and competence is to open the way for consideration of displaced children's involvement in military-type activities that is unencumbered by assumptions that this is necessarily the consequence either of individual incapacity in intellectual and moral reasoning or of adult trickery and coercion. As I shall argue, within the particular sociopolitical settings of displacement, the motivations for older children's engagement in such activities should be explored in relation to their specific experience. This, in turn, requires attention to the innumerable factors that mediate the meanings derived from that experience. Leaving aside complex issues surrounding the influence of biology and genetics that would necessitate a far more extensive discussion, I shall focus on three mediating factors, all of which have appeared as significant in the context of displacement camps as noted by myself and other researchers. These factors are (1) the camp as social space, (2) social transition and (3) politicisation. I shall discuss each of these in turn.

The Camp as social space

Different disciplinary approaches and streams of thought conceptualise displacement camps in very different ways. For example, there have been a number of philosophical reflections on the figure of the camp as an abstracted institution within the state, postmodernity or global geopolitics (Augé, 1995; Agamben, 1998; Diken, 2004). For scholars of international relations the camp is commonly seen as a 'warehouse' in which politically and economically marginalised populations are left in limbo while international agencies and governments search for long-term solutions (Loescher and Milner, 2004). Increasingly, the camp is seen in problematic terms as a breeding-ground for violence: the location in which the so-called 'refugee warrior' is housed or even forged (Zohlberg et al., 1989; Lischer, 2005).

An alternative perspective on the camp emerges from a central concern with the lived experience of displaced populations typically pursued by anthropologists. Accordingly, the camp is located in an historical trajectory linking causes of displacement with the present life of residents and their imaginings of and efforts to secure a particular future. In contrast to the perspective from international relations, which tends to see the emergence of violence in monocausal terms – for example, as a response to the violence of displacement or due to the actions and inactions of states and the international community (Adelman, 1998; Lischer, 2003) – such an approach encourages consideration of political violence as a product of the complex interplay between past experience, current circumstances and collective aspirations.

Liisa Malkki's (1995, 1996) well-known account of Burundian Hutu refugees in Tanzania not only locates the camp within an historical trajectory but also reveals how, within this space, residents engage continually in memorialisation. Moreover, such narration of the past is linked to the imagining of a common destiny. As this author observes:

> The most unusual and prominent social fact about the camp of Mishano was that the refugees who had lived within its confines for so many years were still in 1985-6 continually

engaged in an urgent, collective process of constructing and reconstructing a true history of their trajectory as 'a people'....The culminating chapter in the refugees' historical narratives of the Burundian past amounted to a vast and painful documentation of the mass killings of people belonging to the Hutu category by Burundi's (mainly Tutsi) army – and, eventually, by Tutsi civilians – in 1972. So many years later, the historical and personal memory of the apocalyptic violence and terror of that era still had a sharp and shocking salience in people's everyday lives.

These historical narratives were ubiquitous in the camp, forming ... an overarching historical trajectory that was fundamentally also a national history of the 'rightful natives' of Burundi. The camp refugees saw themselves as a nation in exile. And they thought of exile as an era of moral trials and hardships that would enable them to reclaim the 'homeland' in Burundi at some moment in the future. (Malkki, 1996, p 380)

Malkki's concurrent research with self-settled Burundian refugees living in an urban setting revealed little evidence of such collective narration. This finding further illustrated the specificity of Mishano Camp as a space within which a common history linking past, present and future was constructed.

My own research in Hussein Camp in Jordan – home to roughly 50,000 Palestinian refugees – in the late 1990s did not discover quite such deliberateness in the processes of constructing history as described by Malkki. This was, perhaps, a consequence of the longer existence of Hussein Camp and other Palestinian camps in comparison to Mishano. Nevertheless, among neighbours, within the home, in school and at the local youth club, everyday practices and conversations constantly invited camp residents to consider their past and to remember their difference – as a group – from the native Jordanian population (see Sayigh, 1977, 1998; Farah, 2003). Moreover, in spite of the failure of the Oslo Peace Process to properly address the Palestinian refugees from 1948, notions of 'return' remained strongly salient, if differently inflected, among successive generations.

Into this space, thousands of children have been born over more than 50 years, each receiving innumerable prompts from their social and physical environment that connect them to processes of differentiation and historicisation. Explaining to me how it is that children in the camp, from an early age, come to understand that they are refugees from

Palestine, parents and teachers alluded to the physical environment of the camp: the narrow, regimented streets and uniform housing units. In their estimation, the young soon perceive the difference between this layout and that of surrounding areas, prompting a process of questioning that leads them to an understanding of their lives within a distinct historical trajectory. As one young man from Hussein Camp explained, 'we only have to see the blue [UN] flag over the school to remember that we are Palestinians'.

As well as such visual cues from their physical surroundings, I found that children in Hussein Camp learned explicitly about their homeland – often acquiring detailed information about the particular villages in which their grandparents lived prior to expulsion in 1948. Furthermore, they were encouraged to join older generations in considering the challenges and privations of their present circumstances as the consequences of injustice, indifference and hypocrisy on the part of numerous governments and global institutions.

Like many other Palestinian camps in urban settings, Hussein Camp is encircled by large areas of residential housing. In the case of this specific camp, many of the surrounding homes are also inhabited by Palestinians displaced in 1948 or 1967 and their descendants. Yet, the shared connection to Palestine and history of exile were expressed far more often within the camp. Why should this be? First, there was an intensity of social interaction in Hussein Camp. This was partly the function of the layout of the camp already mentioned, with rows of small, terraced dwellings laid back to back along narrow streets. Thus, residents were compelled into a physical proximity with one another generally considered more appropriate for kin than for unrelated neighbours.

Out of this enforced intimacy and the challenges of survival, strong neighbourhood bonds emerged. Particularly for boys and adolescent males, the neighbourhood (*haara*) was a vital location of social interaction where most free time was spent. As I have argued elsewhere (Hart, 2008), the local peer group served as a source of information and in the development of attitudes and behaviour, and was also an immediate model for a wider 'imagined' community, enabling identification with the camp as a whole and, by further extension, the community of Palestinians in exile.

In addition to this physical proximity and the social networks to which it gave rise, there was also strong awareness – among residents and Palestinians living outside the camp – of Hussein Camp as a moral and political space. For leaders of the nationalist movement this camp, like the other camps, was the heartland of the Palestinian struggle for return and statehood. Children growing up in the camp were referred to collectively by such terms as *jeel al-awdeh* ('generation of return') – an expression of the hopes vested in them that they would achieve redemption of the entire population in exile through reclaiming Palestine.

The awareness that children in Hussein Camp had of themselves as members of a distinct community-in-exile has sometimes found collective expression. There have been several occasions in the recent history of this particular camp when both boys and girls left their classrooms and massed in the main street to demonstrate – often violently – outside the police station. This symbol of Jordanian authority became a proxy for Israel in their protest against particular actions in the Occupied Territories, such as the 2002 incursion into Jenin Camp. These were collective activities that demonstrated and reinforced a sense of membership both of an immediate cohort of peers and of the larger refugee community. While Palestinian children living outside Hussein Camp have also participated, the camp and its young population have always been central to such actions. Moreover, such events became part of a common vocabulary within the camp as peer and family groups recalled together their involvement and the excitement experienced. For example, I was party to a conversation in one family when the particular courage and determination of the daughters of the house in fighting the Jordanian police was remembered in a tone of amused pride by their brothers and parents.

Social transition

Different societies manage the transition of children into the roles, responsibilities and status associated with 'adulthood' in very different ways – through education, various forms of apprenticeship, the conduct of particular rites and so on. Conflict and resulting displacement often undermine the processes by which transition is conventionally effected. Not only do certain forms of apprenticeship and ritual action become unsustainable but the constraints on movement may make it impossible for teenagers and their families to secure the resources required for marriage, completion of formal education, construction of a separate home or other acts that are commonly requisite. The obstacles to physical movement and socioeconomic advancement should therefore also be considered for the frustration they may cause the young in their efforts to achieve adult status.

Standard views of globalisation as embodying the free and rapid movement of commodities, ideas and people often pay insufficient attention to the increasing restrictions on the travel of certain people in particular locations. Although displacement, by definition, involves some measure of movement, the actual routes open to refugees and the internally displaced are increasingly constrained. Even when displacement camps are not physically bounded and inhabitants fenced in, the possibilities for establishing a viable life are curtailed by border controls, asylum policies, restrictions on employment, and systems of surveillance increasingly justified in the name of security post-September 11th. Thus, displaced young people are liable to find their scope to cross immediate national borders, let alone enter the wealthy nations of Europe, North America, East Asia and Australasia, drastically curtailed. With such restrictions are lost important routes to economic and social advancement.

The sources of frustration for displaced adolescent girls may well differ from their male peers. Given the close proximity of unrelated neighbours in most camps – Hussein included – families often fear the consequences of their daughters' early engagement in sexual activity. In some locations there are additional fears of sexual violence and trafficking. As a result, girls are often married off at a very early age or, at the least, kept largely within the home once past puberty. Thus, there may be very particular frustrations for adolescent girls, denied access to education and to any possibility of independence (Hoodfar, 2008).

The pursuit of social adulthood may be further hindered by the inability of camp residents to undertake the rites and practices through which young people conventionally achieve transition. Humanitarian agencies may exert their best efforts to prevent activities considered risky or otherwise unsuitable. The consequent frustration of young people can be further compounded by the introduction of interventions that stress their vulnerability rather than their strengths and competencies. Writing about displacement camps in Eastern Africa, Hirut Tefferi (2007, p 301) offers the following observation:

> [I]n relation to humanitarian interventions, adolescents in displacement situations must regularly recast themselves as vulnerable, dependent children in order to escape legal punishment or gain priority for relief assistance. Furthermore, while young people are, under normal circumstances, expected to perform a considerable amount of productive work and take decisions on certain matters, they are expected by humanitarian agencies to sit in classrooms, usually with children much younger than themselves. Their roles in defending their communities and properties

are consistently delegitimised, and they are discouraged from taking part in training or from exhibiting skills that relate to the defence of themselves and their communities. Agencies usually offer services to them only if they are seen as vulnerable, according to such labels as 'unaccompanied children' and 'demobilised child soldiers'....

Politicisation

As I have suggested, there is growing support for the view that environment plays a significant role in intellectual and cognitive development. We may suppose, therefore, that children who grow up in a politically fragile environment are liable to gain an understanding of 'politics' at an earlier age than their peers living in a relatively stable society.

Yet the assumption that children develop 'political consciousness', potentially leading to purposive action, carries the risk of providing an adultist rationale for processes that are not necessarily experienced in that manner by the young. Such notions as 'politicisation', 'political life' and 'political consciousness' seem to rely on the view that the 'political' exists as a self-evident and distinct domain of thought and activity that children engage with or not. This view is manifest in studies of children and politics conducted in Western countries in which the 'political' relates to knowledge of and interest in such matters as voting or the structure and functioning of government (for example, Connell, 1971; Stevens, 1982; Pirie and Worcester, 2000; White et al., 2000).

I would suggest that what is conceptualised by such an approach as 'political' may be experienced in a more visceral, less delineated manner by children living in settings of armed conflict and displacement. In such situations, where the effects of sharp asymmetries of power are experienced directly by the young within everyday life – in terms of danger, containment, marginalisation, disempowerment and so on – it is questionable whether 'politics' constitutes a discrete arena that a child chooses to engage with or not. Rather, the effects of asymmetrical relations of power, operating in routine fashion at levels including and far beyond the domestic, and experienced by children as violating their physical or moral integrity, function, I would suggest, to prompt questioning, reflection and discussion that inform cognitive and intellectual development. Understanding and action that we label 'political' grow out of the connection made by young people between their own experience and society-wide crisis. As Henrik Vigh (2008, p 16), quoting Sorokin, has recently written:

> [I]t is 'when people find themselves ruined, uprooted,
> mutilated and their routines of life upset' that they 'ask
> themselves why and how this has come about' (1963:3).
> Habituation leads to the establishment of social facts, yet
> when paired with chronic crisis we see a continuous critical
> assessment of the social, its movement, one's position and
> the possibilities of action available within it.

To be clear, ruin, uprooting, mutilation and the upset of routines of
life are not in themselves the causes of such awakening of critical
consciousness: after all, such things might equally result from a natural
disaster as the oppressive workings of asymmetrical power relations. The
spur to such awakening, I would argue, comes from the degradation
experienced when fellow human beings deliberately inflict such
damage on one other with intent to harm (Soyinka, 2004, p 1000). This
point is made clearly by Axel Honneth (1995, p 132): 'for each of the
negative emotional reactions that accompany the experiences of having
one's claims to recognition disregarded holds out the possibility that
the injustice done to one will cognitively disclose itself and become a
motive for political resistance'.

Thus, the key questions are, first, whether or not the young are
capable of feeling the pain of humiliation, and second, if so, might this
spur thought and action that could be considered 'political'? A recent
study undertaken by Rita Giacaman and colleagues (2008) involving
nearly 3,500 Palestinian 10th and 11th Grade students found a strong
correlation between exposure to 'humiliating events' that gave rise to
feelings of 'having been unjustly treated or debased' and the reporting
of 'subjective health complaints' – a term that encompasses conditions
such as gastrointestinal complaints, musculoskeletal pain, tiredness, sleep
problems, fatigue, and mood changes that have no clear physiological
aetiology. On the basis of such findings these authors caution that:

> The more worrisome aspect is the potential link between
> the indignities of humiliation and the 'hunger for retaliation'
> that may lead to a desire to strike back whenever possible.
> When humiliation is widely experienced, such feelings can
> lead to disastrous results not only among young people....
> (Giacaman et al., 2008, 570)

The following quote, taken from an observational report by the Israeli
human rights organisation *MachsomWatch* [Checkpoint Watch] of
Qalandiya checkpoint in the West Bank, illustrates a moment when

humiliation appears to provoke such retaliation from two teenage brothers, with severe consequences for both of them:

1st November, 2004

> There were a lot of detainees whose i.d.'s were taken from them for inspection.... They were waiting a long time. The older soldier casually put the blue i.d.'s in a pile on the concrete block. No one checked them. They simply lay there. The detainees saw this and were burning mad. One of them, a young boy approached one of the soldiers and requested his i.d. back. He was tired, hungry and wanted to go home. The soldier felt threatened and shoved him with his two hands. The boy lost his cool and pushed the soldier back. ... within minutes, soldiers fell upon him, pushed him to the ground and started beating him. The brother of the young man who was in the line of those waiting leaped at the sight of his brother being hit, and the two of them were mercilessly beaten. There was a tumultuous outburst with people running out of the line to the site of the happening, some of them wanting to intervene, others worried, all of them shouting and the older soldier shot his pistol in the air. Everyone was running.
> ... At last, the two (young) men who tried to defend themselves and hit back at the soldiers gave in. When they stood on their feet, they were led by the soldiers, they were bleeding and one of them was simply torn apart. (www. machsomwatch,org)

Fighting with Israeli soldiers at a checkpoint would presumably constitute a 'political' act in most people's estimation. However, these boys' behaviour should not be seen as necessarily the result of some preceding and deliberate process of 'politicisation'. While the decision of the first boy to request the return of his ID and then to fight back occurred in a moment, inevitably it was informed by previous experiences both as recipient and as witness of such treatment by Israeli soldiers. It is precisely in encounters like this, taking place as a matter of course within daily life, that children's 'claims to recognition' – to use Honneth's (1995, p 132) phrase – are 'disregarded' and thereby, I would contend, emerges the motivation to understand and to counter the relations of power that enable such disregard to be expressed routinely.

Life in many of the world's refugee and internally displaced person (IDP) camps is likely to entail not only physical privation but also humiliation that, I would suggest, may be experienced by the young as simultaneously both an individual and a collective experience resulting from drastically asymmetrical relations of power. Moreover, camp residence itself can, in some cases, be seen as the consequence of such inequity: part of a trajectory of discrimination or global indifference. While there are certainly numerous examples of militants within displacement camps seeking to mobilise young people, there is growing evidence to suggest that they are often providing an outlet for teenagers who share the frustration and resentment of older generations.[3] This has been seen recently, for example, among young Bhutanese refugees in Nepal.[4] For those development and humanitarian practitioners seeking societal transformation through children's participation there is a challenge to attend to the 'voices' of children who may actively choose the language of violence to express their frustrations or pursue their aspirations. Can such children be attended to with the same earnestness as those who speak in the language of peace and democracy?

Conclusion: from politics to policy (and back again)

Much of the literature on displaced children living in situations of conflict tends towards an assumption that they are vulnerable to recruitment by virtue of a combination of their immaturity (for example, Brett and Specht, 2003; Singer, 2005) and their residence within a camp (for example, Reich and Achvarina, 2006). Such views sidestep serious questions about displaced children's own motivations for engagement in armed conflict: questions that would highlight the politics and economics that shape and constrain their lives. Avoidance of political-economic context in this manner is not an inevitability. Indeed, from an historical perspective we can see that the longstanding involvement of teenagers in armed conflict has only come to be considered in these depoliticising terms relatively recently: the literature on children's involvement in political violence in earlier times clearly shows how the young were seen – and saw themselves – as part of the collective struggle (for example, Read, 2001; Van Emden, 2005).

Although we should all be concerned to avoid the risks associated with children's involvement in political violence, it is doubtful whether the current trend in writing and advocacy that marginalises consideration of displaced children's own motivations and concerns can ultimately serve this purpose. I would argue that preventative efforts need to be informed by two clear but interrelated conceptual moves in order to become more effective.

First, there is a need to assert the historicity of displacement and the lives of displacees. It is important to locate camps themselves within their specific historical trajectory. In this way we can supplement the view of encampment as somehow causative of political violence with appreciation of the ways in which such encampment is also an effect of violence – structural as well as physical. In addition, challenging the tendency to see camps as 'non-places' that are simply 'there to be passed through' (Augé, 1995, p 104), attention must be paid to the ongoing construction of meaning within such settings both by and for the young. Thus, the anger and frustration of young camp residents may be understood not simply as a response to their current conditions but in relation to an extended, even intergenerational, experience of oppression and marginalisation.

Second, we need to develop research based on appreciation of displaced young people's potential to engage purposively in actions that may be labelled 'political'. Moving beyond a view of 'politicisation' in which the young are construed simply as the receptors of adult efforts to impart ideology, we should examine the ways that displaced children's thought and action are informed by everyday experience within power relations that are profoundly asymmetrical and threatening both morally and physically.

Expanding research efforts in line with these two considerations – the historicity of displacement and the intentionality of displaced children – may enable us to challenge the current tendency to recast profoundly political matters as issues of policy. Questions are hereby opened up about the actions and inaction that perpetuate displacement and the associated marginalisation of the young. For example, we are led to enquire into the effects of the increasingly restrictive asylum policies of most Western states on the social and economic prospects of displaced young people in the global South. We may also be encouraged to ask about the ways in which young people interpret the foreign policies of powerful Western governments. In the final analysis, our hope of ending displaced children's engagement in political violence may depend in no small measure on challenging those forces that lie behind the current tendency to see 'child recruitment' through the narrow and decontextualised lens of policy.

Notes

[1] This text was first published in *Conflict, Security and Development*, 8(3), pp 277-93, and is reproduced here with kind permission of the publisher.

[2] Such infantilisation is neatly illustrated in Singer's (2001) use of the term 'tots' to describe child soldiers.

[3] At the same time, we need also to be attentive to young people's exercise of agency in terms of resisting the efforts of would-be recruiters. This has been reported in various locations, including within refugee camps in Uganda. (Christina R. Clark-Kazak, personal communication).

[4] Roz Evans, personal communication.

References

Ackermann, L., Feeny, T., Hart, J. and Newman, J. (2003) *Understanding and Evaluating Children's Participation: A Review of Contemporary Literature*, Woking: Plan International.

Adelman, H. (1998) 'Why refugee warriors are threats', *Journal of Conflict Studies*, XVIII(1), www.lib.unb.ca/Texts/JCS/bin/get.cgi?directory=SPR98/&filename=adelman.html

Agamben, G. (1998) *Homo Sacer: Sovereign Power and Bare Life*, Stanford, CA: Stanford University Press.

Augé, M. (1995) *Non-Places: Introduction to an Anthropology of Supermodernity*, London: Verso.

Boyden, J. (2007) 'Children, war and world disorder in the 21st century: a review of the theories and literature on children's contributions to armed violence', *Conflict, Security & Development*, 7(2), pp 255-79.

Brett, R. and Specht, I. (2003) *Young Soldiers: Why they Choose to Fight*, Boulder, CO: Lynne Reiner Publishing.

Cole, M. (1996) *Cultural Psychology: A Once and Future Discipline*, Cambridge, MA: Harvard University Press.

Connell, R.W. (1971) *The Child's Construction of Politics*, Melbourne: University of Melbourne Press.

Diken, B. (2004) 'From refugee camps to gated communities: biopolitics and the end of the city', *Citizenship Studies*, 8(1), pp 83-106.

Farah, R. (2003) 'Palestinian refugee camps reinscribing and contesting memory and space', in C. Strange and A. Bashford (eds) *Isolation Places and Practices of Exclusion*, London and New York: Routledge.

Ghobadi, B. (2004) In interview with Brandon Judell, in *New York Theatre Wire*, www.nytheatre-wire.com/bj05025t.htm

Giacaman, R., Abu-Rmeileh, N., Husseini, A., Saab, H. and Boyce, W. (2008) 'Humiliation: the invisible trauma of war for Palestinian youth', *Public Health*, 121, pp 563-71.

Gordon, D., Nandy, S., Pantazis, C., Pemberton, S. and Townsend, P. (2003) *Child Poverty in the Developing World*, Bristol: The Policy Press.

Hart, J. (2008) 'Dislocated masculinity: adolescence and the Palestinian nation-in-exile', *Journal of Refugee Studies*, 21(1), pp 64-81.

Honneth, A. (1995) *The Struggle for Recognition: The Moral Grammar of Social Conflicts*, Cambridge: Polity Press.

Hoodfar, H. (2008) 'The long road home: adolescent Afghan refugees in Iran contemplate "return"', in J. Hart (ed) *Years of Conflict: Adolescence, Political Violence and Displacement*, Oxford: Berghahn Books.

Keesee, D. (2001) *Too Young to Die: Boy Soldiers of the Union Army 1861-1865*, Huntington, WV: Blue Acorn Press.

Kohlberg, L. (1976) 'Moral stages and moralization; the cognitive-developmental approach', in T. Lickona (ed) *Moral Development and Behavior: Theory, Research and Social Issues*, Austin, TX: Rinehart and Winston.

Lave, J. (1990) 'The culture of acquisition and the practice of understanding', in J. Stigler, R. Shweder and G. Herdt (eds) *Cultural Psychology: Essays on Comparative Human Development*, Cambridge: Cambridge University Press.

Lischer, S. (2003) 'Collateral damage: humanitarian assistance as a cause of conflict', *International Security*, 28(1), pp 79-109.

Lischer, S. (2005) *Dangerous Sanctuaries: Refugee Camps, Civil War, and the Dilemmas of Humanitarian Aid*, Ithaca, NY: Cornell University Press.

Loescher, G. and Milner, J. (2004) 'Protracted refugee situations and state and regional insecurity', *Conflict, Security and Development*, 4(1), pp 3-20.

Machel, G. (2001) *The Impact of Armed Conflict on Children*, London: Hurst & Co.

Malkki, L. (1995) *Purity and Exile: Violence, Memory, and National Cosmology among Hutu Refugees in Tanzania*, Chicago, IL: University of Chicago Press.

Malkki, L. (1996) 'Speechless emissaries: refugees, humanitarianism, and dehistoricization', *Cultural Anthropology*, 11(3), pp 377-404.

Murphy, X. (1990) *The Boys' War: Confederate and Union Soldiers Talk about the Civil War*, New York, NY: Clarion Books.

Peters, K. and Richards, P. (1998) 'Why we fight: voices of youth combatants in Sierra Leone', *Africa*, 68(2), pp 183-210.

Pirie, M. and Worcester, R. (2000) *The Big Turn-Off: Attitudes of Young People to Government, Citizenship and Community*, London: Adam Smith Institute.

Prout, A. (2005) *The Future of Childhood*, Abingdon and New York, NY: Routledge Farmer.

Read, K. (2001) 'When is a kid a kid? Negotiating children's rights in El Salvador's civil war', *History of Religions*, 41(4), pp 391–409.

Reich, S. and Achvarina, V. (2006) 'No place to hide: refugees, displaced persons and the recruitment of child soldiers', *International Security*, 31(1), pp 127–64.

Rogoff, B. (1981) 'Schooling and the development of cognitive skills', in Triandis, H. and Heron, A. (eds) *Handbook of Cross-Cultural Psychology: Developmental Psychology Volume 4*, Boston: Allyn and Bacon.

Rosen, D. (2005) *Armies of the Young: Child Soldiers in War and Terrorism*, Camden, NJ: Rutgers University Press.

Santos Pais, M. (2000) 'Child participation and the Convention on the Rights of the Child', in R. Ranjani (ed) The Political Participation of Children, Cambridge, MA: Harvard Center for Population and Development Studies, Harvard University.

Sayigh, R. (1977) 'Sources of Palestinian nationalism: a study of a Palestinian camp in Lebanon', *Journal of Palestine Studies*, 6(4), pp 17–40.

Sayigh, R. (1998) 'Palestinian camp women as tellers of history', *Journal of Palestine Studies*, 27(X), pp 42–58.

Singer, P.W. (2001) 'Caution: children at war', *Parameters*, 31(4), pp 40–56.

Singer, P.W. (2005) Children at War, New York: Pantheon Books.

Soyinka, W. (2004) *Climate of Fear: The BBC Reith Lectures 2004*, London: Profile Books.

Stevens, O. (1982) *Children Talking Politics: Political Learning in Childhood*, Oxford: Martin Robertson.

Tefferi, H. (2007) 'Reconstructing adolescence after displacement: experience from Eastern Africa', *Children & Society*, 21(4), pp 297–308.

Van Emden, R. (2005) *Boy Soldiers of the Great War*, London: Headline Book Publishing.

Vigh, H. (2008) 'Crisis and chronicity: anthropological perspectives on continuous conflict and decline', *Ethnos*, 73(1), pp 5–24.

Vygotsky, L. (1978) Mind in Society: The Development of Higher Psychological Processes, Cambridge, MA: Harvard University Press.

White, C., Bruce, S. and Ritchie, J. (2000) *Young People's Politics: Political Interest and Engagement amongst 14-24 year olds*, York: Joseph Rowntree Foundation.

Zohlberg, A., Suhrke, A. and Aguyayo, S. (1989) *Escape from Violence: Conflict and the Refugee Crisis in the Developing World*, Oxford: Oxford University Press.

FIVE

Between a rock and a hard place: negotiating age and identity in the UK asylum system[1]

Heaven Crawley

Introduction

The experiences of separated children who seek asylum in the UK and attempt to negotiate the complex array of individuals and institutions with whom they come into contact is increasingly well documented (Bhabha and Finch, 2007). Less often considered is the extent to which the success – or otherwise – of these children in securing refugee status and access to appropriate housing, welfare and educational support is determined not only by their individual experiences and abilities, but also by a particular conceptualisation of 'childhood' that pervades the asylum process. This chapter examines the ways in which children's experiences of conflict, human rights abuse and loss are assessed and interpreted, through reference to the particular experiences of children whose physical appearance and account of what has happened in their lives lead them to be 'age disputed' and treated as adults. For this group of children, a conceptualisation of 'childhood' that requires them to be apolitical and without agency has concrete and significant implications for their ability to access international protection and rebuild their lives in the UK.

Understanding the context: the UK asylum system

The past decade has seen considerable changes in policy and practice in the UK's system for determining asylum applications and for providing support to individuals and families awaiting a decision on their claims for protection. These changes include measures aimed at reducing the number of asylum applications, decreasing the costs of supporting asylum seekers, and forcibly removing individuals and families from the

UK who are considered to be at the end of the process (Home Office, 1998, 2001, 2005). While the use of welfare support as an immigration control mechanism is nothing new, the extent to which 'internal controls' have been utlilised is unprecedented (Cohen et al., 2002). Also unprecedented is the extent to which asylum and immigration policy in the UK has developed a discourse of exclusion for those who are not seen as 'legitimate' beneficiaries of support (Walters, 2004; Schuster, 2005; McDonald and Billings, 2007).

Separated children[2] seeking asylum in the UK had, until relatively recently, been protected from the worst aspects of these changes. Separated children are, by definition, children who have been deprived of their family environment and are therefore recognised as requiring particular kinds of support. The UK, like other European countries, has seen an increase in the number of separated children arriving and claiming asylum over recent years. In 1999, the Home Office reported that there were a total of 3,350 applications for asylum made by separated children in the UK. In 2002, this number had nearly doubled to 6,200 (Home Office, 2006). As the number of applications has increased, there has been a growing expectation within central government that those responsible for providing care and support to children should play a role in new procedures for controlling immigration. This has been associated with growing tensions between laws and policies designed to protect and support children in the UK and the experiences of children who are subject to immigration control (Crawley, 2006).

The government's overall approach towards separated asylum-seeking children can be seen most recently in its consultation on proposed changes to the system of support. This process, which has become known as the UASC Reform Programme,[3] is significant because of its systematic and wide-ranging scope and its attempt to subordinate welfare services provided to separated children to the objectives of immigration control. An explicit aim of the programme is to realign immigration and childcare systems and ensure that care systems acquire an immigration focus. Mostly implicit, but sometimes explicit, in the documentation relating to the proposed reforms is an assumption that most separated children are not genuinely in need of protection, but are exploiting a loophole in the UK asylum system to secure support:

> We must safeguard the asylum system from abuse and do more to identify and deter those who are not in genuine need of asylum, while at the same time ensuring the best possible response to those with a well-founded fear of persecution in their country of origin. To help achieve this

we will highlight, in the key countries where asylum seeking children tend to come from, the United Kingdom's rigorous asylum application process so that we dissuade children from travelling here needlessly. (Home Office, 2007, para 23)

The experiences of asylum-seeking children whose stated age is disputed can only be understood in this context. As noted above, the number of separated children claiming asylum in 2002 stood at over 6,000. By 2005 this number had fallen dramatically to 2,965 cases, but for the first time the Home Office also published statistics on age-disputed cases, which showed an additional 2,425 applications from applicants claiming to be children but whose age the Home Office disputed (Home Office, 2006). This means that in 2005 nearly half (45%) of all applications made by those presenting as separated asylum-seeking children were age disputed (Crawley, 2006, 2007). Many of these disputes remain unresolved, with implications for the Home Office, social service departments, legal representatives, voluntary sector practitioners and, most importantly, separated children and young people themselves.

Not only does the number of age-disputed children appear to have increased, so too does the political significance and salience of this issue. In the period since 2004, age disputes and the process of age assessment have risen rapidly up the policy agenda, in many ways becoming a 'touchstone' issue for a wide range of other concerns about the government's approach to asylum seekers in general, and towards separated asylum-seeking children in particular. This is partly a reflection of increasing litigation challenging current policy and practice, particularly in relation to unlawful detention. But it also reflects increasing concern about the assumptions that underlie the determination of age and a particular conceptualisation of 'childhood' that fails adequately to reflect the lived experiences of children and young people in search of protection.

Understanding disputes over age

In the UK, adulthood is defined as occurring at the age of 18. Turning 18 is accompanied by the assumption of 'adult' rights and responsibilities, and structures and institutions have been designed to distinguish between those who are under and over this age. There is, of course, no necessary transformation of an individual's ability to look after themselves or to behave in 'adult' ways upon turning 18. Indeed, the fact that childhood is socially constructed is reflected in the fact that it is through law, rather than simply as a result of the ageing process per se, that people achieve 'adulthood' (James and James, 2004).

Whether or not an asylum seeker is under or over 18 years of age therefore has very significant implications for the services and support to which they are entitled and for the way in which the application for protection will be dealt with by the immigration system. If a child's stated age is disputed and they are either not formally age assessed or are incorrectly assessed by social services as being over 18 years of age, that child will enter the adult asylum determination process. Age-disputed applicants do not benefit from any of the concessions available to children whose age is not in dispute. There are also different systems of welfare, social and educational provision for adults and children. Where an asylum seeker is defined as a separated child, they will be provided with accommodation and support by a local authority under the 1989 Children Act. By contrast, where the applicant is treated as an adult, has no funds of their own, and are not detained, they will be accommodated by the National Asylum Support Service (NASS) under powers contained in the 1999 Immigration and Asylum Act.

Understanding the reasons why age is disputed is a complex task, not least because of the wide range of circumstances in which such disputes occur. Although most arise when an asylum seeker first applies for asylum, usually at a port of entry or screening unit, age may also be disputed by a social services department as a result of a formal or informal process of age assessment. The dispute may reflect or confirm the Home Office's initial decision to dispute age, or may arise as a result of a needs assessment. In some cases social services may decide to dispute a child's age, even though the applicant has not been age disputed by the Home Office and is being treated as a separated child for the purpose of the asylum process (Crawley, 2007).

From the perspective of the Home Office, the reasons for age disputes are straightforward and are 'illustrative of a serious level of abuse of the system' (Home Office, 2007, para 24) by adults claiming to be children in order to access the benefit that this brings.[4] This has been the prevailing view for a number of years. For example, the Home Office's 2002 White Paper addressed the 'need to identify children in genuine need at the earliest possible stage, to sift out adults posing as children and to deter those seeking to abuse the system' (Home Office, 2002, para 4.55) The White Paper went on to note (at para 4.56) that Home Office staff were 'already taking steps to challenge older applicants and divert them to the adult asylum process so that adults posing as children do not become a problem for local authorities'. There is evidence that some social workers also hold the view that increasing numbers of separated asylum-seeking children who they accept are under 18 years of age are claiming to be younger than they actually are in order to access the immigration and welfare-related benefits that this brings (Crawley, 2007).

From the perspective of those advocating on behalf of children and young people, the reasons why age disputes occur are very much more complex and require an appreciation of the ways in which 'childhood' – and therefore the chronological age associated with being a 'child' or an 'adult' – is constructed in different contexts. This, in turn, has implications for what it means to be a child, the experiences of children and how children look and behave. As Stainton Rogers (2001) suggests, there is no *natural* distinction that marks off children as a certain category of person; the category of child is just that, a category. Moreover,

> [T]here is no benchmark of undisputed 'truth' that tells us what children are; there are merely different categories, each of which tells us a different truth about what children are. These categories 'work' for us in the way that they do – they make sense to us – only within the context of the society and culture in which we live.... In another place or at another time the concept of 'childhood' – which seems so self-evidently real to us – would be something different. Or it might even be quite meaningless. (Stainton Rogers, 2001, 27)

Although this may appear self-evident, immigration officials and social workers dealing with asylum seekers frequently fail to recognise that the meaning and experience of childhood is often significantly different in the politically, socially, culturally and economically different countries from which asylum seekers come.

At the very simplest level, the significance given to chronological age is itself a reflection of the particular context in which we live. As Hockey and James (1993) note, the precise chronologisation of ageing in relation to lifecourse identities is a relatively recent phenomenon of modernity, a byproduct of the rationalisation and categorisation of all aspects of life that industrialisation brought with it. While an individual's chronological age has huge implications for the asylum process and for the provision of welfare and education support, it is much less significant for those children and young people who come from countries and cultures that do not attach the same importance to chronological age. In many of the countries, birthdays are not marked. This may reflect the social and cultural context from which children originate, or conditions of poverty and/or conflict that render such celebrations impossible. Children may also have grown up in economic and political contexts where being a child does not confer any particular rights or privileges, or indeed may be a distinct disadvantage in the fight for resources or even survival. These children are forced to grow up very quickly because there is no advantage to be gained from remaining 'childlike' or dependent for longer than absolutely necessary.

The insignificance of chronological age is reflected in the fact that many separated asylum-seeking children do not know their date of birth, or even their age. When asked how old they are, many children calculate or guess their age on the basis of events that have happened in their lives, or information that has been given to them by others prior to their departure (Crawley, 2007). It is also reflected in the fact that children are often unable to produce documentary evidence of their stated age. Issues relating to documentation, including birth certificates and ID cards, can be a significant factor in the decision to dispute age, and one that may be exacerbated by the use of different calendars in some countries of origin (for example, Iran and Afghanistan). Issues of documentation may also be tied in with the perceived credibility (or otherwise) of the child's account. For example, if forged documents are produced, this may be perceived (by the immigration officer, social worker or immigration judge) as undermining the veracity of the child's account, regardless of their content and despite the fact that this may have been the only way of securing passage.

All of these difficulties are compounded by the problems associated with assessments of age based on physical appearance. There is evidence that much of what currently passes for 'age assessment', particularly at screening units and ports but also among some social workers, legal representatives, immigration judges and other practitioners, is essentially a rapid visual assessment, which concludes that an individual *doesn't look like a child* (Crawley, 2007). Yet even among children who grow up in the same social and economic environment and come from similar ethnic backgrounds, there are significant physical and emotional differences, as well as differences in needs and vulnerability, between children of the same age. Separated asylum-seeking children come from cultures and contexts in which childhood is defined in different ways and where the social, economic and political circumstances in which they live make it impossible for them to do the things that we expect children living in the UK to be able to do. These children are much less likely to go to school – the taken-for-granted 'norm' of childhood in our society – and much more likely to work, involve themselves in political activities, be caught up in conflict and fight for their communities or even their survival. Many separated asylum-seeking children have been brought up in conditions of poverty. Some have worked or have been forced to work. Others have been effectively 'aged' by their experiences before arriving in the UK. Bekham[5] described his life in Afghanistan and the fact that his face and hands had been weathered by his outdoor life as a shepherd. He observed that it was not possible to compare his physical appearance with that of a child of a comparable age who had been brought up in the UK because of their different life experiences:

> 'When I went to the Home Office they told me I was over 18 even though I had a hard and a difficult life in Afghanistan. I worked for the family as a shepherd and it was a tough life. That's why my face looks much older than I am.... Last time I went to the Home Office I told them that I am now 16 and they looked at my hands and said "no, you are not 16". But I am not like a British child. They don't work. My fingers and my hands, they have all got hard and old and soiled by work. That's why it's different.' (Bekham, aged 15, Afghanistan)

Because the process of reaching 'adulthood' does not necessarily reflect processes of bodily maturation, and because physical development varies hugely between individuals, it is virtually impossible to assess chronological age even using scientific or medical assessment processes. These methods (which involve x-rays of wrists, teeth and the clavicle to assess bone length and density) are widely accepted as having a margin of error of at least two years in either direction. In other words, a child or young person may actually be up to two years older or younger than the estimated chronological age. Age assessment is particularly difficult for those who are aged between 15 and 20 years of age and yet this is where the assessment of age – and the outcome of the process – is most critical (Crawley, 2007).

Few of these complexities are recognised in the UK's asylum system. Instead, children are routinely required to negotiate a process of age assessment that is based on a series of assumptions about how children should look and behave. These assumptions, particularly when they operate in tandem with an asylum determination process based on notions of 'credibility' and 'genuineness', undermine the ability of children to explain what has happened to them and their reasons for seeking protection in the UK.

The experiences of children who are age disputed

It is difficult for asylum seekers, regardless of their age, to provide an account of their experiences. For separated children, the requirement of the asylum system for a narrative that is coherent, chronologically consistent and brings to the fore those aspects that are most relevant to the claim for international protection can be particularly problematic. As Kohli (2005, this volume) suggests, refugee and asylum-seeking children often remain silent or talk in guarded ways about their lives and circumstances. Silence and limited talk are used as powerful protective shields when asylum-seeking children feel that their sense of safety and belonging are threatened in hostile environments. Kolhi (2005) concludes that while silence is a complex phenomenon in relation to children and forced migration, the refusal or inability of children to articulate a clear and 'thick' story about their experiences can cause suspicion among decision makers in the asylum process.

Many children experience the asylum process and the various interviews with which it is associated as intensely hostile, reflecting a 'culture of disbelief' that pervades the asylum process generally. There is widespread doubt and cynicism about the legitimacy or otherwise of their applications for asylum, with separated children variously described by immigration officers as 'rolling in', 'turning on the waterworks' and 'pretending to be stupid' (Crawley, 2007). These difficulties are exacerbated for those whose age is disputed. Not only are these children treated as adults – therefore not benefiting from child-focused interviewing techniques, legal representation or the presence of an appropriate adult – but they may also experience particular hostility because of assumptions that they have lied about their age and, by default, their experiences. Desta is from Ethiopia and was 16 when she was interviewed for her asylum application:

> 'After four hours she called me. I got there around 9am and I was waiting and waiting and at around 2.30pm she called my number and then she took me to the backroom. She was asking me, and shouting at me. When she asked me "when did you start school?", I couldn't remember properly. She just kept shouting at me. I was crying, I couldn't remember. She was shouting "You're lying aren't you? When did you start school, when did you finish school?" She just kept shouting and I told her that I couldn't think. She told me she would throw me out if I didn't tell her. After that she just wrote down some things. She had a bad attitude, some

problems, because she is putting you on the spot and you can't think straight and you have all these things in your head and you are angry at the same time so you can't think.' (Desta, aged 16, Ethiopia)

Although children become upset and confused, interviews are not stopped. Joseph described how his nationality as well as his age had been disputed because he chose to speak in English rather than French or Kinyarwanda at his asylum interview, and also slipped into the dialect of his uncle, with whom he had lived on the Congolese border after his parents were killed during the genocide. During the interview Joseph became very stressed and anxious, and was unable to describe what had been very difficult experiences in Rwanda:

> 'The first interview was a week after I came and I was just on my own....The interview didn't go well. When I came for my interview they just put me in a room and that was it. They didn't really tell me I was applying for asylum. They just started asking questions....The guys who were doing the interview kept laughing at me. I had my education in Kenya and I couldn't work out the years because I was so stressed ... I missed some questions and I felt bad because they would just laugh at me. They kept saying "why are you crying? This won't help you."' (Joseph, aged 14, Rwanda)

There are obvious consequences of being treated in this way, for children themselves and for the success or otherwise of their applications for asylum. For many children the difficulties of being a refugee, of being separated from family members and of being in an unfamiliar setting with no sense of what will happen in the future are directly associated with, or exacerbated by, the experience of being age disputed. This is because disputes over age bring into question the child's past and identity in a way that goes beyond the asylum process itself.

Many children express a deep sense of 'being wronged' when their age is disputed by immigration staff or by social services staff. Others describe feeling bewildered and sometimes intimidated by the way in which their age comes to be disputed, often as a result of a cursory visual assessment conducted through a glass screen or at some distance. Hassan was 16 years old when he arrived at Heathrow airport and claimed asylum. He described how he left Iran after his parents had separated and he was forced to live with his father who was abusive towards him. He was taken to Thailand by an agent and then on to China. His hair was bleached blonde in Thailand and his head shaved in China. In neither place was he allowed to leave the room in which he was staying. It is unclear why he had spent time in each country and he was unwilling to elaborate. What is clear, however, was that he was deeply troubled by the way in which he was treated by immigration officers when he arrived at Heathrow airport and his age was disputed:

> 'The worst thing I can remember they made me sit there and like a slave market other immigration officers were told to look at me and guess my age. It was like I'm going to be sold. One would say 24, another would say 21. I was told to stand up and down. Then they said "you are over 18".... When they were deciding my age in that place it was like they are going to buy you. It was the worst point.'
> (Hassan, aged 16, Iran)

Hassan's age was disputed and he was taken to Oakington Reception Centre in Bedfordshire where he was detained for eight days. He was subsequently formally assessed by social services who accepted that he was the age he said he was and took him into their care.

Being treated as an adult also clearly has implications for the kinds of information that is collected during the asylum interview. Because age-disputed children are not able to talk about what happened to them, their experiences *as children* are not properly taken into account during the decision-making process. Just as significantly, there is evidence that even where children are able to talk about their experiences, their agency and political identity is negated. What children do and what is done to children is often not considered 'political'. Where evidence of political activity is accepted, this may be taken as further evidence that the applicant must be an adult. Children's political activity or involvement is perceived as being incompatible with the claim to be a child.

Children's engagement in 'politics' and political processes

Although the poor quality of decision making in cases involving children has been noted elsewhere, this problem is often explained by reference to problems in the quality of asylum decision making more generally and the absence of appropriate procedures for responding to the particular needs and vulnerability of children (Bhabha and Finch, 2007). Evidence from research with age-disputed children suggests that it also reflects a failure of the asylum process to acknowledge and respond appropriately to children's political identity and agency. Children's applications are rarely considered in detail, nor are they granted rights under international law: more often than not, children are simply granted leave on a discretionary and temporary basis. In 2005, only 5% of cases involving separated asylum-seeking children were granted full refugee status. By contrast, 69% of these cases were granted exceptional or discretionary leave to remain, compared with just 10% of adults (Home Office, 2006). Many children have difficulty in securing a proper assessment of their experiences before they turn 18 – and when the application is assessed after they turn 18, their experiences *as children* are no longer considered relevant. They are then liable to be deported and removed from the UK.

The failure to recognise children's agency, in particular their political agency, is of course not unique to the asylum process. Children are commonly considered to be 'apolitical' in that they have no political rights of citizens, and are typically neglected in thinking about politics (see also Hart, Smith, this volume). Much of contemporary policy and politics is based on assumptions that children and young people do not ordinarily inhabit the civic or political sphere. A growing body of literature points to the fact that the dominant characteristics of modern Western childhood obscure any notion of children as competent social actors – properly in and of the social world – and thus able to participate in the world of politics (Wyness et al., 2004; Berti, 2005; Hess and Torney, 2005).

Despite these efforts to exclude children from the public world of politics, children are not secluded from political life, nor are they shielded against the fall-out from political processes (James and James, 2004). Evidence suggests that while young people are reasonably interested in politics and political issues, they are cynical about politicians and formal mechanisms for political participation (Howard and Gill, 2000). Debates about children and politics habitually fail to consider areas where young people *are* active. Children engage with 'politics' and political processes in different ways from those associated with adults. O'Toole (2003) suggests that children and young people politically participate in distinctive ways, preferring to get involved on the lowest level, in concrete issues and on a short-term basis. If this is the case for children and young people brought up in the UK, it seems even more likely to be the case where participation in formal political structures is either actively prevented or brings risks to personal safety and well-being. In many of the countries from which asylum seekers come, children play a key role in their community's struggle although this role is sometimes different from the more 'formalised' or 'institutionalised' role taken by adults in those settings. Moreover, the ways in which 'childhood' is constituted in societies is itself a political process involving relations of power. Children who refuse or fail to conform to notions and ideas about how they should behave *as children* are effectively engaging in inherently political processes.

The failure to recognise the ways in which children engage with politics and express their political identities has significant implications for those seeking asylum in the UK. Although very few children and young people participating in the ILPA research (Crawley, 2007) could be described as conventional political activists – there were no party members, few were members of single-issue groups and no one was a political campaigner in the conventional sense – most were directly engaged in the issues affecting themselves and their communities and deeply interested in effecting change. These children and young people cannot be characterised as apolitical. In fact, most were highly articulate about the political issues that affected them, both in their countries of origin and in the UK, as well as about the disconnection between these issues and mainstream politics. As in O'Toole's research, their responses demonstrated the ways in which politics was for them very much a lived experience – rather than a set of distinct arenas that they chose to enter or avoid (O 'Toole, 2003).

This gives rise to a highly contradictory situation where asylum-seeking children find themselves effectively 'caught between a rock and a hard place'. On the one hand, the failure to recognise children's political agency leaves them without rights or status: they are given leave on a discretionary basis but their experiences are not properly or fully considered. On the other hand, where their agency and activities are acknowledged, their status and identity *as children* are likely to be contested. For many, the very essence of childhood, at least in contemporary Western terms, prohibits political participation such that the 'political child' is seen as the 'unchild', a counter-stereotypical image of children that does not fit with the way we commonly view childhood (Wyness et al., 2004). And as Aitken (2001) suggests, there are particular consequences and implications for 'the unchildlike child'.

The implications of being an 'unchildlike child' can be seen in the case of Erbil, a Kurd from Iran who was 14 years old when he arrived in the UK. Erbil described how he had become involved in a local incident, which led to a statue of an important Islamic leader being destroyed. He believed that the Iranian army would try to arrest him, as had happened to others involved in the event. When his case was considered by the Home Office, it was determined that Erbil was unlikely to have been involved in these activities or to be at risk if returned because he was a child:

> 'There was a group of children. The leader of them, he disappeared, and others disappeared. They have their nails taken off.... So that's why I escaped and came here to the UK.... The Home Office looked on the internet about my case and they saw that there was a problem. But they said "you are too young and the government wouldn't kill you if you go back". They say I'm not young. It's not true.'
> (Erbil, aged 14, Iran)

Ironically, his age was disputed by a social services department who considered that both his physical appearance (particularly his height and the fact that he had facial hair) and his political activities while in Iran were adult- rather than child-like. At a subsequent appeal hearing, the immigration judge accepted that Erbil was the age he claimed to be but concluded that this very fact made it unlikely that Erbil would have been involved in any political activity or that the Iranian authorities would be interested in him. His claims to political agency were dismissed as 'youthful bravado' and 'unworthy of belief':

> 'Your immaturity was accepted as an indication of your age but also makes it unlikely that you were politically involved as claimed ... he shared no serious interest in or real knowledge of politics, as of course would be expected of most boys of the age he was then.... We regard his claim that he helped people to topple the statue ... as no more than youthful bravado and to be unworthy of belief.'
> (Immigration judge)

Other children are unable to secure refugee status because the significance of familial relationships in situations of conflict and political unrest is not appreciated. Faela, a 15-year-old girl from the Democratic Republic of the Congo (DRC) described how she had been detained because of the political activities of her father. Although she was not aware of the detail of her father's activities, it is clear that the persecution she experienced was a direct result of her relationship to him:

> 'My father had been a journalist writing for the newspaper. In our country there are two main parties, the actual President's one and the opposition. My father's party [the

opposition] went into exile. After some time the leader wanted to come back.... My father went to the airport to wait for him with the other party members. People weren't scared of going there. They were sure he was going to come. So they went to the airport. I was there with my father and my brother. We were singing. Suddenly the President's soldiers came to chase everybody. That's when it all started. Some people were killed there. They took me to a prison with some other people. I was there about one month. There were many girls there. They were really horrible to us.... Because they knew I was my father's daughter they wanted to get me. But I didn't have any idea what he was doing. They asked many questions but I didn't know the answers.' (Faela, aged 15, DRC)

While the exclusion of children from the public sphere frequently serves to undermine their participation in formal political processes and institutions, this does not mean that children do not have agency or that they do not have political identities, either of their own making or imposed on them by others as a result of their relationship with politically active family members. Indeed, the very exclusion of children and young people from formal mechanisms for exerting political power and influence means that it is almost inevitable that this should be the case.

Policy and practice implications

There is a growing body of evidence that children who are separated from their parents or primary carers, and who claim asylum in the UK, struggle to negotiate an asylum system designed for adults and a child protection system focused on children who live in their own community within their own families. This chapter has explored two key aspects of these negotiations: the overreliance on physical appearance and issues of credibility in determining the age (and needs) of an individual asylum seeker; and the failure of immigration officials to recognise the political agency and identities of children in the countries from which they come. It has been suggested that in the context of tightening immigration and asylum policies, these issues are associated with a significant increase in the number of separated children whose stated age is disputed and who are treated as adults. This is partly because current procedures fail to take into consideration the broken narratives of children, the difficulties they have in expressing a coherent account of their experiences, and child-specific experiences of persecution (Kohli, 2005 and Chapter Six, this volume). For children who are age disputed, the silences and limited talk are interpreted as 'proof' that they are lying about both their experiences and their age. But it is also because political agency, where it is acknowledged, may be interpreted by decision makers as 'unchildlike' and as confirmation that an asylum seeker is not the age that he or she claims to be.

Despite this evidence, the Home Office maintains a highly simplistic view of the reasons for the growing number of age disputes. The proposed policy solution – the introduction of dental x-rays – is equally simplistic (Crawley, 2007). Although significant lobbying and campaigning against the government's plans to introduce x-rays has at least led to an acknowledgement that '[t]here is presently a lack of consensus among stakeholders about the merits of x-rays as a means of accurately assessing age' (Home Office, 2008, para 5.3), proposals in relation to age disputes continue to show a failure to recognise the socially constructed nature of childhood and to engage with debates about the ways in which information about the experiences and identities of children and young people is gathered and interpreted. In particular, the Home Office's statement (at para 5.1) that '[f]ailing to detect those who lie about their age has serious consequences', implies that there is some 'truth' in relation to whether an individual is a child or an adult that can simply be collected and recorded.

Disputes over the age of asylum-seeking children can and should be understood as part of a broader set of policy changes taking place to control and regulate migration (and particularly asylum migration). But they also need to be understood as part of a broader process of contestation over what it is to be a 'child' in society. As James and James (2004, p 32) suggest, the particular and often exclusionary ways in which childhood comes into being is not simply the result of the messy and chaotic path of history or random chance, 'rather it represents the culminated history of the various cultural determinants and discourses of childhood being encoded in particular political policies and particular kinds of social practices'. It is perhaps not surprising that immigration law and policy reflect the ways in which 'childhood' has come to be institutionalised in Western society. Disputes over age have become a 'touchstone' issue not simply because of the numbers of children and young people affected or the seriousness of the consequences, but because of the ways in which the construction of boundaries between those who are or are not perceived as 'childlike' is part of a much bigger struggle over the agency or otherwise of children and over the rights that they wish to assert on this basis. To this extent, disputes over age can be seen not only as a key site of contestation over the rights and entitlements of asylum seekers, but also as the ways in which 'childhood' is constituted and regulated – and how this changes over time and geographical space.

Notes

[1] This chapter is based in significant part on the findings of research, funded by the Nuffield Foundation, which was undertaken by the author for the Immigration Law Practitioners' Association (ILPA) in 2005-06 and launched at the House of Commons in June 2007. The full report entitled *When is a Child not a Child? Asylum, Age Disputes and the Process of Age Assessment* (Crawley, 2007) can be downloaded at www.ilpa.org.uk/publications/ILPA%20Age% 20Dispute%20Report.pdf

[2] 'Separated children' is the term used in most countries to describe those children who are outside their country of origin and separated from their parents or legal or customary carer. In some cases they arrive on their own; in others they may be accompanied by an adult who is not their parent or legal or customary carer.

[3] The Home Office uses the term 'unaccompanied asylum-seeking children' (UASC) when referring to separated children seeking asylum in the UK.

[4] Although the level of support is viewed by many as inadequate, separated asylum-seeking children will generally not be detained or subject to the fast-track procedures, those whose asylum claims are refused are only removed from the UK if adequate care and reception arrangements are in place in their country of origin, and separated children benefit from being looked after by local authorities under the 1989 Children Act.

[5] The names of children have been changed to protect their identity.

Acknowledgements

The author would like to thank all those who contributed to ILPA's research into age disputes and the process of age assessment, on which this chapter is largely based. Particular thanks are due to the children and young people who took part in the project, and to Susan Rowlands (formerly General Secretary of ILPA).

References

Aitken, S.C. (2001) *Geographies of Young People: The Morally Contested Spaces of Identity*, London: Routledge.

Berti, A.E. (2005) 'Children's understanding of politics', in M. Barrett, and E. Buchanan-Barrow (eds) *Children's Understanding of Society*, Hove: Psychology Press, pp 69-104.

Bhabha, J. and Finch, N. (2007) *Seeking Asylum Alone: United Kingdom*, Harvard, MA: Harvard University Press.

Cohen, S., Humphries, B. and Mynott, E. (eds) (2002) *From Immigration Controls to Welfare Controls*, London: Routledge.

Crawley, H. (2006) *Child First, Migrant Second: Ensuring that Every Child Matters*, London: ILPA.

Crawley, H. (2007) *When is a Child not a Child: Asylum, Age Disputes and the Process of Age Assessment*, London: ILPA, www.ilpa.org.uk/publications/ILPA%20Age%20Dispute%20Report.pdf

Hess, R.D. and Torney, J. (2005) *The Development of Political Attitudes in Children*, Chicago, IL: Aldine Transaction.

Hockey, J. and James, A. (1993) *Growing Up and Growing Old: Ageing and Dependency in the Life Course*, London: Sage Publications.

Home Office (1998) *Fairer, Faster and Firmer: A Modern Approach to Immigration and Asylum*, London: Home Office.

Home Office (2001) *Secure Borders, Safe Haven*, London: Home Office.

Home Office (2002) *Secure Borders, Safe Haven: Integration with Diversity in Modern Britain*, London: Home Office.

Home Office (2005) *Controlling Our Borders: Making Migration Work for Britain – Five-Year Strategy on Asylum and Immigration*, London: Home Office.

Home Office (2006) *Asylum Statistics United Kingdom* 2005, London: Home Office.

Home Office (2007) *Planning Better Outcomes and Support for Unaccompanied Asylum Seeking Children: A Consultation Paper*, London: Home Office.

Home Office (2008) *Better Outcomes: The Way Forward: Improving the Care of Unaccompanied Asylum Seeking Children*, London: Home Office.

Howard, S. and Gill, J. (2000) 'The pebble in the pond: children's constructions of power, politics and democratic citizenship', *Cambridge Journal of Education*, 30(3), pp 357-78.

James, A. and James, A.L. (2004) *Constructing Childhood: Theory, Policy and Social Practice*, Basingstoke: Palgrave Macmillan.

Kohli, R. (2005) 'The sound of silence: listening to what unaccompanied asylum-seeking children do and do not say', *British Journal of Social Work*, 36, pp 707-21.

McDonald, I. and Billings, P. (2007) 'The treatment of asylum seekers in the UK', *Social Welfare and Family Law*, 29(1), pp 49-65.

O'Toole, T. (2003) 'Engaging with young people's conceptions of the political', *Children's Geographies*, 1(1), pp 71-90.

Schuster, L. (2005) 'A sledgehammer to crack a nut: deportation, detention and dispersal in Europe', *Social Policy and Administration*, 39(6), pp 606-21.

Stainton Rogers, W. (2001) 'Constructing childhood, constructing child concern', in P. Foley, J. Roche and S. Tucker (eds) *Children in Society: Contemporary Theory, Policy and Practice*, Basingstoke: Palgrave Macmillan, pp 26-41.

Walters, N. (2004) 'Secure border, safe haven, domopolitics', *Citizenship Studies*, 8(3), pp 237-60.

Wyness, M., Harrison, L. and Buchanan, I. (2004) 'Childhood, politics and ambiguity: towards an agenda for children's political inclusion', *Sociology*, 38(1), pp 81-99.

SIX

Understanding silences and secrets when working with unaccompanied asylum-seeking children

Ravi Kohli

Introduction

In making claims for sanctuary, asylum seekers tell stories of their persecution and flight, which they hope will get them through whatever border stands between them and an ordinary life outside their homeland. Sometimes, when they have to, they embellish their experiences, rewrite their scripts, polish up the presentation and talk of persecution in compelling ways. They sometimes pluck out a series of linear events even when their lives and trajectories are wayward and untidy, because the ways in which asylum receptors accept stories are often in linear form, with a sequence of suffering making the links in a chain of events. As they smooth and order their disordered lives, and use mechanical means to contain and structure the organic nature of living precariously, they learn to choose what to say, what not to say, and how to blend events into narratives that are purposeful and credible – ones that assessors and helpers in the country of asylum will buy into and believe. In that respect, people seeking asylum are acting no differently to anyone else who seeks to make the best of themselves in a testing situation. However, the contrast is that theirs is a strategy of survival, rather than one that seeks an extension of established comforts.

So, the focus of inquiry in this chapter is on how asylum seekers' lives are displayed through the stories they provide, in order to bridge potential credibility gaps and to optimise their claim for protection. In particular, I focus on the lives of unaccompanied asylum-seeking children (UASC) who have come to industrialised nations with stories to tell – and stories to hide. I develop the argument that our purpose as receivers of their narratives is to understand the amalgamations that children sometimes use in these circumstances, in order to enable them to experience us as fair, trustworthy and helpful people. Moreover, I suggest that there are advantages for the storyteller and the listener in working with silences, fractured narratives, and their complex underbellies, in that, over time, multiple stories can co-exist, allowing the sometimes solitary and neat 'truth' about an asylum claim to fit within a broader frame of a life experienced as coherent, fluid and whole. This chapter is based on research published elsewhere (Kohli, 2006), reporting on the relationships that social workers in the UK have with unaccompanied children. Here, I summarise and elaborate on some of the thoughts expressed in the earlier paper.

Unaccompanied asylum-seeking children

The meaning of the term 'refugee' is relatively clear, certainly within international conventions. For example, according to the 1951 United Nations Convention related to the Status of Refugees, it is someone who makes a successful claim in a chosen country of asylum, on the basis that in their country of origin s/he has:

> a well founded fear of being persecuted for reasons of race, religion, nationality, membership of a particular social group or political opinion, is outside the country of his (or her) nationality and is unable or, owing to such fear, is unwilling to avail himself (or herself) of the protection of that country.... (Article 1a[2])

Asylum seekers are those who have made a claim and are awaiting a decision by the authorities in their country of sanctuary. Therefore, UASC are children and young people below 18 years of age who 'are separated from both parents and are not being cared for by an adult who, by law or custom, is responsible to do so' (UNHCR, 1994, p 121), and who have made an application for refugee status and been granted temporary admission to the host country while their claim is considered. In this chapter the terms 'asylum seeker' and 'refugee' are used interchangeably in reference to unaccompanied minors, because their circumstances have substantial overlaps, even though refugee status is only granted to a small minority of cases in the UK. In 2006, there were 3,200 unaccompanied minors looked after in England out of a total of 60,300 children and young people (DfES, 2006). About two thirds were male, and one third female. Some 2,000 of them were in London, and another 460 in South East England, with some indications that in the Midlands (440 UASC) and in the North of England (270 UASC) numbers of looked-after UASC had increased steadily between 2002 and 2006. Contemporary reports estimate, in the absence of reliable data, that there were 100-200 UASC in Scotland in 2006 (Hopkins and Hill, 2006) and about 70 UASC in Wales in 2003 (Hewett et al., 2005). These bald figures contain much variability in terms of age, gender, country of origin and circumstances of arrival at the door of welfare services. Whatever their trajectory, and however precisely visible they are to those maintaining demographic data, they bring with them generous portions of complexity as they come face to face with providers of welfare services. It is this complexity that is visible in the stories that they show and tell over time about their movement to the asylum country, and into systems of care and protection.

Not seeing or showing the ordinary past

There is little indication in the existing literature that much is known about the pre-departure histories of asylum-seeking and refugee children and young people now living in Western industrialised nations. I have said elsewhere that the opportunities to consider the ebb and flow of ordinary lives – that is, before extraordinary events overtook asylum-seeking children – have not been taken up, in part because the lens through which children such as these are seen is constructed after the cataclysmic event. In one sense, the lens distorts their lives and refracts their trajectories, and in some respects this is useful all round. For the child to present themselves, and to be seen, as an asylum seeker has an advantage for all parties, and some diagnostic and bureaucratic value and function, where the assessor and the assessed try and keep each other in focus through the asylum lens. In that respect, forced migration and its ripples lead to:

> the creation of a compacted identity, where what is most visible is the label on the outside of 'refugee' and 'asylum seeker'. It is by the presentation and judgement of this outside packaging, that the terms of entry into host nations are negotiated. In a sense, children and young people who are forced migrants make the journey away from harm, yet at the same time the journey makes them, as they shift from a full and detailed life to a regulated, scrutinised and labelled existence, however extensive or short lived the transition. While these labels have an administrative utility, it

> is through their usage that individuality and ordinariness are compromised.... (Kohli and Mitchell, 2007, pp xiii–xiv)

These compromises are displayed in different ways when being marshalled by these powerful forces. The day-to-day aspects of history are occluded, and the pressure is on to package that history into shapes that 'sell' well within the negotiated spaces made for asylum seekers within the countries of refuge. It is in this process and from this context of the storytelling that the flavour and colour of what is said and unsaid establishes itself sometimes weakly, at other times robustly, but always within a sense of contingency, fear and hope.

Not talking: why some unaccompanied young people are silent about their lives

Jaworski's (1993) systematic exploration of varying aspects of silence confirms its power as a form of communication. He notes that 'silence occurs and means something all of the time. Some instances of silence are more easily recognised and identified than others that appear concealed in a multitude of words' (Jaworski, 1993, p 8). If we apply this proposition to refugee and asylum-seeking children, some specific reasons emerge for the maintenance of silence and, by association, secrets. Here, silence and secrets are largely attributed to the processes of becoming refugees. For example, the commonest response in the clinical and research literature that considers the emergence and maintenance of silences is that asylum-seeking and refugee children are sometimes too frightened to talk about experiences that have been unmanageable. Melzak (1992) proposes that war silences children, and that the silence is a way of dealing with deep disturbance – in some ways an attempt to survive intolerable loss. She also notes that it is not just that these children do not talk about their experiences, but that they can also forget them – wipe them out of conscious memory – or become confused about what happened when and lose the capacity to talk about what has happened to them as a sequence of events. Herlihy et al. (2002), in a study designed to investigate the ways in which people seeking asylum remember and tell their stories, similarly found that under the stresses created by forced migration people tended to tell stories that were fractured or inconsistent over time. Bögner et al. (2007) have also explored these 'faults of memory' among people who have experienced sexual violence within their broader experiences as refugees, concluding that there is a significant association between people feeling ashamed and the ways in which they show and tell their stories, sometimes denying or hiding fuller accounts to avoid loss of face, and stepping over or around the emotional landmines associated with those feelings. Overall, it is possible to assert that if the memories of their lives become jumbled or smudged, then the stories they tell about themselves as they move are likely to lose order and precision, as they would for anyone in such strained and complex circumstances. Sometimes the viscosity of grief, combined with the tempo of rapid and irredeemable change, creates a need to manage different speeds of living and experiencing life, and perhaps only the hardiest manage this multi-speed living simultaneously. Green's (2000) research with unaccompanied minors in Denmark confirms and extends this view. She notes that, at times, asylum-seeking and refugee children carry 'unclear losses' (Green, 2000, p 4), in that they may not know what has happened to the people they left behind, or whether there is any point in hoping for eventual reunion. Taking these perspectives together, we see that reasons for silence are related both to past events and to current circumstances and worries about the future. This view of refugee lives as brimming with loss and danger has been revisited from a psychotherapeutic perspective with a little hope. For example, in re-examining why people are silent when they lose their sense of home through becoming refugees, Papadopoulos (2002) offers a more positive appraisal for the presence of silence in their lives, in a way that appears to take into account both vulnerability and resilience as refugees attempt to manage mercurial changes and leaden losses in their lives. He starts with the proposition that through forced migration people lose their homes as well as a *sense* of home, that there are losses in both the outside and inner worlds – and that while the outside changes can be sudden, the transitions to adjusting to those changes can be prolonged. In that context he suggests that refugees are sometimes purposefully silent, and that this silence allows healing to take place over time. He asserts that forced migration leaves people temporarily disorientated, as if they were frozen – a type of 'psychological hypothermia' – and that they need to thaw out in order to proceed again with ordinary living. The maintenance of silence by refugees is seen to have protective functions, rather than necessarily psychopathological ones, in that it allows them a psychological space to reflect on their experiences and make some sense of them, before using their emotional energy to move on in their new worlds.

Taking all these views together, one can see the emergence and maintenance of silence and secrets as part of a process of healing, as well as a way of concealing and managing the confusion and disorder generated by forced migration. As such, it is a process that is both burdensome and protective. This combination of cost and benefit is also seen within other strategies for being economical with the truth, which are maintained by unaccompanied minors as they begin to talk a little about their experiences.

Telling a 'thin' story: unaccompanied children and a constructed narrative

When unaccompanied minors do talk, they sometimes do so reluctantly and cautiously, with a distrusting eye. Ayotte's (2000) study of the lives of 218 cases of children seeking asylum in Western Europe confirms that sometimes, when they are asked about the reasons for seeking sanctuary, they give tailored reasons – reasons that fit the criteria that the country of sanctuary uses to determine asylum claims. There is some evidence that these stories are rehearsed with parents or agents prior to departure in order to maximise the chances of acceptance, no matter where in Europe they appear (Anderson, 2001). Anderson's (2001) study, based in Germany, recognises these special circumstances for unaccompanied minors and takes into account that all the children who have left their homelands, for whatever reason, have to wear silence or 'economy of truth' as a protective carapace in order to arrive in relative safety. She notes that they may have been told to attend to 'what the interrogators want them to hear' (Anderson, 2001, p 196) and to try and appease their listeners by sticking to a simple and digestible storyline, which may not be the whole truth but which shadows it closely enough to be credible. The children's experiences, according to these expositions, are complex – in a sense, one could say that they have what White (1997) would call 'thick stories' (the *ordinary* stories of a wish to succeed in the world following forced migration), which are presented to the receiving authorities as 'thin stories' (the *extraordinary* stories of a particular sort of suffering) in order to obtain citizenship. While the thick stories might be multilayered and complex, it is the simpler, thin stories that are perceived as being admissible to the receiving authorities. The thin stories are therefore purposefully constructed as an acceptable amalgam in compliance with international conventions related to the status of refugees. They act as the key to entry into the destination country, based on its immigration policies. Once past the country's outer border, these stories then reappear in the explanations given to other officials who may be responsible for their care and protection. Particularly if the officials and helpers are identified with 'the authorities' and mistrusted, to repeat a story of suffering is rational and purposeful when sanctuary is sought.

'Thick' explanations for 'thick' and 'thin' stories

Researchers into the lives of refugees (being themselves examples of a particular type of interrogator) have also faced silence and distrust, and some of their reflections on the meanings of these aspects of their relationships with refugees are worth considering. For example, Bertrand (2000) observes that refugees and asylum seekers often present stories to the outside world that are highly selective. When gathering refugee stories, he suggests that the researcher is empathic and non-directive, even if the contrived story that the refugee tells is a mask that is presented to the researcher in the same way that it is to any figure perceived to be in authority. Jacobson and Landau (2003) make a similar point when they observe that refugees consciously construct a shielding narrative to survive, on the basis that a story told in a compelling way to a researcher might help them in some way to reach their longed-for destination of acceptance within a host country.

Both these studies emphasise that what researchers find when entering the lives of refugees is a type of functional distrust that maintains a level of integrity but allows the refugee the best chance of survival in a potentially hostile encounter, very similar to the functional aspects of silence. Moreover, these descriptions of the types of stories that are told, and interpretations of why they are told in the ways that they are, link well with the notion of getting to 'thick description' via a naturalistic study as developed within ethnography by Geertz (1973), working within the view that social phenomena have multiple explanations and that they can and should be viewed from a variety of perspectives. These researchers, in considering the many meanings that are attached to the maintenance of silences and secrets, identify not just that they exist, but also that they are purposeful, complex and understandable. A little like the move by Papadopoulos (2002) from seeing silence as a pathological fact to an understandable form of reconstruction, this sense of digging out explanations of resilience that emphasise imagination, creativity and purposefulness about the stories that refugees use allows a little light among the gloom.

While ethnographic researchers have concentrated on the emergence of many-layered 'thick' explanations of secrets and silence, others (Hall, 1997; Parton and O'Byrne, 2000) have also begun to dwell on the meanings of thick and thin stories. Firmly based on ideas derived from narrative therapy (White and Epston, 1990), itself embedded within a wider social constructionist frame (Burr, 1995), their approach suggests that the way people use and tell thicker, perhaps more capable stories about themselves can help in reconstructing their lives, particularly when they have become trapped in thin narratives of victimhood. In that sense, their emphasis on helpers understanding, uncovering and using stories of survival, capability and resilience to work alongside users of services fits very well with some aspects of clinical practice with unaccompanied minors as described in the literature. As Melzak (1995, p 112) says when writing about her therapeutic work with refugee children, her aim is to let children tell their stories in their full and complex dimensions, as constellations of connected experiences – 'to tell the story of memories connected with shame, guilt and extreme emotions such as fear and rage, and memories connected with feelings of pleasure, and deep feelings of well-being connected with home and community'.

This 'whole' approach – where the value of a thicker story for a refugee child is emphasised – characterises important aspects of practice, and those elements within it that reinforce the idea of a worker and an unaccompanied minor *companionably* being involved in the co-management of a process within which trust in the relationship is built up over time to create the right conditions for thin stories to be understood, thicker stories to emerge, capabilities to be harnessed and psychological and practical aspects of resettlement to occur.

Showing and knowing stories by UASC

The study from which the findings below are extracted was conducted with social workers. It examined the types of assistance offered by social workers that aided resettlement for UASC. Twenty-nine social workers in four local authorities were interviewed in relation to young people in their care. Each was asked to tell the story of one young person they were working with. One of the aims of the study was to see how well the social workers knew the young people, particularly in terms of their past lives, in the context of silence and mistrust. The practitioners themselves were not research-minded, in the sense of being consciously aware of the studies above, yet as they told their stories of the stories that they knew, their ways of practising echoed and embellished some of the findings available within the literature.

Knowing history

Without exception, the young people whom the social workers were looking after were reported to be only 'foggily' known. A consistent pattern described by the social workers was of the young people's reluctance to talk openly about their past lives. Some never talked at all. Others talked only when prompted by the workers. Silence about the past was an organising feature for many of them. The social workers gave various reasons for the existence of silence, which resonate with the ones noted in the literature:

- First, some of the young people were too shocked to talk. This particular silence, like any other silence associated with grief and trauma, had its own viscosity that slowed the young people down in their acts of ordinary living and was the most worrying of silences for the social workers.
- Second, social workers reported that many of the young people had been told to be quiet by those who had sent them, so that their applications for asylum were not jeopardised by revealing fragments that might have undermined their formal claim. Also, they were said to be worried that their families would be traced and put at risk in some way, if their whereabouts were known.
- Third, despite everything, some young people were perceived as wanting to get on with the practicalities of resettlement, occupied, like any other adolescents, in dealing with their day-to-day lives, and not so concerned with looking backwards or forwards in detail.
- Fourth, fear about the future meant that some young people were too unsettled in the present to reflect on the past. In these instances, the practitioners emphasised that the young people could only open up about their full past lives when they were offered some degree of settlement about their asylum applications.

From the varied accounts given by the respondents, there was a clear sense of the young people carrying their version of Pandora's Box, with 'thick' stories wrapped in silence. Particularly for those who had come to the UK several years ago, extensive silence appeared to have eroded the capacity to remember anything much beyond the story given to the Home Office, as if this learning by rote of thin stories had obliterated other experiences and memories.

Stories of leaving home

The social workers knew some of the details about the events leading to the flight from home. About one in five of the young people's stories were recorded in great detail via copies of the statements that had been made to the Home Office in the asylum applications. Another fifth were sketched out. From another one third of the young people, social workers knew that they had not witnessed traumatic events or been personally subject to torture. For the rest of the young people the trigger events were unknown, because they had not disclosed them to the social workers, or because the workers had not asked. The social workers described four ways in which the young people talked about departure, when they did talk about it:

- First, there were young people who knew what was happening to them and spoke about it openly. They had been part of the planning process of escape, were clearly attempting to get away from persecution and were not afraid to talk.
- Second, there were young people who knew, but did not say, and for these the workers struggled to identify the boundaries between privacy and secrecy.
- Third, there were young people who had little idea of what was happening to them and had explained their bewilderment openly. Sometimes they were too young to understand, and had come with older siblings who 'held' the story. Others simply did not know which country they had landed in.
- Fourth, there were those whom the social workers thought knew little about why they had been chosen as the ones to go, and now were stuck in a confused silence, being unable to give reasons to themselves or others for their departure. One young person confessed to having 'lost the steering wheel of my life', without knowing how this had happened, or why those in charge of his life prior to departure had made the decisions that had so radically affected him.

These stories were about sudden and catastrophic events that led to exodus, or about a prolonged period of attrition in which safety and belonging were eroded over months or years. The noose became tighter, freedom became restricted, the family was threatened, family members were killed, and arrangements were made with agents for flight and put into effect in dramatic fashion. The workers knew that a minority of the young people had survived intense difficulties, including being raped, beaten, trapped, frightened and confused.

Lives in the present: responding to silence, listening to talk

The social workers made three types of responses to whatever the young people said or did not say about their lives. First, they focused on the practical aspects of helping the young person to find their way in their day-to-day living. They said they were puzzled and sceptical about the asylum stories that they had heard repeatedly, or what they perceived to be inconsistencies within individual narratives. While none of the social workers in this study appeared to act like border guards, the ones who expressed some degree of scepticism were also the ones who were least likely to know anything about the young person's life before leaving. Instead, they worked with the asylum story and its practical and legal consequences for the young person, shepherding the asylum claim towards a decision that would allow some clarity about resettlement for the future. They thought that the young people lied sometimes, not just that they told thin stories, and that silence could sometimes be a cover for secret lives within which contacts with people whom they knew in the UK were hidden from the authorities. They also suggested that scepticism could build up into suspicion, and that suspicion could lead to cynicism. For example, they reported instances of other social services personnel becoming cynical about claims made by some young people being younger than they appeared, and worrying that their services were being exploited and their resources drained. Similarly, some practitioners were concerned that, on the basis of becoming familiar with asylum stories that all sounded the same, some of their colleagues had became hostile over time, and rudimentary in terms of helping beyond the immediate needs of the young person for shelter and food. However, none of these respondents identified themselves as being part of the culture of cynicism, even where they felt sceptical. On the contrary, many offered a sympathetic 'I believe what they say' approach to the young people's claims, based in part on seeing the young people as deserving of help. For both parties, forgetting appeared to be a better strategy than remembering, within which the possibility of being released from the burdens of the past could be achieved by burying thicker stories.

Second, some of the respondents noted that a movement forward towards resettlement could not be achieved without looking back to the past. Here, social workers appeared to be attuned to the meaning of silence, and adopted a broadly therapeutic approach in their work. First, there was the issue of timing. In many instances these social workers said that they had to wait before history and its impact was clear to them from the young people's own accounts of what happened to make them leave. A commonly expressed view here was that the young people were 'totally lost and abandoned and frightened' by the flight and entry into the UK and used silence productively, as suggested by Papadopoulos (2002), watching and listening to others as well as in processing the impact of their presence on others in the new context. In building up thick explanations for silence, these practitioners hypothesised that *not* talking had a link to the management of distress that they needed to understand rather than try and puncture in any premature way before the young person was prepared to do the talking. The rhythm and evolution of talking was considered to be an important part of their engagement with the young people, even though silence and monosyllabic answers were frustrating in some instances. When the timing was right, this second set of respondents sat with the young people as they tried to put words to their experiences. They described deep sadness being expressed in different ways. For a few of the young people there was a fearful watchfulness that would slowly blend into loss of appetite, headaches, lack of sleep, recurrent nightmares, and tears. There was anger in some others that would be launched if little things did not go according to plan, or if they were denied in some way. Some just cried. In these instances the social workers showed a capacity that encouraged the young people to remember people who were no longer accessible in the real world. They acted as mediums in the sense of having a keen intuitive understanding of the meaning of loss and the importance of communion with people who were dead or missing. Remembering and mourning the dead and missing, at a time and at a pace that the young people could tolerate, became components of a collaborative way of thinking about the past and its impact on the present (Summerfield, 1995).

A third set of social workers took neither the role of practical helper nor therapeutically minded practitioner. They aimed for, and sometimes became, the young people's trusted *companions* over time, absorbed into their friendship networks. These social workers, about one in four of the respondents, appeared from the outset to be interested in the young people not just as asylum seekers, but as adolescents having to reclaim and reinvent their lives in deeply uncertain circumstances. They recognised that a complex set of reasons had led to departure from the homeland – for some clearly associated with civil unrest and persecution, and for others with economic fragmentation in the country of origin. In any case, they saw that wanting to get away from poverty, get an education or make money, could co-exist with asylum stories and be legitimate reasons for departure. A basic shared proposition among these practitioners, exactly paralleling the description of 'thin' stories in the literature, appeared to be that some people lied about their reasons for coming to the UK because only lies would fit the narrow channel that was generated by the current legal definition of asylum. Furthermore, they said that in not being able to be honest about the whole of their contexts of departure, some of the young people were trapped inside these stories. These social workers did not appear to view lying in itself as problematic, only the burden that the lies created for the young people, who could not talk of other reasons that had led them to come to the UK without fear of being summarily ejected. In this respect, they came to reframe 'the problems *of* asylum seekers' as 'problems *for* these young people'. Their own position was presented within the research interviews as one of sympathetic understanding, rather than the narrower pursuit of acceptability of the asylum story. A particular feature of these workers was a capacity to look beyond the given story that they had heard many times before and to see a storyteller who was frightened about telling the story for themselves for the first time to a social worker. They hypothesised that once they had decided to 'really listen' to a story – to take into account the stage, the play, the actors and the script, so to speak – there would be the possibility of dilating the channels of communication with the young people that had been constricted by fear or mistrust. One of these practitioners, reflecting the point made by Anderson (2001) and others, said: 'I look back and can see now that they're told to say that [asylum] story. That's what they have to say. If I were in their place, I'd say the same thing, and even if I'd heard it a thousand times, they don't know that I've heard it a thousand times.'

These social workers tended to make the young people feel welcome. They hoped that the 'thin' asylum story would be transformed in time into a less rehearsed and more honest account of motivations, circumstances and past lives, within which multiple explanations could co-exist. As trust grew, these practitioners said that the young people told stories of ordinary lives before leaving, of growing up in families and communities of belonging that they now longed to recover or re-grow. For example, the young people were reported as missing their families, and the sights, sounds, smells and textures of living in their childhood environments. They were said to be angry at their parents for making decisions that had led them so far away; they were grateful for having got away; they felt guilty and worried about those left behind, particularly other siblings; and they wanted to succeed, knowing the material and psychological investment that had been made in them by the family left behind. These workers also reported that the young people were determined and resolute survivors, sufficiently elastic not to have been broken by the events they had faced. They told stories of survival in the face of adversity. One social worker offered the following characteristic glimpse of a young man's journey towards a self-contained flat she had found with him:

'After he'd arrived in the UK, he had one bag. When I picked him up from his first placement and took him to the next he had three bags and when I took him from the last foster carers I could hardly get his stuff into my little Ford car. He had so much stuff he'd accumulated. And he wanted to take his little wardrobe with him....'

These practitioners appeared to be fond of the young people, and offered a reliable, enduring companionship to them. As they came to know the stories of their ordinary lives, and to recount them in the research interview, the young people became 'real' to them, to the extent that the labels of 'asylum seeker' and 'refugee' dissolved, and the young people came to be 'storied' as multidimensional people, not just asylum seekers and refugees.

Conclusion

Through harvesting some key findings in the literature that focuses on secrets and silences in the lives of refugees generally, and the lives of UASC in particular, we can assert that silence is a complex phenomenon in relation to children seeking asylum-forced migration. It appears to show that the maintenance of silence can both constrict and defend particular positions that unaccompanied minors adopt at particular times along their journeys of seeking sanctuary. Moreover, in relation to the reasons for silence, it is beginning to be shown that people who have to adjust to rapid and at times catastrophic circumstances use silence and restricted talking as 'buoyancy aids' as well as experiencing their leaden effects. The study of contemporary social work practice in the UK that is used here illuminates some of the ways in which unaccompanied minors and their helpers co-manage silence and 'thin' stories, how they give 'thick' explanations for these behaviours, and how they uncover thicker lives together. Their ways of co-existing and of managing what can be known and shown at particular times in the journey of resettlement appears emblematic of the ways in which people who are strangers to one another can manage to communicate about and around lives that are hidden, where flashes of light make only some things visible. In the meantime, chiming with the research and clinical literature (although perhaps not directly informed by it in practice), the practitioners' stories illuminated some of the complexity within their encounters. Overall, from both research and practice, we can derive clear messages about the ways in which silence and secrets modulate, and ebb and flow, through refugee lives. These messages are that silence is not always destructive, that selective stories are understandable, and that the kindness of trustworthy, powerful, protective strangers is a necessary precursor to a safe life for unaccompanied minors who have risked many things in their bid for sanctuary.

References

Anderson, P. (2001) '"You don't belong here in Germany....": on the social situation of children in Germany', *Journal of Refugee Studies*, 14(2), pp 187-99.

Ayotte, W. (2000) *Separated Children Coming to Western Europe: Why they Travel and How they Arrive*, London: Save the Children.

Bertrand, D. (2000) 'The autobiographical method of investigating the psychosocial wellness of refugees', in F.L. Ahern (ed) *Psychosocial Wellness of Refugees: Issues of Qualitative and Quantitative Research*, New York, NY: Berghahn Books.

Bögner, D., Herlihy, J. and Brewin, C.R. (2007) 'Impact of sexual violence on disclosure during Home Office interviews', *British Journal of Psychiatry*, 191, pp 75-81.

Burr, V. (1995) *An Introduction to Social Constructionism*, London: Routledge.

DfES (Department for Education and Skills) (2006) *Children Looked After in England (Including Adoptions and Care Leavers) 2005-06*, First Release, 16th November, London: DfES.

Geertz, C. (1973) *The Interpretation of Cultures*, New York, NY: Basic Books.

Green, E. (2000) *Unaccompanied Children in the Danish Asylum Process*, København: Danish Refugee Council.

Hall, C. (1997) *Social Work as Narrative: Storytelling and Persuasion in Professional Texts*, Aldershot: Ashgate.

Herlihy, J., Scragg, P. and Turner, S. (2002) 'Discrepancies in autobiographical memories – implications for the assessment of asylum seekers: repeated interviews study', *British Medical Journal*, 324, pp 324-7.

Hewett, T., Smalley, N., Dunkerley, D. and Scourfield, J. (2005) *Uncertain Futures: Children Seeking Asylum in Wales*, Cardiff: Wales Programme of Save the Children.

Hopkins, P. and Hill, M. (2006) *This is a Good Place to Live and Think about the Future: The Needs and Experiences of Unaccompanied Asylum-Seeking Children in Scotland*, Glasgow: The Glasgow Centre for the Study of Child and Society/Scottish Refugee Council.

Jacobson, K. and Landau, L. (2003) *Researching Refugees: Some Methodological and Ethical Considerations in Social Science and Forced Migration*, Geneva: UNHCR Evaluation and Policy Unit.

Jaworski, A. (1993) *The Power of Silence: Social and Pragmatic Perspectives*, London: Sage Publications.

Kohli, R.K.S. (2006) 'The sound of silence: listening to what unaccompanied children say and do not say', *British Journal of Social Work*, 36, pp 707-21.

Kohli, R.K.S. and Mitchell, F. (2007) *Working with Unaccompanied Asylum Seeking Children: Issues for Policy and Practice*, Basingstoke: Palgrave Macmillan.

Melzak, S. (1992) *Secrecy, Privacy, Survival, Repressive Regimes, and Growing Up*, London: Anna Freud Centre.

Melzak, S. (1995) *What Happens to Children when their Parents are Not There? The Challenge of Holding a Developmental and Child Focussed Perspective within Organisations that Offer Therapeutic Work with Survivors of Torture and Organised Violence*, London: Medical Foundation for the Care of Victims of Torture.

Papadopoulos, R.K. (ed) (2002) *Therapeutic Care for Refugees: No Place like Home*, London: Karnac.

Parton, N. and O'Byrne, P. (2000) *Constructive Social Work: Towards a New Practice*, Basingstoke: Macmillan Press.

Summerfield, D. (1995) 'Raising the dead: war, reparation, and the politics of memory', *British Medical Journal*, 311, pp 495-7.

UNHCR (United Nations High Commissioner for Refugees) (1994) *Refugee Children: Guidelines on Protection and Care*, Geneva: UNHCR.

White, M. (1997) *Narratives of Therapists' Lives*, Adelaide: Dulwich Centre Publications.

White, M. and Epston, D. (1990) *Narrative Means to Therapeutic Ends*, New York, NY: Norton.

SEVEN

Doing Britishness: multilingual practices, creativity and criticality of British Chinese children

Li Wei, Zhu Hua and Chao-Jung Wu

Introduction

Sociolinguists have long argued that language plays a crucial role in revealing and constructing a speaker's identity (for example, Edwards, 1985; Le Page and Tabouret-Keller, 1985). Recent public debate in the UK over what constitutes Britishness provides new impetus to the line of research where linguistic practices are seen as both markers and makers of individuals' as well as groups' identities. So far, attention has mainly been paid to how specific ethnic and sociocultural identities are constructed through distinctive ways of language use or how speakers borrow features of another ethnic or social group's language to index particular identities (for example, Rampton, 1995; Fought, 2006). In this chapter, we investigate a distinctively multilingual phenomenon, that is, codeswitching – the alternation of languages within the same episode of interaction – and argue that codeswitching is used strategically and creatively by multilingual, minority ethnic children in Britain to negotiate a complex and multidimensional identity, to challenge conventional values and attitudes and to construct a new sense of Britishness.

The data for this chapter come from two related research projects on the multilingual practices of British Chinese children. One focuses on the complementary schools context and the other on intergenerational conflict talk. We will first outline the sociolinguistic situation of the Chinese community in the UK, focusing on recent changes within the community. We then introduce the two contexts in which we conducted our research. Particular attention is given to the Chinese complementary schools, a major educational and cultural institution that has hitherto received relatively little research attention. The main body of the chapter is devoted to an analysis of codeswitching practices by Chinese-English bilingual children in the Chinese complementary school classrooms and at home with their parents. We will show that the tensions between different ideologies, between ideologies and practices, between different generations and their linguistic proficiencies and between competing sociocultural values all manifest in this particular multilingual practice. We conclude the chapter with a discussion of the implications of multilingual practices such as codeswitching for identity construction and negotiation, and for the notion of Britishness.

The changing linguistic landscape of the Chinese community in Britain

The Chinese are one of the largest and longest-established diasporic communities in the UK. Sizeable Chinese settlement can be traced to the 19th century. The current UK Chinese community is predominantly made up of post-Second World War immigrants, their British-born children and more recent immigrants from mainland China. Due to the historical connections with Hong Kong and other Cantonese-speaking areas of south-eastern China, Cantonese has been the dominant language of the UK Chinese community. Since the return of sovereignty of Hong Kong to China in 1997, more and more Cantonese speakers have started speaking or learning to speak Mandarin, the dominant language variety of mainland China. In addition, the number of Mandarin-speaking mainland Chinese immigrants has risen significantly in recent years. There are no official statistics regarding the number of speakers of different varieties of Chinese, but it is generally believed that Cantonese speakers make up over 90% of the UK Chinese population, with about 5% Hakka speakers and the rest speaking various other languages. The number of native Mandarin speakers remains small, probably around 2%. But the number of people who speak Mandarin in addition to Cantonese and other Chinese varieties is estimated to be about 60% of the Chinese population in Britain overall (see further Li, 2007).

Like other diasporic communities in the UK, the Chinese face, on the one hand, the sociolinguistic dilemma of maintaining their ethnic languages and, on the other hand, developing proficiency in English. Previous studies of British Chinese communities revealed an ongoing three-generational language shift, with the grandparent generation remaining typically Chinese monolingual, the parent generation using Chinese as their primary language of communication but having some English for specific domains and the British-born generation, who make up a quarter of the UK Chinese population, becoming English dominant (Li, 1994). However, important changes are taking place within the Chinese communities, as more Chinese first-language speakers arrive in the UK to take up residency and more British-born Chinese become parents and even grandparents (Li, 2007).

Unlike other minority ethnic children in Britain, Chinese children rarely constitute more than 3% of the school population in any given area. This is partly due to their scattered settlement pattern. The children spend most of their time with English speakers and use English as their primary language of communication. While most of the British Chinese children understand Chinese and can speak it with varying degrees of fluency, their Chinese shows clear signs of English language influence (Li and Lee, 2001) and their literacy level in Chinese is low.

Chinese complementary schools

Since the 1970s, there has been a major educational and cultural initiative to set up weekend schools and classes to teach literacy and other cultural customs to British Chinese children. The Chinese complementary schools, as they are generally known in the UK, have a clear policy that only Chinese should be used in this context (see further Li and Wu, 2008). Significant differences exist between the teachers' and the pupils' linguistic proficiency and preference: the teachers tend to be native speakers of Chinese, have had a substantial monolingual experience as Chinese speakers and prefer to use Chinese most if not all of the time; the pupils have had limited and context-specific input in Chinese, have high proficiency in English and use English as the *lingua franca* with their peers.

The establishment of complementary schools has attracted public debates vis-à-vis government's involvement in educational management, and challenged the dominant ideology of uniculturalism in the UK. Yet, their own policies and practices have rarely been questioned (see Li, 2006). For instance, one of the principal objectives of the complementary schools is the maintenance of linguistic knowledge and cultural identity among the British-born generations. How successful have the complementary schools been in achieving this objective? More importantly perhaps, what is this 'cultural identity' that the schools and communities wish to maintain? Do parents and children share the same idea and vision about their identities?

While it is understandable that the complementary schools want to insist on using community languages in this particular domain, the consequence of such compartmentalisation is an issue of concern. In this chapter, we wish to argue that complementary schools provide a unique space for multilingual creativity and criticality. By creativity we mean the ability to choose between following and flouting the rules and norms of behaviour, including the use of language, in the schools. We define criticality in the present context as an ability to use evidence appropriately, systematically and insightfully to inform considered views of cultural, social and linguistic phenomena, to question and problematise received wisdom and to express views adequately through reasoned responses to situations. We will show that the pupils understand very well the policies of the complementary schools and what is expected of them in terms of language choice. They are also fully aware of the discrepancies between their own linguistic proficiencies in the various languages and those of the teachers. We are particularly interested in how the pupils manipulate the discrepancies in language proficiencies to their advantage in the classroom. We will show further that British Chinese children use multilingual practices such as codeswitching as a symbolic and creative resource in interactions with their parents and grandparents to challenge the traditional values, attitudes and practices. In doing so, they are not only building a new identity for themselves but also developing new family dynamics.

Codeswitching by Chinese–English bilingual children

The present chapter draws data from two related research projects. The first investigated multilingual practices in Chinese complementary schools in Manchester, where there are five Cantonese and two Mandarin schools. We undertook extensive ethnographic observations in two of the schools, one Cantonese and one Mandarin, focusing on classroom interaction. Recordings were made in the classroom as well as during break time, and a selection of teachers, administrators, parents and pupils were interviewed. Elsewhere (Li and Wu, 2008), we examined the teachers' use of codeswitching in the classrooms. In what follows we focus on the pupils' codeswitching. All the examples are taken from transcripts of audio-recorded interactions and are given in standard Chinese and English orthography. The English translation of Chinese utterances is given in arrowed brackets (see 'Transcription conventions' at the end of the chapter).

The second project from which we draw our examples investigated bilingual intergenerational conflict talk in Chinese families in Newcastle. Following Grimshaw (1990), 'conflict talk' is used here as a cover term for verbal interactions in which participants take alternative positions, whether reconcilable or mutually exclusive, on issues of common concern. A key feature of conflict talk is the difference in viewpoints and opinions among the participants. Such differences may be caused by a variety of factors. In intergenerational talk, speakers of different life experiences tend to hold different views on issues of mutual concern. In diasporic families, the differences in life experience between members of different generations can be very substantial, resulting in conflicting views and values. We examine below how such conflicting views and values are displayed and managed in Chinese family talk.

Classroom interaction in complementary schools

The first example we look at was recorded in a lesson at the Mandarin school when the teacher tried to explain a famous Chinese legend, *Hou'yi shooting the sun*. The legend goes like this:

> There were 10 suns (symbolising the Heavenly Emperor's sons) in a sea called Dong Hai and they lived in a tree called Fu Sang. At one time, the 10 suns decided to go into the sky all at once and caused havoc in the mortal world. The Heavenly Emperor, Tian Di, asked Hou'yi, the archer, to teach them a lesson. Hou'yi shot down nine suns. At this point the ordinary folks stole his last arrow because they did not want a world without any sun.

Using stories like this to teach literacy is a very traditional method. While the pupils knew that they were learning new words, phrases and sentence structures, they clearly found the story illogical. The teachers, on the other hand, tended to misinterpret the pupils' apparent difficulty with the story as difficulties with the language. This is exactly what happened in the present example. The teacher (T) read the story aloud and then tried to explain it in Chinese. There was little reaction from the pupils. The teacher then started to explain the story with codeswitching.

> ### Example 1 (T: teacher, B: boy)
>
> T: 有人把箭偷了，因为 <Somebody stole the arrow, because> people, they know that they will not survive if there was no sun right? If there is no sun, they will not survive either. So people took the arrow...
> B: 这个后羿不懂啊?
> <And this Houyi didn't know/understand?>
> T: It's a legend.
> B: Oh, it's a legend. Let us just let it go.

At one level, B, a boy aged 12, was following the teacher very well. He knew what the teacher was trying to explain, but seemed puzzled by the logic of the story. When he questioned it, the teacher simply answered that it was a legend. Notice that B's question was in fact in Chinese. But the teacher's answer was in English. B followed it with a rather sarcastic comment, in English. His choice of language seemed to have been made very strategically: his first challenge to the teacher's explanation was softened by his choice of Chinese, the teacher's stronger language and the school's preferred language, whereas his second challenge was more blatant and against the expectation of a respectful Chinese pupil.

The next example comes from a different class of the same school.

> ### Example 2 (T: teacher, B: boy, P: non-specific pupil)
>
> T: 那么中国的朝代啊，可以这样来记。它是一个 诗歌的形式。有兴趣的同学，可以抄下去，最好抄下去。
> <Chinese dynasties, you can remember them this way. It's a form of a poem. Those who are interested can copy it down, it's best that you do.>
> (Teacher shifted the white boards while students talked a little.)
> B1 (seeing what's being written): Oh dear God!
> P1: What's this?
> B1: Something to do with.
> T: 朝代 <Dynasty> (XXX).
> B1: Yes.
> P1: Oh God!
> T: 就通过记住这个，就知道所有中国的朝代了。谁在前，谁在后。
> <If you were memorising these, you'd know all the dynasties in China. Which one was first, which one to follow.>
> B1: We could not go back.
> B2: You could do.
> B1: Yeah. I'd like slaughter a (XXX), they won't be like this hard.
> (Students discussed it.)

...

T: 别讲话了！赶快抄。
<Stop talking! Copy it down quickly.>
B3: I can't (XXX) write down, just (XXX) 朝代歌 <song of dynasties>?

...

B1: How come there were so many 朝代 <dynasties>? Why say 一朝代
<one dynasty>，两朝代 <two dynasties>? What the hell.
(Students copied and talked.)
(There were questions about how to write specific characters. T also read out
what was written on the board.)

...

T: 怎么了？
<What's the matter?>
B1: Demolished, killed, eaten.
T: 王朝到此完，结束了。到清朝以后，就没有皇朝了，是不是？清朝以
后就是民国，然后中华人民共和国。
<That's the end of emperor era, all ended. There was no more emperor after
Ching Dynasty, right? After Ching Dynasty, there was Republic of China, and
then People's Republic of China.>
B1: What? In English. Speak our language, man.
B2: (XXX)
B1: Never mind.
(Students copied and talked.)

The learning objective here is to remember the sequence of the Chinese
dynasties in the correct order. To facilitate learning, the teacher made
it into a rhyme. Yet, the pupils could not see the point of remembering
the names and the sequence of the dynasties in the first place. All the
pupils recorded in this example were boys, who felt that the task was
hard and pointless. In the first half of the example, they merely talked
among themselves and made various comments in English, but not
directly challenging the teacher. It was only when the teacher tried
to stop them from talking that B1 began to challenge her, first with a
question on why so many dynasties, followed by a sarcastic comment
'Demolished, killed, eaten', which signalled an end of the dynasties as
well as his hope to finish the task. The teacher continued to explain
what happened after the Chinese imperial era came to an end. It was at
this point that B1 asked the teacher, very boldly, to 'speak our language'.
This is the clearest example we have in all the recordings of the pupils'
talk that they regarded English as *their* language.

The Chinese pupils we studied not only considered English as the 'we code' (Gumperz, 1982), but also knew that their English skills were much more superior than those of the teachers in the Chinese complementary schools. The teachers are obviously chosen because of their experience and skills in teaching Chinese. Some of them have rather limited English. The next example came from the Cantonese school. The regular class teacher was away. A teaching assistant (TA) was called in. The class had an exam in the first period and then had a break. The TA went into the classroom to tell the class that they could do whatever they liked. The pupils immediately realised that his English was not very good and decided to challenge him.

Example 3 (TA: teaching assistant, B: boy, P: non-specific pupil)

TA (low voice): 這節課自由活動，不要那麼嘈，嘈的話要默書。

<This session is free activity. Don't be so noisy. If you are noisy, we'll do dictation.> Understand? 下節課自由活動。不要那麼嘈，嘈的話要默書。自由活動啦。<Free activity for the next session. If you are noisy, we'll do dictation. Free activity.>

B: Do you speak English?

TA (very low voice): Sort of.

B: What?

TA: Yeah.

P: Yeah.

B (correcting TA): Sometimes.

B's question 'Do you speak English?' is very face-threatening. His correction in the following turn is equally direct. This kind of challenge is rare in our examples. Most of the time, the pupils tried to challenge their teachers' English skills in a more subtle way, as in Example 4.

Example 4 (T: teacher, P: non-specific pupil)

(T was giving pupils a dictation.)

P: (text) 離開了地球 <Leave the earth> … comma.

PI (to another pupil): 你默了，是嗎？

<You've done the dictation, right?>

(Pupils kept talking.)

T: 誰跟不到的舉手。

<Raise your hand if you cannot follow.>

PI: What?

P2: You're too fast.

T: OK.

P3 (exaggerated): Slooooow … down.

T: 我慢慢說，最後一次。。。最後一次了。

<I'll say it slowly, last time … very last time.>

P3 (grandly): Thank you.

In this example, the class was having a mock dictation exam. The pupils were chatting constantly while the teacher repeated the dictation content again and again. At the beginning of the excerpt, one pupil was repeating the dictation content while writing down his answer and the other boys were chatting among themselves. When the teacher asked in Cantonese that anyone who could not follow his reading should raise their hand, the pupils all spoke in English. P3 then said 'slow down' very slowly as if instructing the teacher. T then said in Cantonese: 'I'll say it slowly, last time … very last time'. P3 used a very grand tone of voice in his reply as if he was the master of the school. This strategic use of language turned the teacher–pupil relationship around: the teacher was put in a position where he was asked to follow the pupils' instructions.

It has to be said that the Chinese school teachers all accepted that their pupils' English was much more superior than their own. Many of them used translation, from Chinese to English, in their teaching mainly because they felt that it was the only way they could make the pupils understand the text. Nevertheless, most teachers did not like their authority in the classroom to be undermined. In the interviews we conducted with the teachers, some of them expressed their concerns over the pupils' switching to English. Interestingly, few of them described the pupils' general behaviour as being rude; rather, they considered speaking English to the teachers as rude.

The children also challenged some of the traditional pedagogical tasks typically used in Chinese schools. We mentioned above that there was an overuse of mythology and ancient fairytales in reading and writing. Example 5 below gives a clear example of the pupils' unhappiness with this tradition. Here, L had been disruptive in class. As a punishment, the teacher asked L to copy texts from the textbook. This is their conversation at the end of the lesson:

Example 5 (T: teacher, L: boy)

T: L，我看一下你抄的。

<L, let me see your copy.>

L: 没抄完。

<Didn't finish.>

T: 那你站着，不许走。

<Then you stand here, you are not allowed to leave.>

L: You can't stop me.

T: 坐下来，我看一下你的作业。

<Sit down, let me look at your work.>

L: 三个字。

<Three characters.>

T: 我看一下。… 你为什么没有抄？

<Let me see … why didn't you copy?>

L (low voice): Can't be bothered….

T: 我没有 right punish 你吗？你如果不听讲的话？

<I don't have (the)> right (to) punish <you>? <If you don't listen to the lesson?>

L: I don't care.

T: 为什么不听讲？

<Why didn't you listen in the lesson?>

L: It's too boring. Make it more exciting.

T: 那你说怎么让它更 <Then you tell me how we can make it more> exciting 呢？

L: Stop that mythology and repeating things all over again and again.

T: OK, 那下一次你来教一次课好不好？好不好，我们看一看你怎么 <then next time you can try and teach the lesson for once, alright? Let's see how you can> make it more interesting.

下一次。<Next time.> Let's make a deal. Or you give me some suggestions. OK?

L: Fine.

T: 好，你准备一下，我们下一次要讲的内容是复习12课到20课。

<OK, you get prepared. Our next lesson should be revision for Lesson 12 to 20.>

L: Alright.

T: 你回家的时候准备一下，该怎么教这个课。<When you go home, prepare how you are going to teach the lesson.> Let's make a deal?

L: Fine.

T: 好，我不让你都弄完，你准备一下12到16课，你看看怎么让这个课 <OK, I won't ask to you do all of it, you prepare Lesson 12 to 16. You can decide how to make the lesson> very interesting, very alive, OK?

L: OK.

T: OK? Let's make a deal?

L (faintly): Explain it.

T: Explain it. Just revise it, go over it. OK? Make a deal?

L (very faint): Deal.

(L left.)

The teacher in this example was a very patient and experienced teacher. She did point out to L that she had the right to 'punish' him. But she was willing to take advice and suggestions from him and to try her best to make the lessons more appealing. L stated in very clear terms that he wanted the teacher to stop using mythology in teaching. The teacher then asked him to prepare some lessons and act as the teacher the following week. We know from the teacher that it did not actually happen, as L did not prepare the lesson. But she felt that she made the point clear to him that it was not easy to make this kind of lesson very exciting. Many teachers expressed similar views during our interviews about the textbooks they were using. On the one hand, they were concerned that some of the contents were not suitable for the British Chinese children; on the other, they did not want the textbooks to be too different from those used in China, Hong Kong or Taiwan, as they believed that the latter set the standard for Chinese language teaching.

The tension between the traditional way of teaching and what is appropriate for this particular group of Chinese pupils manifested in many aspects of the school and classroom management. Example 6 below shows how much the pupils were against a particular teaching method that the teacher was using.

Example 6 (T: teacher, G: girl, B: boy, H: a boy)

T: 嗯，不错。能挑出他的错误吗？

<Um, not bad, can you find where he made a mistake?>

G1: Yeah, '涨' (zhang)，他说 zang。

T: 嗯。

<Um.>

B1: '聪' (cong)，他说 chong。

H: Stop picking on people. It's cruel.

G1: 学校门前，他说'学校面前'。

<In front of the school entrance, he said, 'school, face, front'.>

T: 嗯，不过已经很好了。

<Um, but it was pretty good.>

T (T naming the next person to do the exercise): Y.

(Y read fluently.)

...

H: I think she said 'sha' instead of 'shua'.

T (repeated the word): '玩耍' (wan shua)。

H: (teasing) I know. She said it too fast.

It is typical of Chinese classrooms that the teacher asks one pupil to read aloud or write something on the board. The teacher would then ask the whole class to say if the pupil got anything wrong. As we can see in Example 6, the pupils in this class thought it was picking on people, not just the language errors. There are clearly two kinds of cultural values and expectations at work here. What is interesting is that H seemed to know what was expected of the pupils. He first remarked that it was cruel to pick on people, but then he did pick out the mistake by G1 himself. His last remark that the girl spoke too fast was tongue-in-cheek and aimed at mocking the whole pedagogical task.

The examples we have given show that the pupils had little difficulty in understanding what the teachers asked them to do in the classroom. They were very much 'on task'. What they wanted to challenge were: (a) the teacher's authority and (b) traditional ways of Chinese teaching. The examples also show that the pupils' language skills, in both English and Chinese, are highly developed. They are able to manipulate them creatively and strategically to gain control of the classroom and turn the table on their teachers.

Intergenerational conflict talk

We now turn to two examples of intergenerational conflict talk. In Example 7, A is the mother of B, her daughter. A is in her forties and an accountant. She came to England from mainland China some 14 years ago and is fluent in both Mandarin and English. B is in her late teens and has been living in England since she was two and a half. Here, the mother and daughter are arguing about whether the daughter should go to a family friend's home together with the parents. In Example 8, C is the mother of D, a 16-year-old young man who has been living in the UK since he was five. C is in her late thirties and has been working in a government organisation since her family moved to Britain from China about 11 years ago. She is fluent in both Mandarin and English. In this episode, the son is trying to get some money from his mother, but his mother refuses.

Example 7

121	A:	你明天晚上不能出去 <啊。
		<You can't go out tomorrow evening.> (PA)
122	B:	Hey, why not?
123	A:	我们要去马叔叔家,不是跟你说过了吗?
		<We are going to Uncle Ma's house. Haven't I told you before?>
124	B:	When?
125	A:	Tomorrow!
126	B:	Yes, but you never told me.
127	A:	I just told you.
128	B:	Yes, but you didn't tell me before.
129	A:	上次马叔叔他们来,不是说好我们要去吗?
		<The last time Uncle Ma came here, didn't we agree to go there?>
130	B:	But YOU agreed that. I didn't know.
131	A:	Don't shout at me!
132	B:	I'm not shouting.
	{23.0}	
133	B:	我跟Tina 说好要去她们家呢。.
		<I've agreed to go to Tina's house.>
134	A:	去哪儿?
		<Go where?>
135	B:	Tina's house.
136	A:	我不是说了吗? 我们要去马叔叔家。
		<Haven't I said? We are going to Uncle Ma's.>
137	B:	But I don't want to.
138	A:	什么 I don't want to? 我们说好要去的。.
		<What 'I don't want to'? We agreed to go.>
139	B:	可是 I didn't.
		(But)
140	A:	What I didn't?
141	B:	I didn't know we were going.
	{3.4}	
142	A:	人家上次来看我们, 我们说好要去看人家。
		<When they came to see us last time, we agreed to go and see them.>
143	B:	But you didn't tell me.
144	A:	You are here. You know.
145	B:	I didn't! YOU talked about it. Nobody told ME.
146	A:	I told you.
147	B:	I don't want to go.

		{2.0}
148	A:	人家小钢不是也来了吗? 你怎么不能去?
		<Wasn't XiaoGang here too? Why can't you go?>
149	B:	I want to go to Tina's.
150	A:	Go to Tina another day 啦. (PA)
		{4.2}
151	B:	Can you go without me?
152	A:	No.
153	B:	Why not?
154	A:	我们是一家的嘛。人家一家来，我们不一家去，那好吗？
		<We are one family. Their family came. It isn't nice if we don't go together, is it?>
155	B:	Why not?
156	A:	人家还请我们吃饭呢。
		<They also invite us to dinner.>
157	B:	我们不是也请他们吃饭了吗?
		<But we invited them to dinner too, didn't we?>
158	A:	是啊.所以我们得回请。
		<Yes. That's why we should return the invitation.>
159	B:	I don't want to.
160	A:	No.

Both speakers in Example 7 frequently switch from Chinese to English and vice versa. Yet, the positioning of codeswitching is very strategic. For example, at the beginning of this episode (Turn 121), A tells her daughter in Mandarin not to go out the following evening. B responds in English. Her interjection 'Hey' overlapped with her mother's utterance final particle. This overlap may have helped to reduce the potential conflict, as the mother does not react to B's challenge but gives her the exact reason why she should not go out that evening. A does, however, reinforce her demand to the daughter by asking a question, in Mandarin. When B asks her next question in English, A responds in English. In fact, A responds again in English in Turn 127 following the daughter's assertion that the mother never told her about the visit to Ma's family. It seems that the mother uses Mandarin to state and reiterate her position (Turns 121 and 123), but switches to English to respond to her daughter's challenge to her position – B's challenges in English: Turns 124 and 126; A's responses to B's: Turns 125 and 127. This pattern repeats itself again and again in the episode. A's strategic choice and positioning of English is giving the daughter a message that she is the authority figure in the family and she would not allow her position to be questioned.

The conflict in Example 8 is of a different kind. Here, the son, D, makes a request for money. His request is in English. C, the mother, responds in Mandarin. Many studies have found that codeswitching can be used to contextualise 'dispreferred' responses in bilingual conversation in a similar way as pause, hesitation and other structural complexities in monolingual conversation (Auer, 1984; Li, 1994). In the present example, the mother is clearly using her choice of Mandarin as a dispreference marker. The son evidently understands this and tries to negotiate through Mandarin. In fact, the son speaks Mandarin most of the time in this episode. He only uses English in Turns 11 and 17 when he makes the request, in Turns 19 and 30 to answer C's English questions, Turns 28 and 38 to display his positions and a single word reply in Turn 36. The mother, on the other hand, uses English to challenge the son in Turns 18, 29 and 31, and with one English word each in Turns 37 and 39. Significantly, all these turns are in question form.

Example 8

11	D:	Mum, can I have some money?
12	C:	干吗?
		\<What for?\>
13	D:	出去一下。.
		\<Go out for a moment.\>
14	C:	几点了? 你要上哪儿?
		\<What time is it? Where do you want to go?\>
15	D:	你就别管了。
		\<You don't need to interfere.\>
16	C:	这么晚了，你要去哪儿?
		\<It's so late. Where do you want to go?\>
17	D:	不是现在。 \<Not right now.\> Can I have some money?
18	C:	Where's your money?
19	D:	I haven't got any.
20	C:	我给你的钱都上哪儿去了?
		\<Where did the money that I gave you go?\>
21	D:	你什么时候给我了?
		\<When did you give it to me?\>
22	C:	不要老'你''你'的。.
		\<Don't always say 'ni', 'ni' (*informal* form of you).\>
23	D:	哎呀'您'行了吧?
		\<(Interjection). 'Nin' (*respectful* form of you). Is that OK?\>

		{2.0}
24	D:	给点钱行吗? Please?
		<Can you give me some money?>
25	C:	你爸给你的钱呢?
		<Where's the money your dad gave you?>
26	D:	他哪儿给我了?
		<Where did he give it to me?>
27	C:	你不老说你的钱都是你爸给的嘛?
		<Don't you always say that it is your dad who gives you money?>
28	D:	哎呀, he doesn't give me anything.
		(Interjection)
29	C:	So give you?
30	D:	You.
31	C:	You.
32	D:	您.
		<*vou* form of *you*.>
		{1.3}
33	C:	这么晚了你要上哪儿?
		<It's so late. Where do you want to go?>
34	D:	不是现在去。明天。
		<Not going now. Tomorrow.>
35	C:	明天? 上哪儿呀?
		<Tomorrow? Where to go?>
36	D:	School.
37	C:	School 你要什么钱呀?
		<Why you need money to go to school?>
38	D:	I want to buy something.
39	C:	Buy 什么?
		<Buy what?>
40	D:	哎呀, 真麻烦。.
		(Interjection) <Really troublesome.>
		(B walks away)

In both Examples 7 and 8, the mothers' English utterances are considerably shorter than their Chinese utterances. This could not simply be due to their relative proficiencies in the two languages. In fact, their use of English, in short form, is very effective, as the children in both examples evidently understand the implicature. As far as the mothers are concerned, getting the message across is most important and there is no point in engaging in an elaborate argument when they have made their positions clear.

One important aspect of these two examples concerns 'talk about social, cultural and linguistic practice'. Many researchers argue that language practice is a sociocultural practice (see, for example, Zhu et al., 2007). Language practice can reflect one's social and cultural orientation and, at the same time, reinforce, change and mediate one's social and cultural orientation. On occasions, conversation participants make explicit comments on social, cultural and linguistic practices. These comments are an important and useful source of data for the analyst to understand the sociocultural values of the speakers. In intergenerational talk in diasporic families, such comments may well index changes in sociocultural values. An important cause of the dispute between the mother and the daughter in Example 7 is that the daughter believes that she was never told about the return visit to Uncle Ma's family, whereas the mother claims that the daughter knew about it because she was present when the matter was discussed and agreed. The daughter strongly rejects the mother's claim in Turn 130: 'But YOU agreed that. I didn't know'. Here, it is not simply the choice of language that is significant, but her emphasis on the distinction between 'you' (the mother) and 'I'. As the mother makes it clear in her subsequent turns, she considers the whole family as a unit and the daughter part of it. To her, when the family agreed to pay a return visit to their friends, everybody in the family, including the daughter, would be included. The daughter, on the other hand, takes a more individualistic view and believes that she was not party to that agreement even though she was present. This sharp difference in cultural perspective is made explicit by the contrasting choice of words in Turns 138 and 139. The mother uses the inclusive Chinese first person plural pronoun 我们 (we), whereas the daughter chooses to use the specific English first person singular *I*. Indeed, the daughter makes it even more explicit in Turn 145 where she says to the mother 'YOU talked about it. Nobody told ME'.

Clearly, the dispute here goes way beyond the choice of pronouns. It is really about the concepts of 'family' and 'self'. As Bond (1991) points out, the traditional Chinese notion of family is a vague but extremely powerful one; it could include anyone related to the same surname. It also sets a moral and behavioural norm that everyone in the family is expected to follow. In the traditional Chinese culture, the individual does not exist without reference to the family or some other social group. The mother in Example 7 is evidently following this tradition. The daughter, however, appears to have developed a more independent and individualist sense of self.

What is remarkable is that the mother does seem to understand her daughter's perspective. But she is taking the opportunity to give the daughter a lesson on family values and the cultural principle of reciprocity. However, the daughter overtly challenges her mother's argument that the *whole* family should act together. Apparently she does not have any problem with her parents' repaying the visit. What she cannot understand or accept is why everyone, including her, has to do the same. In her explanation, the mother brings up the issue of dinner. What she wants to convey to the daughter is that Ma's family are being very generous; it is not simply an invitation to visit but also to dinner, which would obviously incur cost to the host. This, however, adds to the mystery and frustration the daughter is experiencing. To her, it all seems a bit redundant.

Turning to Example 8, we find another example of talk on social, cultural and linguistic practice, this time about the use of politeness markers. In Chinese, there are two forms of the second person singular pronoun, that is, 'ni' 你 and 'nin' 您, similar to the *tu*/*vous* distinction in French. The former is used informally between people of equal status. The latter, 'nin', is a polite and formal form, usually used to show respect and to elevate the hearer. It is useful to note that while Chinese speakers tend to avoid using *ni* altogether – a general tendency to omit personal pronouns in the discourse of pro-drop languages – they often overuse *nin* to show politeness.

In the family context, children are expected to use the polite form *nin* when speaking to their parents and other adults. In Example 8, the son uses *ni* in Turn 21. The mother finds it offensive and tells him off. The son makes a self-repair, albeit rather reluctantly. Interestingly, when the son uses the English 'you' in Turn 30, the mother finds it equally unacceptable and demands a repair. The son makes the correction with the Chinese *nin* in Turn 32. What we have here, then, is an example of cultural values being carried over by the mother into linguistic practices in a different language. One may also speculate that part of the reason that the mother in Example 7, Turn 131, said to the daughter 'Don't shout at me!', when the daughter was not actually shouting at all, may be because she finds the daughter's use of 'you' in English in the previous turn similarly offensive.

To sum up, the examples of talk about social, cultural and linguistic practices in Examples 7 and 8 reveal interesting differences in cultural values between the two generations in diasporic Chinese families. While one cannot predict precisely what might happen to traditional cultural values among the younger generations, we can be certain that the family dynamics will be affected by the changing values and practices.

Summary and conclusion

Societies change their ideologies, values and practices all the time. Diaspora and minority ethnic communities are probably experiencing such changes more than other communities. The examples we have examined in this chapter provide clear evidence of such changes in the Chinese communities in Britain. In particular, we have shown that contrary to the stereotype of the obedient Chinese child, the children in our examples challenge their parents' and teachers' positions and display very different behaviours from the traditional cultural norm. They do so through strategic use of their linguistic resources such as codeswitching.

The examples also illustrate the tensions and conflicts between the dominant language ideologies and policies, on the one hand, and individual speakers' actual practices, on the other. The Chinese complementary schools, for example, promote a particular kind of monolingualism – Chinese only. However, as our evidence shows, both the teachers and the pupils use a great deal of English and they codeswitched frequently in and out of the classroom. We have shown how Chinese pupils use their language skills to simultaneously follow and flout the rules and norms of behaviour in the school. They use codeswitching to challenge the teacher's authority in the classroom and traditional ways of Chinese teaching. They are highly skilful in manipulating the discrepancies in language proficiencies between themselves and the teachers to gain control of the classroom and turn the table on their teachers. The pupil's behaviours provide further examples of the kind of argument Heller and Martin-Jones (2001) put forward that multilingual practices are a symbolic resource of contestation and struggle against institutional ideologies.

The British Chinese children's multilingual creativity is perhaps the most significant finding of the present study and a point that we wish to highlight. Creativity in our view is about pushing and breaking the boundaries between the old and the new, the conventional and original, and the acceptable and the challenging. It goes hand in hand with criticality – the ability to judge what can or cannot be challenged and in what way. The examples we have seen in this chapter show that while the children are fully aware of the rules and expectations of the school, the teachers and the parents, they make full use of their linguistic and cultural resources to gain an upper hand in the classroom and negotiate their positions and identities in the family.

Globalisation intensifies the multilingual norm across the world today. Nevertheless, public policies and popular perception tend to interpret multilingualism in simplistic ways as different communities speaking distinctive languages. The fact is that multilingual speakers alternate and mix their languages all the time. Being able to switch between languages is part of being multilingual and part of being a global citizen today. The Chinese children we have seen in the examples of this chapter are a new group of British citizens: they are British Chinese. Codeswitching between Chinese and English is part of their identity and their Britishness. Their multilingual practices present a challenge to the traditional values of the Chinese communities and families as well as ideology of monolingualism and uniculturalism, which still dominates in British society. It is hoped that this chapter demonstrates the significance of systematic studies of language use, including talk about social, cultural and linguistic practice to researchers, policy makers and the multilingual individuals and communities themselves.

Transcription conventions

For examples 1-6:

...	short pause
(plain font)	additional information
(XXX)	inaudible
P	pupil – not specified
B/G	boy/girl – not specified
T	teacher

For examples 7 and 8:

{n}	number of overlaps in the extract

Acknowledgements

We gratefully acknowledge the support of the Economic and Social Research Council of Great Britain for the project 'Investigating multilingualism in complementary schools in four communities' (ESRC, RES-000-23-1180) from which this chapter draws its examples. Apart from Li Wei and Chao-Jung Wu, the research team of the project includes Angela Creese, Taşkın Baraç, Arvind Bhatt, Adrian Blackledge, Shahela Hamid, Vally Lytra, Dilek Yagcioglu-Ali and Peter Martin. We wish to thank all the pupils, teachers and parents at the Chinese schools in Manchester for their contribution to the project. We also acknowledge the award to Zhu Hua (SGDMI/PID134128) from the Arts & Humanities Research Council, UK under its Diasporas, Migration and Identities programme.

References

Auer, P. (1984) *Bilingual Conversation*, Amsterdam: Benjamins.

Bond, M.H. (1991) *Beyond the Chinese Face: Insights from Psychology*, Hong Kong: Oxford University Press.

Edwards, J. (1985) *Language, Society and Identity*, Oxford: Blackwell.

Fought, C. (2006) *Language and Ethnicity*, Cambridge: Cambridge University Press.

Grimshaw, A. (1990) 'Introduction', in A. Grimshaw (ed) *Conflict Talk: Sociolinguistic Investigations of Arguments in Conversations*, Cambridge: Cambridge University Press, pp 1-20.

Gumperz, J. (1982) *Discourse Strategies*, Cambridge: Cambridge University Press.

Heller, M. and Martin-Jones, M. (eds) (2001) *Voices of Authority: Education and Linguistic Differences*, Westport, CT: Ablex.

Le Page, R. and Tabouret-Keller, A. (1985) *Acts of Identity: Creole-Based Approaches to Language and Ethnicity*, Cambridge: Cambridge University Press.

Li, W. (1994) *Three Generations, Two Languages, One Family: Language Choice and Language Shift in a Chinese Community in Britain*, Clevedon: Multilingual Matters.

Li, W. (2006) 'Complementary schools: past, present and future', *Language and Education*, 20(1), pp 76-83.

Li, W. (2007) 'Chinese', in D. Britain (ed) *Language of the British Isles*, Cambridge: Cambridge University Press.

Li, W. and Lee, S. (2001) 'L1 Development in an L2 environment: the use of Cantonese classifiers and quantifiers by young British-born Chinese in Tyneside', *International Journal of Bilingual Education and Bilingualism*, 4(6), pp 359-82.

Li, W. and Wu, C. (2008) 'Codeswitching, ideologies and practices', in He, A.E. and Xiao, Y. (eds) *Chinese as a Heritage Language: Fostering Rooted World Citizenry*, Honolulu, HI: National Foreign Language Resource Centre, University of Hawai'i, pp 225-38.

Rampton, B. (1995) *Crossing: Language and Ethnicity among Adolescents*, London: Longman.

Zhu, H., Seedhouse, P., Li, W. and Cook, V. (eds) (2007) *Language Learning and Teaching as Social Interaction*, London: Palgrave.

EIGHT

Closings in young children's disputes: resolution, dissipation and teacher intervention

Amelia Church

Introduction

As other contributors to this volume have shown, children's communications are often misheard or unheard. One reason is that in many settings children are powerless to make themselves heard. Another is that adults do not have sufficient understanding of how children communicate. For example, young children are active participants in constructing their own social worlds, yet adults may impinge on this process without a full understanding of how children go about creating rule-governed environments in which they are capable agents. This chapter shows how conversation analysis can be a tool for understanding how children communicate and engage, how they deal with conflict and how adults can support their autonomy rather than undermine it.

Children's arguments are a productive site for researchers to investigate children's competencies and this chapter explores how young children resolve verbal disputes with peers. Examples of spontaneous arguments between four-year-old children illustrate that although disputes are not always resolved, there are three very distinct possible outcomes: resolution, abandonment and teacher intervention. Conversation analysis of these three dispute 'closings' reveals that very specific linguistic resources are used by young children to manage disagreements with peers. Linguistic research shows us that we go about responding to other speakers in very particular ways. Preference organisation is a concept which explains that responses – to requests, invitations and so on – are normally performed in one of two ways (preferred or dispreferred) and that these 'turn shapes' are marked consistently throughout all types of discourse. This concept of preference is introduced later in the chapter, but is brought to the reader's attention here as it proves to be a governing principle in young children's disputes with peers.

It stands to reason that once an argument has begun there are only two possible outcomes: continuation or dissipation. In other words, once children have engaged in verbal conflict, the only alternatives are to sustain the dispute or to arrive at some sort of ending. It is the closing of disputes that is of particular interest here, because the *continuation* of conflict is essentially defined by the *absence* of a conclusion. Throughout this chapter, an analysis of closings in children's spontaneous peer disputes is documented, namely by distinguishing three possible closings: resolution, abandonment and teacher intervention.

Background

Oppositional talk provides an opportunity for children to construct and negotiate their own social world, simultaneously reflecting and constructing their particular cultural experiences. Indeed, 'conflict among children latently functions to develop their sense of social structure and helps reproduce authority, friendship, and other interactional patterns that transcend single episodes of dispute' (Maynard, 1985b, p 220). Conflict fosters the acquisition and refinement of social skills (Hay and Ross, 1982, p 112) and is related to social acceptance (Putallaz and Sheppard, 1995, p 346). Far from causing permanent rifts or discord, arguments between children tend to be quickly forgotten. As remarked by a 10-year-old boy: 'That stupid Mr. Dan gonna come up there and say "Y'all better come on and shake hands." Don't mean nothin cuz we be playing together next day anyway' (Goodwin, 1982, p 87).

As children acquire language for multiple purposes, they are learning to argue (Maynard, 1986; Eisenberg, 1987). Far from being a disordered activity, in adversative discourse children are 'playing with structures of embedding and ellipsis in return actions, providing disclaimers disarming the illocutionary force (Austin, 1962) of a prior speaker's talk, and formulating logical proofs – all without creating rifts in relationships' (Goodwin, 1982, p 91). Verbal disputes, then, provide children with an opportunity not only to manipulate or persuade their play partners but also to use increasingly complex language to do so. Viewing verbal conflict as an activity best avoided, one to be ended as quickly as possible (see Sackin and Thelen, 1984), fails to acknowledge the opportunity afforded by adversative discourse for children to pay close attention to talk-in-interaction. Indeed, dispute contexts provide children with far greater motivation to quickly produce creative structures than could be constructed by the teacher for pedagogic purposes (Goodwin and Goodwin, 1987).

'Oppositional talk' (Corsaro and Maynard, 1996) and its various guises (conflict, argument, dispute, adversarial discourse and so on) is fundamentally identified through opposition to some prior objectionable utterance or event. Elsewhere, opposition is described as 'overt disagreement' (Miller et al., 1986, p 544), expressing an 'adversary position' (Coulter, 1990, p 185) or 'counter-assertion' that rejects, denies or contradicts the prior assertion (Phinney, 1986, p 48). 'Protest, resistance, or retaliation' (Hay and Ross, 1982, p 107) are also used to describe the onset and progress of opposition. Conflict, then, denotes an articulated form of disagreement where 'one party impedes the satisfaction of the wants of the other' (O'Keefe and Benoit, 1982, p 163). It should be noted that disagreement is not necessarily overt; persuasion (Miller et al., 1986, p 544) is also proposed as a defining characteristic of conflict.

A core, defining feature of conflict is the performance of adversary positions (Coulter, 1990, p 185) maintained by at least two people (Hay, 1984, p 2; Garvey and Shantz, 1995, p 94). Consequently, disputes are defined as spontaneously co-constructed by the children themselves (Eisenberg and Garvey, 1981, p 150). For the purposes of this chapter, we are concerned with non-pretend, non-ritual, non-joking adversative discourse (see Garvey and Shantz, 1995). As a working definition, conflict 'begins with overt opposition between individuals and continues until opposition ceases. Moves within conflict either continue the opposition or address it with attempts at conciliation or resolution' (Ross and Conant 1995, p 154).

It is the attempts at *conciliation* or *resolution* of disputes that concerns us here. Earlier research on child conflict illustrates the type of verbal strategies produced (for example, Eisenberg and Garvey, 1981), and provisional attempts have been made to describe sequences of these strategies. Consideration of the outcomes of children's disputes is generally made only in passing. Although most studies specify the boundaries of conflict episodes – disputes 'end with either clear settlements, physical movement of dispute participants from the interactive scene, or a shift away from the disputed event to a new topic or activity' (Corsaro and Rizzo, 1990, p 26) – attention to the form of closing sequences has been limited.

An undisputed feature of conflict endings is that the conclusion is brought about by the collaborative effort of the parties involved. The successful resolution of conflict depends on the acquiescence of both or all parties. Vuchinich (1990) states that the end of a conflict episode is dependent on the mutual participation of all participants. This is reached in one of two ways: either one child achieves a dominant position (which necessitates the resignation of the other child) or both parties negotiate an acceptable end to the disputing. As Eisenberg and Garvey (1981, p 168) point out, the 'successful resolution of an adversative episode is a mutual endeavor: a child is more likely to win if he considers his opponent's intentions *and* more likely to concede if his own desires are taken into account'.

Yet, attempting to isolate successful examples of conflict resolution is complicated by the claim that in many children's disputes a clear outcome does not exist:

> The majority of disputes, however, are terminated without any sharp indication that either position has 'won' or 'lost'. In general, the end of an argument occurs when one of the two disputing parties does not tie his talk to the topic of the prior dispute, but instead produces an action that breaks the argument frame ... and his adversary accepts this shift. Although compromise is seldom reached, nor sought as a goal of the interaction, by shifting to noncompetitive talk (between former disputants), parties cooperate in bringing about the closure of the dispute. (Goodwin, 1982, pp 87–8)

Given the contention that resolution is not readily achieved in children's disputing, further investigation of conflict outcomes is warranted. If children are not always 'winning' or 'losing' arguments, how is it that arguments are brought to a close? And where disputes are resolved, how is this achieved? Other than the termination sequences identified above, what features of talk are implicated in outcomes? The body of existing research in children's conflict presents a thorough account of what children argue about and the types of strategies children use during disputes. Essentially, *what* children do in disputes is well established. But questions remain as to *how* children co-construct conflict closings. The purpose of this chapter is to further detail types of closings in young children's arguments and illustrate how it is that children go about 'doing resolution'.

The data

The data consist of audio- and video-taped dispute sequences produced spontaneously by four-year-old children in two day-care centres in inner-city and inner-suburban Melbourne, Australia. Video and audio recordings were carried out during morning free play sessions over a period of two months in each centre. Each group consisted of more than 10 children who attended the centre at least three days a week with approximately equal numbers of boys and girls. All children were aged between three years, eleven months and five years, three months and – with one exception – all children participating in the study would be enrolled in formal schooling the following year. The children involved in the study spoke English as a first language or had developed near-native fluency. The two preschools selected for inclusion in the project were private providers (that is, fee-paying rather than wholly government funded) and children attending were predominantly from middle-class families (as indicated by socioeconomic measures of residential suburb).

The database consists of 60 spontaneous disputes recorded during the morning free play sessions in both day-care centres. The dispute episodes were transcribed using conventions developed by Gail Jefferson among others (see Sacks et al., 1974; Atkinson and Heritage, 1984). The transcripts are faithful to a conversation analytic methodology and capture distinctive features of the interaction constructed – and oriented to – by the participants themselves. Conversation analysis (see Schegloff, 2007; ten Have, 2007) was employed as a methodology as it proves particularly useful in research with young children given the insistence on naturally occurring data, a preoccupation with data-driven analysis and the very features of talk that participants attend to (Church, 2007). Following a conversation analytic paradigm of 'unmotivated looking', the analysis uncovers sequential features of closings in children's disputes.

Three types of dispute closings: resolution, abandonment and teacher intervention

Analysis of the 60 spontaneous disputes between four-year-old children uncovered three distinct types of dispute closings where (1) acceptance of the outcome denotes 'resolution', (2) unacknowledged dissipation distinguishes disputes that are 'abandoned' and (3) 'teacher intervention' is imposed where children are seemingly unable to co-construct resolution. Essentially, mutual acceptance implies that some sort of resolution has been achieved, that the conflict is recognised as finished by the involved parties (even where one party may be dissatisfied with the outcome). However, disputes may also come to an end without overt acknowledgement by either party – a cessation of disputing despite any clear conclusion. We shall see that the fundamental distinction between resolution and abandonment of disputes lies in the maintenance of established play partnerships. That is, children continue to play together once a dispute is resolved, but do not when a dispute is abandoned. Alternatively, where the children are seemingly unable to orchestrate some sort of conclusion themselves, one may be imposed through teacher intervention. The differentiation between these three types of closing in children's peer disputes will become apparent in the extracts taken from data collected in the two preschool environments.

Resolution

In resolved episodes, a clear conclusion of the argument is arrived at, one that is mutually acceptable to all participants. As almost half of the disputes recorded in the two observation environments were heard as resolved, outright resolution appears more common than has been suggested in earlier research (for example, Goodwin, 1982). Given that frequency of occurrence is not accounted for in this naturalistic data, we should be wary of any quantitative claims; close attention to the performance of conflict resolution, however, is possible.

A form of resolution identified as a distinct win/loss outcome arises when one child is successful in imposing their wishes on another party, understood either in the non-verbal acquiescence of the other party or through vocal acceptance. In Extract 1, for example, Luke concedes with a non-verbal move following Sam's imperative in line 9 (see 'Transcription conventions' at the end of the chapter).

Extract 1

Participants:	LUK Luke, SAM Sam
Situation:	LUK is banging a wooden block on his own head.

1	LUK:	look Sam (0.3) ow ow.=
2	SAM:	=don't do that (.) that's-,
		(0.8)
3	SAM:	don't do that Luke¿.
4	LUK:	i want to crack it.
		(2.2)
5	SAM:	if you crack heads you'll ↓die: (0.3) do you want to ↑die::
		(0.3) and then your mummy will cry:?
		(1.3)
6	LUK:	°yes°.
		(1.5)

7	SAM:	don't you like your mummy.
8	LUK:	°yes i do°.
		(0.3)
9	SAM:	then don't (0.3) then don't die yourself.
10 →	%act:	LUK stops hitting his head with the block.

Resolution can also be achieved in a more face-saving manner, where a child agrees with the proposal made by the prior speaker. This agreement promotes the speaker to the role of collaborator, although it should be noted that it is the preceding turn that creates the opportunity for collaboration. Typically, this type of acknowledgment of the opposing position is performed with an agreement token (for example, 'yeah'), as exemplified by John in line 6, Extract 2.

Extract 2

Participants:	JON John, TES Tess
Situation:	JON and TES are playing with the magnet fishing game. The fish are seven different colours. TES 'catches' a blue fish even though the blue 'boat' is in front of JON.

1	JON:	oh you got my one (.) x ing it.
2	TES:	↑no: we are sharing John?
3	JON:	no (0.3) no you got my ↑blue one.
		(0.4)
4	TES:	but we (0.3) but (0.5) but we are just sharing.
		(0.8)
5	TES:	that one goes in there [John].
6 →	JON:	[°°yeah] oh yeah coz°°-,

Alternatively, resolved dispute closings incorporate a modified acceptance of the opposing position or introduce an alternative proposal. The first of these (modified acceptance) is similar to the outcome of the previous examples, in that one party's position supersedes another. In this instance, however, the acquiescing party incorporates some condition of their own (for example, line 12, Extract 3). That is, disputes are resolved where the acceptance of the other's position is implied rather than overtly stated. In these cases the child is essentially accepting the position of the other party but imposing some of their own conditions.

Extract 3

Participants:		MIR Miranda, CAZ Caroline
Situation:		MIR and CAZ are playing in the spaceship. MIR is holding two plastic lids.

1	MIR:	we ↑both have two.
		(1.2)
2	MIR:	see?
		(0.8)
3	CAZ:	no: (0.3) (i've got these).
4	MIR:	then give one to me Caroline because you've got lots there.
		(1.0)
5	CAZ:	i'm not giving any of these to you¿
		(1.8)
6	MIR:	(if you don't) then i'll just take it then.
	%act:	reaches to grab plastic lid
7	CAZ:	STO::P!
		(0.3)
8	MIR:	gimme one of them.
		(0.2)
9	CAZ:	i am not going to.
		.... (5.6)
10	%com:	utterances inaudible
11	MIR:	let's just be nice and understand okay?
		(1.9)
12 →	CAZ:	but we have to just type into the computer.
	%com:	MIR takes up this suggestion and both girls return to playing with the keyboards in the spaceship.

Resolution may also be achieved by an absence of response, achieved through silence and resumption of collaborative interaction with no further opposition. In other words, disputes may be seen to be resolved where no further challenge is made to the prior speaker. The absence of a vocal opposition implies silent acquiescence to whoever produces the final turn. A defining feature of resolution in these episodes is that the children continue to play together after the zero response.

Extract 4

Participants:	LUK Luke, SAM Sam
Situation:	Pack-up time. The children are pretending to be cranes and are placing blocks next to Adam who has been given the responsibility of stacking the blocks on the shelf.

I	LUK:	0 ((%act: puts a block on the shelf))
2	SAM:	leave them there (0.3) ↑Adam's (.) Adam's in charge of putting them away (0.3) Luke?
		(5.7)
3	LUK:	i saw you: put one away¿=
4	SAM:	=that doesn't matter cause it wasn't a block it was a cylinder.
→	%com:	LUK makes no further comment.

Resolution can therefore be achieved indirectly, effectively accommodating the claims of the other party in the next turn without overtly acknowledging them. A child may ignore the prior speaker's contribution, yet if they do not actively reject the content of this contribution, the dispute is resolved. A common feature of these varieties of closings is that one party decides *not* to continue the dispute.

Where disputes are resolved, the single most important defining feature is the resumption of collaborative (or at least parallel) play. In each of the episodes identified above as resolved, the children were able to continue playing together once the dispute had closed. While the outcome might not have been gratifying to all involved, it was acceptable to each of the children, evident in resumed shared activity. This outcome is therefore distinct from abandoned disputes where one of the participants typically left the play area or at least refrained from any further interaction with the opposing party.

Abandonment

Disputes must be resolved if conversation or interaction is to continue. Without active resolution of a dispute, collaborative play cannot be resumed. An outcome described in this research as *abandonment* denotes the interruption of cooperative interaction. When an argument is not resolved by the children themselves, or through the teacher as an arbitrator (see below), the abandonment of the argument results in the breakdown of shared activity. Where disputes are abandoned, collaborative or parallel play is *not* resumed.

Failure to respond was seen as a final move in some resolved disputes, where a zero response (that is, no further challenge) functioned as tacit acceptance of the other party's position. Yet, in *abandoned* disputes, zero responses can also mark the end of the episode. Unlike resolved episodes, however, an absence of further opposition in abandoned disputes precedes a breakdown in collaborative play. Where zero responses were implicated in resolution, the participants continued to play together. In abandoned disputes, on the other hand, one party made no further challenge *and* no further attempt to engage the other party in any activity (see Vuchinich's [1990] *withdrawal* format).

A failure to respond resulting in abandonment of the dispute may be accompanied by one party physically removing themselves from the shared play space.

Extract 5

	Participants:	FEL Felicity, CHE Cherie, NAN Nancy
	Situation:	FEL and CHE are using the only two available fishing rods to catch the magnetic fish. NAN has been watching them for some time.
1	NAN:	i want a turn of that fish.
		(2.1)
2	NAN:	Cherie.
		(0.8)
3	FEL:	wha:[t]?
4	NAN:	[i wan] i wanna tu:rn (0.7) i wanna turn of that.
		(0.4)
5	FEL:	well ↑we (0.3) got here fi:rst?
		(0.3)
6	NAN:	we have to share (0.6) have to [share].
7	CHE:	((*sings quietly to herself*)) [get the] little fishies out (0.2) in the little box.
8	CHE:	((*to FEL*)) (these [are yours]).
9	FEL:	([fishes]),
		(0.5)
10	CHE:	you put them in.
		(2.6)
11	NAN:	you have to sha:re (.) don't get away.
		(1.2)
12	CHE:	we (.) ↑a:re.
		(0.6)

13	NAN:	no you're not °sharing° (.) you're (0.4) taking a long time.
		(3.4)
14	FEL:	mmm.
15	NAN:	don't say mmm.
		(1.1)
16	FEL:	mmm.
17	NAN:	don't (0.3) don't say THAT!
		(0.2)
18	FEL:	mmm.
		(0.4)
19	NAN:	DON'T SAY THAT!
20	CHE:	put the [little fishies],
21	NAN:	[you don't have] to sa:y tha:t.
		(0.6)
22	NAN:	you don't have to sa:y that (0.7) anyway.
		(2.3)
23	NAN:	don't say that °to me° (0.3) [anyway].
		(0.4)
24	FEL:	[MMM].
		(0.5)
25	NAN:	D[O::N'T (.) ((whimpers)) i don't] like it.
26	CHE:	[fishes (0.2) they're your fishes]
→	%act:	CHE and FEL move with their fishing rods to the other side of the room.

Abandonment brought about by a failure to respond (ignoring) and moving away from the opposing party may be achieved in a number of ways. Physical removal from the shared play space can be initiated by either the final speaker or the opposing party. In Extracts 6 and 7, the final speaker abandons his attempts to engage or convince the other party, giving up in the first example and defying the challenge of the other party in the second. In sum, the difference between zero responses in resolved and abandoned disputes lies in a distinction between unspoken acceptance (resulting in resolution) and ignoring the opposition (abandonment).

Extract 6

Participants:	NIG Nigel, SIM Simon
Situation:	It has been raining and all children have been inside. Three minutes prior to this episode the assistant teacher had gone outside, which meant that the children could now go outside and play under the veranda. NIG did not see the teacher move outside.

1	SIM:	i'm going outsi:de.
		(0.3)
2	NIG:	no you're not allowed to¿
		(1.0)
3	SIM:	wha:t?
		(0.3)
4	NIG:	you're not allowed to go outside,
5	SIM:	yea:h¿
		(0.3)
6	NIG:	no you're not,
7	SIM:	i a::m?
→	%act:	SIM opens door and goes outside.

Extract 7

Participants:	ADM Adam, KOY Koyo
Situation:	Pack-up time. The children are trying to put blocks on the shelf. ADM has made something with the blocks on the shelf, KOY accidentally knocks it as he puts another block on the shelf.

1	KOY:	0 ((%act: knocks block off shelf))
2	ADM:	((*whines*)) NO:: (.) YOU'RE BREAKING IT.
		(0.2)
3	KOY:	BECAUSE YOU'RE NOT PACKING UP.
		(0.6)
4	KOY:	↑no (.) you're not packing¿=
5	ADM:	=YES I AM.
→	%act:	KOY walks away to collect more blocks.

Teacher intervention

We have seen that the closings described as resolved or abandoned are constructed by the children themselves. A third possible dispute closing, however, is reached through external intervention. The intervention may be sought by the children (for example, Extract 8) or initiated by the teacher (for example, Extract 9). In the episodes where intervention was sought by one of the participants, children appealed to the teacher as a figure of authority to support their own position (see Maynard, 1985a). Notably, teacher interventions are generally seen as an avoidance rather than a valid strategy to resolve conflict (Newman et al., 2001, p 398). To this end, appeals to the teacher, and even teacher-initiated intervention, were not heard in the beginnings of the disputes, but instead were produced when other persuasion attempts had failed.

Extract 8

Participants:	PAU Paul, WIN Winnie, YYY Teacher
Situation:	WIN and LOU [who is LOU?] are building garages with the wooden blocks. PAU has joined them. WIN picks up a plastic ladder made from connector pieces.

1	WIN:	i've got a great idea what we can do with this¿
		(2.5)
2	PAU:	give it to me!
3	WIN:	i [found it].
4	PAU:	[no i-](.) no i had i:t.
5	WIN:	i found it¿
6	PAU:	no i had it a while ag[o]?
7	WIN:	[no].
		(0.5)
8	PAU:	i had it a while ago.=
9	WIN:	=no you did[n't].
10 →	PAU:	[well] i'm telling on you.
		(0.7)
11 →	WIN:	excuse me [YYY].
12	PAU:	[no],
13	PAU:	um Caroline gave it to me.
	%com:	Caroline is not present
		(0.5)
14 →	WIN:	excuse me [YYY].
15	PAU:	[Caroline] gave it to me.
	%yyy:	teacher intervenes but response is inaudible.

Extract 9

Participants:		HIL Hilary, TES Tess, YYY Teacher
Situation:		HIL and TES are sitting at a table, each placing coloured pieces into mesh frames. HIL has quietly been singing a popular tune about 'Barbie'. Before the dialogue is picked up by the audio-tape (prior interaction is obscured by the conversation of other children closer to the microphone) TES had started to sing the same song. HIL had told TES that she was not allowed to sing this particular song.

1	TES:	everybody can sing it (0.5) not just you:?
		(4.6)
2	HIL:	well i sing my song if i <u>wa</u>nt.
		(1.7)
3	HIL:	it's my: so:ng¿
4	TES:	it's my song <u>too</u>: and it's not <u>yo</u>ur song.
		(0.2)
5	HIL:	it <u>is</u> my song.
		(0.5)
6	TES:	NOT <u>YOU</u>R: SONG.
		(0.6)
7	TES:	EENGHH ((*screeches in frustration*)) .hhh (.) IT'S NOT <u>YOUR</u> SONG Hilary.
		(1.5)
8	YYY:	Tess are you okay?
		(1.3)
9	TES:	Hilary just said the <u>song</u> is <u>hers</u> and it's not it's <u>mi</u>:ne.
		(0.9)
10	HIL:	well it <u>is</u> mine <u>too</u>:.
		(3.8)
11 →	YYY:	↑girls (0.4) what's the problem.
		(1.5)
12	HIL:	it is my song <u>too</u>:.
13	TES:	it's <u>not</u> <u>you</u>:r song too::¿
		(0.2)
14	HIL:	it is.
		(0.4)
15	TES:	no:.
		(2.5)
16	HIL:	<u>i</u> heard it on the radio.
		(0.4)
17 →	YYY:	okay what's the matter over here.
%yyy:		teacher goes on to explain that songs belong to everybody.

Notably, these disputes feature repetition of turns as each speaker restates their objection without any significant modification of the turn. In this exchange of repeated objections with little novel content, an appeal to an external authority imposes an endpoint for an otherwise interminable cycle. As such, resorting to staff intervention represents a stalemate between the children.

Each of the three types of closings identified in this chapter – resolution, abandonment and teacher intervention – are fundamentally characterised by whether the children were able to bring the dispute to a close and whether collaborative play resumed once the dispute ended. It remains to be seen how it is that children arrive at each of these endings. In the final section of this chapter, we move beyond defining dispute closings to explain how it is that these closings are co-constructed.

Characteristics of closings

Analysis of turn shapes in all of the data collected in this project (60 spontaneous disputes) uncovered a universal pattern: turns (utterances made by the children) were overwhelmingly produced in one of two ways. Opposition turns were either (i) short, immediate and direct or (ii) delayed and accompanied by a reason for the opposition.

Returning to the children's spontaneous disputes, examples of the first sort of turn shape (i) identified in the data are:

Extract 5

14	FEL:	mmm.
15 →	NAN:	don't say mmm.

Extract 6

6	NIG:	no you're not,
7 →	SIM:	i a::m?

Extract 7

5	KOY:	↑no (.) you're not packing¿=
6 →	ADM:	=YES I AM.

Extract 8

8	PAU:	i had it a while ago.=
9 →	WIN:	=no you did[n't].

Extract 9

3	HIL:	it's my: so:ng¿
4	TES:	it's my song <u>too</u>: and it's not <u>your</u> song.
		(0.2)
5	HIL:	it <u>is</u> my song.
...		
13	TES:	it's <u>not</u> <u>you</u>:r song too::¿
		(0.2)
14 →	HIL:	it is

Examples of the second type of turn type (ii) heard in the children's disputes are:

Extract 1

		(2.2)
5 →	SAM:	if you crack heads you'll ↓die: (0.3) do you want to ↑die::
		(0.3) and then your mummy will cry:?

Extract 2

		(0.4)
4 →	TES:	but we (0.3) but (0.5) but we are just sharing.

Extract 3

11	MIR:	let's just be nice and understand okay? (1.9)
12 →	CAZ:	but we have to just type into the computer.

Extract 4

3	LUK:	i saw you: put one away¿=
4	SAM:	=that doesn't matter cause it wasn't a block it was a cylinder.

These features are strikingly characteristic of preference organisation (Pomerantz, 1984; Sacks, 1987); a universally organising principle of talk. Although the function of preference organisation in adversative discourse has been detailed elsewhere (Kotthoff, 1993; Church, 2004), it is necessary to briefly introduce the concept to illustrate how it is that children go about resolving disputes.

Turn-taking in conversation is necessarily ordered. Not only does one turn occur after another (one speaker at a time), there are also expectations about what sort of turn can occur after another (Schegloff,

2007). Questions are followed by answers, greetings are followed by greetings, invitations are followed by acceptance or declining and so on. The second pair part (for example, answer) – the turn that follows the first pair part (for example, question) – may not always be forthcoming, but nevertheless there is a *preference* for a particular type of action. The concept introduced here is linguistic rather than psychological; the speaker expects but does not always 'want' a particular type of response. Preference organisation is universal in conversation – it is one of the mechanisms that ensures the efficiency of talk-in-interaction. The example that is invariably used to demonstrate preference is pairs of invitation and acceptance/rejection sequences published in Atkinson and Drew (1979, p 58), where extract (i) provides a preferred response and (ii) a dispreferred response:

| (i) | B: | Why don't you come up and see me some[times |
| | A: | [I would like to |

(ii)	B:	Uh if you'd care to come over and visit a little while this morning I'll give you a cup of coffee.
	A:	hehh Well that's awfully sweet of you, I don't think I can make it this morning .hh uhm I'm running an ad in the paper and – and uh I have to stay near the phone.
	B:	Well all right.

The preference is not personal (speaker A in the first example may not really like to visit speaker B) but instead is the term that is used to describe the fact that turns are marked in very particular ways. Preferred turns are produced immediately and directly – that is, the speaker's intention is clear and the utterance produced without delay. Dispreferred turns, on the other hand, are delayed by pause or markers such as 'but' or 'well' and accompanied by some account for why the preferred response is not provided (if you refuse an invitation, a justification for that refusal is expected). Speakers are so sensitive to these preference markers that when we hear a brief pause, we automatically expect a dispreferred response.

While it has been claimed that there is a dispreference for disagreement (see Sacks, 1984) – indeed, conflict is something speakers work to avoid – once disputes are established, preferred responses in the preschool context are turns of explicit opposition. If we return to the children's disputes and the prevalence of either preferred or dispreferred turn shapes, we consider how these turns may function in the outcome of disputes.

All of the examples of preferred turn shapes listed above (Extracts 5-9) were heard in disputes that were abandoned or closed through teacher intervention; these turn shapes are characteristic of exchanges where children were unable to collaboratively resolve the dispute. The immediate, short and explicitly oppositional turns in the disputes ('no you didn't'; 'yes I am') invariably served to sustain the argument. These sort of turn shapes typically provoked sequences of preferred responses. Preferred turns ensure the continuation of the dispute; in other words, immediate and overt opposition invites or expects a next turn of immediate opposition.

On the other hand, where children produced turns that were delayed and accompanied by an account or reason for opposition ('but we are just sharing'; 'that doesn't matter 'cause it wasn't a block, it was a cylinder'), resolution was possible. Although utterances in dispreferred turn shape were not always successful in closing the dispute, they were the only way in which resolution could be secured. This analysis extends beyond the notion of 'compromise' used effectively by children in disputes (for example, Eisenberg and Garvey, 1981), to illustrate that children not only construct but also orient to highly rule-governed norms of conversation.

Through studying preference features in children's disputes, characteristics of sustaining and non-sustaining turns have been identified. Essentially, the more overt the opposition, the more likely the dispute will continue. Conversely, where children account for their opposition (that is, providing novel content), a mutually acceptable outcome becomes possible. Overwhelmingly, the more objective the child's position or justification, the more likely resolution will be secured.

In the 60 recorded disputes – examples of which have been provided throughout this chapter – three distinct types of dispute closings were identified: resolution, abandonment and teacher intervention, and turn shapes in the closings in each type of dispute were markedly – and consistently – different. I argued at the beginning of this chapter that a prediction of dispute outcomes should be based on a pattern of discourse constructed by the participants and demonstrated as universal by the researcher. The findings reported here point to consistent sequences in the interaction: short, direct and overt opposition never leads to resolution, but where children mitigate their opposition through delay, hesitation markers and accounting for their position, they create the opportunity for resolution.

This chapter has examined arguments between four-year-old children as an opportunity to detail communicative competencies in preschool exchanges, by focusing on turn shapes that influence the outcome of young children's verbal conflict. More broadly, however, research of this kind draws attention to children's competencies in social interaction. Specifically, it shows that close attention to features of talk-in-interaction affords a rich understanding of children's linguistic and interpersonal abilities, and can illuminate specific ways in which young children exercise autonomy and competence, which may not be immediately apparent to adult observers.

One application of these findings is the opportunity for teacher intervention in young children's conflict to be informed by the processes of the *children's* talk-in-interaction – talk that is locally organised and constructed by the children themselves. Typically, teachers are not privy to the ongoing interaction – not the context of the dispute prior to intervention, nor the fallout from their interjection or support. This work adds to our understanding of how young children negotiate conflict closings, which has implications for our understanding of dialogic (and pedagogic) exchanges between children and teachers.

As adults, we are not usually privy to the social organisation of children's peer relationships and interactions. Closer attention to children's voices not only allows more effective participation by children in 'adult' worlds, as argued elsewhere in this book; it can also permit more sensitive participation by adults in children's own settings, and more effective support for children's autonomy and competence.

Transcript conventions (see Sacks et al., 1974)

.	Falling terminal contour
,	Continuing contour (incomplete)
?	Strongly rising terminal contour
¿	Rising terminal contour
!	Emphatic/animated utterance terminator
-	Abrupt halt
[ ]	Overlapping speech
=	Latching (contiguous stretches of talk)
(0.7)	Pause measured in tenths of a second
(.)	Pause timed less than 0.2 seconds
___	Stress on the word/syllable/sound
:	Lengthening of previous sound
CAPS	Increase in volume

° °	Decrease in volume
↑ ↓	Significant rise or fall in intonation
> <	Faster than surrounding talk
< >	Slower than surrounding talk
.hhh	Audible inhalation
$	Laughing while talking (smile talk)
( )	Uncertain words (best guess)
(( ))	Comments e.g. quality of speech or intended hearer
x	Unintelligible speech
%act	Identifies (accompanying) nonverbal action
%com	Observer comment
text	Feature of interest

References

Atkinson, J.M. and Drew, P. (1979) *Order in Court: The Organisation of Verbal Interaction in Judicial Settings*, London: Macmillan.

Atkinson, J.M. and Heritage, J. (eds) (1984) *Structures of Social Action: Studies in Conversation Analysis*, Cambridge: Cambridge University Press.

Austin, J.L. (1962) *How to Do Things with Words*, Oxford: Clarendon Press.

Church, A. (2004) 'Preference revisited', *RASK: International Journal of Language and Linguistics*, 21, pp 111-29.

Church, A. (2007) 'Conversation analysis in early childhood research', *Journal of Australian Research in Early Childhood Education*, 14, pp 1-10.

Corsaro, W.A. and Maynard, D.W. (1996) 'Format tying in discussion and argumentation among Italian and American children', in D.I. Slobin, J. Gerhardt, A. Kyratzis and J. Guo (eds) *Social Interaction, Social Context, and Language: Essays in Honor of Susan Ervin-Tripp*, Mahwah, NJ: Lawrence Erlbaum Associates.

Corsaro, W.A. and Rizzo, T.A. (1990) 'Disputes in the peer culture of American and Italian nursery-school children', in A.D. Grimshaw, (ed) *Conflict Talk: Sociolinguistic Investigations of Arguments in Conversations*, Cambridge: Cambridge University Press.

Coulter, J. (1990) 'Elementary properties of argument sequences', in Psathas, G. (ed) *Interaction Competence*, Lanham, MD: University Press of America.

Eisenberg, A.R. (1987) 'Learning to argue with parents and peers', *Argumentation*, 1, pp 113-25.

Eisenberg, A.R. and Garvey, C. (1981) 'Children's use of verbal strategies in resolving conflicts', *Discourse Processes*, 4, pp 149-70.

Garvey, C. and Shantz, C.U. (1995) 'Conflict talk: approaches to adversative discourse', in C.U. Shantz and W.W. Hartup (eds) *Conflict in Child and Adolescent Development*, New York, NY: Cambridge University Press.

Goodwin, M.H. (1982) 'Processes of dispute management among urban black children', *American Ethnologist*, 9, pp 76-96.

Goodwin, M.H. and Goodwin, C. (1987) 'Children's arguing', in S. Philips, S. Steele and C. Tanz (eds) *Language, Gender, and Sex in Comparative Perspective*, New York, NY: Cambridge University Press.

Hay, D.F. (1984) 'Social conflict in early childhood', *Annals of Child Development*, 53, pp 105-13.

Hay, D.F. and Ross, H.S. (1982) 'The social nature of early conflict', *Child Development*, 53, pp 105-13.

Kotthoff, H. (1993) 'Disagreement and concession in disputes: on the context sensitivity of preference structures', *Language in Society*, 22, pp 193-216.

Maynard, D.W. (1985a) 'How children start arguments', *Language in Society*, 14, pp 1-30.

Maynard, D.W. (1985b) 'On the functions of social conflict among children', *American Sociological Review*, 50, pp 207-23.

Maynard, D.W. (1986) 'The development of argumentative skills among children', in P.A. Adler and P. Adler (eds) *Sociological Studies of Child Development*, Greenwich, CT: JAI Press.

Miller, P.M., Danaher, D.L. and Forbes, D. (1986) 'Sex-related strategies for coping with interpersonal conflict in children aged five and seven', *Developmental Psychology*, 22, pp 543-8.

Newman, R.S., Murray, B. and Lussier, C. (2001) 'Confrontation with aggressive peers at school: students' reluctance to seek help from the teacher', *Journal of Educational Psychology*, 93, pp 398-410.

O'Keefe, B.J. and Benoit, P.J. (1982) 'Children's arguments', in J.R. Cox and C.A. Willard (eds) *Advances in Argumentation Theory and Research*, Carbondale, IL: Southern Illinois University Press.

Phinney, J.S. (1986) 'The structure of 5-year-olds' verbal quarrels with peers and siblings', *Journal of Genetic Psychology*, 147, pp 47-60.

Pomerantz, A. (1984) 'Agreeing and disagreeing with assessments: some features of preferred/dispreferred turn shapes', in J.M. Atkinson and J. Heritage (eds) *Structures of Social Action: Studies in Conversation Analysis*, Cambridge: Cambridge University Press.

Putallaz, M. and Sheppard, B.H. (1995) 'Conflict management and social competence', in C.U. Shantz and W.W. Hartup (eds) *Conflict in Child and Adolescent Development*, New York, NY: Cambridge University Press.

Ross, H.S. and Conant, C.L. (1995) 'The social structure of early conflict: interaction, relationships, and alliances', in C.U. Shantz and W.W. Hartup (eds) *Conflict in Child and Adolescent Development*, New York, NY: Cambridge University Press.

Sackin, S. and Thelen, E. (1984) 'An ethological study of peaceful associative outcomes to conflict in preschool children', *Child Development*, 55, pp 1098-102.

Sacks, H. (1984) 'Notes on methodology', in J.M. Atkinson and J. Heritage (eds) *Structures of Social Action: Studies in Conversation Analysis*, Cambridge: Cambridge University Press.

Sacks, H. (1987) 'On the preferences for agreement and contiguity in sequences in conversation', in G. Button and J.R.E Lee (eds) *Talk and Social Organization*, Clevedon: Multilingual Matters.

Sacks, H., Schegloff, E. and Jefferson, G. (1974) 'A simplest systematics for the organization of turn-taking for conversation', *Language*, 50, pp 696-735.

Schegloff, E. (2007) *Sequence Organization in Interaction: A Primer in Conversation Analysis*, Cambridge: Cambridge University Press.

ten Have, P. (2007) *Doing Conversation Analysis: A Practical Guide* (2nd edition), London: Sage Publications.

Vuchinich, S. (1990) *Problem Solving in Families: Research and Practice*, Thousand Oaks, CA: Sage Publications.

NINE

Keeping connected: textual cohesion and textual selves, how young people stay together online

Julia Davies

Introduction: Generation 'Text'

In this chapter I draw on observations from research spanning the last decade, in which I have been tracing paths that children, young people and adults have made through their online interactivity. Some of the data I analyse are drawn from the activities of those 'early adopters' who have pioneered the use of technology as a way of connecting socially (Wildfyre, 1997a; Verdi, 2004). Others whose texts I consider have been part of a generation of youngsters who have taken part in online activities alongside their peers and friends as part of a more recent popular culture interest in social networking sites (www.bebo. com; www.facebook.com; www.myspace.com), or who have used the internet as a way of developing confidence having lost friends and confidence through illness (www.AYME.org.uk). My research is rooted in literacy, language and education, and I conceptualise the internet as the single most transformative invention for these areas since the introduction of the printing press. The latter similarly increased the production of texts, therefore providing greater access to and dissemination of information; like social networking, it empowered individuals and brought social change (Vincent, 2000). We now inhabit a world where a woman from Iraq can keep a blog in English, accessible to a wide and internationally dispersed readership – enemies and sympathisers (Riverbend, 2003-07), and we are able to compare this with a female American soldier's images on a photosharing site and her blog that tells us of her life in base camp (tommigodwin, 2005). We inhabit a world where photographs can be taken on a mobile phone and be disseminated globally even before a journalist arrives (Wikinews,

July 2005); in the same world, and using the same technology, we can play on a photo-sharing website, sending a wig backwards and forwards in a transatlantic online game (jenny, 2006). We can see Dylan Verdi's video blog where she regularly uploaded short films of her everyday life as a 12-, 13- and 14-year-old (Verdi, 2004), Wildfyre's websites and discussion boards about life as a teenage witch (Wildfyre, 1997b) and the schools and hospitals set up by others for cyber 'babyz', which they emailed to each other and wrote about in elaborate role-plays well into their teenage years (Davies, 2004). These examples demonstrate just some of the ways in which the internet can empower individuals to disseminate their voices, often blending the playful and serious, and how the young have found this particularly seductive, being quick to seize opportunities and to explore the boundaries of possibility.

In my tracings of online happenings, I have been fascinated by how so many people, not least young people, find pleasure from embracing what has been called 'the digital revolution', producing and consuming digital texts and viewing this as a central, even vital, part of their everyday lives. Indeed, it has now become almost superfluous to point out how digital technologies are embedded in the fabric of our lives, no longer novelty or 'add-on' but often constitutive of social life. In their study of young people's uses of technology, Lewis and Fabos (2005, p 47) argue that young people are increasingly unable to envisage their lives without access to digital technologies, and that 'When technology becomes "normal" in this way, it is no longer complicated, nor is it notable to its users. It is a fact of life, a way of being in the world, a producer of social subjects that find it unremarkable – so unremarkable that it seems "everybody does it"'.

There are many ways in which people can make links with each other in online spaces; one way is to continue online conversations that began in 'real time' or face to face. Benkler (2006) argues how online interactivity 'thickens' existing social ties, and boyd (2006, p 1) posits:

> The digital era has allowed us to cross space and time, engage with people in a far-off time zone as though they were just next door ... [and] ... network us all closer and closer every day. Yet, people don't live in a global world – they are more concerned with the cultures in which they participate.

Other studies with young people have produced extensive corroborating evidence (Bortree, 2005; Buckingham and Willett, 2006; Hannon and Green, 2007) both in the UK and internationally. In recent interviews carried out for a small-scale project in a UK secondary school, one girl told me: 'I use the computer to centralise everything that's going on in my life', and another explained: 'It's a well-known fact that people do stuff especially so they can take photos of it to put on Bebo. You can even have Bebo parties and that'. These comments demonstrate, as I have shown elsewhere (Davies, 2009), how digital connectivity often blends people's on- and offline lives; things happen offline because of events that have occurred online and vice versa. Another boy explained: 'My Mum goes mad; she says I spend all day with people at school and then talk rubbish to them on Bebo all night'. Dowdall (2006) reports that MySpace now has 87 million members and Bebo has 22 million – both of them social networking sites mainly patronised by teenagers, who use these online spaces to send instant messages, keep blogs, upload photographs, listen to music and much more. Lewis and Fabos (2005) claim that many young people feel they have been 'born into' technological practices, where their social lives are closely bound within their text production and consumption, and Carrington (2005, p 13) writes of how children are being '"naturalized" into new textual landscapes'.

At a time when national and international commentators express concern at low levels of literacy, it is notable that this is coupled with criticism levelled at young people's attraction to online social networking. It is also paradoxical, because online networking depends on abilities to consume and produce complex multimodal texts, which rely, not simply on the linguistic mode, but also on the use of sound, images, icons and even textual layout to signify meanings (Davies, 2006). Young people's skills in manipulating complex multimodal texts are often learned through hours of frustrated concentration (Gee, 2004). They invest a lot of time in developing their skills, possibly reflecting the fact that these also constitute social activities. These new literacy practices are not just about explaining, describing and reporting; they often constitute social events. One young person told me: 'You cannot afford not to go online. You have to read what the others read. Watch the YouTube stuff your mates see. You have to be part of what everyone is saying'.

In this chapter I argue that such networking is about text-making and meaning-making, and that young people are drawn to this process as a way of distributing their voices, being social and performing acts of self. This is literacy as a social practice – a social practice that many young people see as vital in their lives, perceiving non-participation as socially marginalising.

The new literacy studies

I align myself theoretically with what has become known as the 'New Literacy Studies', where reading, writing and meaning are seen as always situated within specific social practices and discourses (Street, 2003; Gee, 2005). Thinking in terms of literacy practices redefines literacy from being purely about the mastery of correct spellings and punctuation, locating it as social, as culturally situated and concerning human relationships (Barton and Hamilton, 1998; Cope and Kalantzis, 2000). For Gee (2005, p 46), 'the traditional view of literacy as the ability to read and write rips literacy out of its sociocultural contexts and treats it as an asocial cognitive skill with little or nothing to do with human relationships'. Gee argues that literacy is primarily concerned with human interactions and relationships. Being literate therefore involves being aware of all kinds of social 'stuff' that surround texts; one needs to decode cultural and social contextual clues, as Lankshear and Knobel (2006, p 13) argue:

> From a sociocultural perspective it is impossible to separate out from text-mediated social practices the bits concerned with reading or writing (or any other sense of literacy) and to treat them independently of all the non-print bits, like values and gestures, context and meaning, action and objects, talk and interaction, tools and spaces. They are all non-subtractable parts of integrated wholes. 'Literacy bits' do not exist apart from the social practices in which they are embedded and in which they are acquired.

This idea of literacy as a social practice fits particularly well when one is looking at online writing, where texts can be jointly authored and meanings challenged, extended, altered and subjected to collaboration, perhaps helping to promote affinities or notions of community. As Cammack (2005) has pointed out, the idea of literacy as a set of practices rather than a narrowly defined list of skills has also pushed literacy studies increasingly in an anthropological direction, as researchers collect data and immerse themselves in settings where literacy practices occur and in individuals' lives, in order to understand those literacy practices as situated in contexts. This has been an approach I have embraced in my work, carefully observing and extrapolating what seem to be socially significant cues and rituals.

Online cultural groups

In my explorations of online interactivity, I view a wide range of online texts, looking at individuals' and groups' communication processes. This includes considering how meanings are constructed through multiple modes, how online communicators present particular kinds of online identity and form connections with each other. In these explorations I realise that I have been watching cultures evolve and develop through meaning-making. I have come to understand how individuals who cluster in online groups can, through a process of collaboration and interactivity, devise and develop particular, nuanced ways of making meanings together that make it possible to define them as a cultural group. As I have previously described (Davies, 2004, 2006, 2007), by communicating with each other on a regular basis, online interactants can, through a process of accretion, develop conventions and rituals that come to acquire specific significance in specific groups so that new meanings emerge. I have been interested in how, on a moment-by-moment basis, culture can emerge through social processes where individuals co-construct meanings through texts. I have seen how social histories are set down and revisited and that these are the fabric of affinities that become cultural rituals, habits and codes that help define and distinguish particular groups. It is these that are the focus of this chapter where I try to describe how affinities are made and developed through online text-making.

Listening in and 'eyeballing' the data

The processes I have outlined above are not exclusive to the internet, for as Carter (2004) and Maybin (2007) have shown, creativity in spoken language works in these ways too. What is particularly useful for the researcher studying the internet is that, because of the nature of much (although not all) online communication, trails are set and threads woven that can be picked up and read again, becoming the object of scrutiny.

In online research it is possible to collect 'raw data' and look at it in its original form, unseparated from its original context. It is not necessary, as when working in other fields, to take the data away from its context in order to analyse it. Such a process is transformative; for example, when transcribing spoken language, the writing process changes the modality of the data, and one must also decide whether to record extra and para-linguistic features and other contextual aspects. Even with online communication, other aspects of context, such as how well people know each other in particular spaces, are not always apparent, so that one cannot know fully the contexts within which the texts are produced.

Important arguments have been made in the past decade or so about really hearing and taking into account what children say, when carrying out research involving children (James and Prout, 1997; Greig and Taylor, 1999; Christensen and James, 2000). In the work I report here, I have 'listened in' to children and young people's voices, seeing them communicate in groups where they have chosen to participate, often *away from the gaze*, as it were, of teachers and parents. In reading texts that young people have chosen to put online, I have seen them represent themselves through different 'voices' in different contexts, experimenting with a variety of ways of being. It is hard to know what an 'authentic voice' actually is, and this may be the researcher's 'holy grail', but I believe it is possible to witness authentic play online, as well as voices that are earnest and serious.

The data

In this account, I draw on data taken mainly from online discussion boards organised and used by and for young people with myalgic encephalomyelitis (ME). For a number of months in 2005 I was granted access to a private discussion board set up by the Association of Young People with ME (AYME). I was granted access for two months, after application to the young board members and the founding director of the charity. My presence and purpose was identified to members via a banner across the bottom of the discussion board, and links to further information and a questionnaire were provided. The so-called AYMERs welcomed me enthusiastically and sometimes asked my views about their discussions – but in the main, my presence was ignored. Data that I use from the boards have been checked first with AYMERs.

Membership of the organisation is carefully screened, and is organised through postal means and limited to those up to the age of 23 who suffer from ME. This illness was for many years contested and unrecognised by medical and other professionals and attracted social stigma. Despite its current recognition by the UK's National Institute for Health and Clinical Excellence (NICE), there is still no clear treatment or mode of diagnosis (Dumit, 2006; Horton-Salway, 2007). Although many people may be severely disabled by the illness, it remains hard to get medical, educational or other intervention, and sufferers are still often regarded as malingerers. The online support given by the AYME site plays a major role in the lives of many young people who would otherwise be left isolated. As one young person explained to me:

> When my condition was worse I relied on the MB [message board] a lot to have contact with other people (as I had lost all my healthy friends) and more importantly other people who could understand how I was feeling and not judge my condition. I found that my main activity would be logging on to the board, it was something I could do whenever I wanted to when I felt up to it. Often it would make my day seem more enjoyable and was a good way of meeting new people or just being entertained! (I often used a laptop in bed at this stage.) (Questionnaire response from a girl aged 16)

The online questionnaire I used provoked discussion among AYMERs about how the organisation had touched their lives. A typical comment came from a 15-year-old girl who said: 'Ayme is everything to me, the support and the wonderful friendships i have made through Ayme have gave me that glimmer of hope so i wont just crawl under a rock and stay there, im part of something! it keeps me going ☺'.

For many AYMERs, the illness hits them at a time when they are just moving into a more independent way of living, moving away from their identity as a child and into adulthood. Many of the young people feel cheated and angry and go through a sense of loss of their independence as well as of friends. The discussion board offers them a place to discuss issues relating to these losses:

I F★★★★★G Hate fridays....

Rasin cake: It's the night when i know all my mates are out and visiting other mates all over the country and generally getting f★★★★d. I'm well pi★★ed. Stupid M.E. Sorry just angry coz i'm sitting on the crap pathetic computer at 9.30 on a friday evening with no life and no boyfriend.

TKatcher: can we be angry together?! I'm also on the net, no friends, no boyfriend with Graham Norton on in the back! I hate fridays too cos their really long and strung out. Not much decent tv cos friends isn't the same! .....
Hope your saturday is better!
Love Lucy XXX

> McTavish: can i join you and TKatcher?friday nights
> can just feel like life's rubbing our nose's in it.

The feeling of isolation is strong, with the young people all expressing
a sense of loss, sensing that life is passing them by. They gaze into their
computer screens, finding some comfort from sharing their feelings but
nevertheless feeling that this is not sufficient. Family television viewing
occurs 'behind their backs', but the programmes have lost their allure
for these teenagers who want to be in a different space. They gaze
outwards to peers they cannot join and who seem to have forgotten
them. The personal computer offers some comfort, but is second best. As
can be seen, AYMERs frequently use their own names as well as their
screennames – Tkatcher signs off her contribution 'Love Lucy XXX',
which seems to signify her making a closer alliance with Raisin Cake
than if she did not use her real name – it is a dropping of the 'public'
face in favour of what might be seen as the 'real' person who wants
to show an affinity. This is an interesting play with multiple identities,
one that actually provides discussion material in other postings where
AYMERs ask the meanings of each other's names. Thus, screen names
are not used to mask identity, but to suggest an aspect of that person's
character to other AYMERS. In this way, there is a sense in which
'multiple selves' are brought to the discussion board; membership is
biologically determined but stronger 'other' identities are brought to
the fore in order to build up a sense of community beyond the illness
itself. As I show below, AYMERs devise ways of creating texts together,
constructing shared understandings and meanings that exclude others,
thus giving them confidence in who they are.

   The discussion board allows people to easily quote each other so
that one person's words are placed into another person's post; thus
Raisin Cake says:

> On 2004-04-02 22:04, TKatcher wrote:
> *can we be angry together?! I'm also on the net, no friends, no*
> *boyfriend with Graham Norton on in the back! I hate fridays too cos*
> *their really long ans strung out. Not much decent tv cos friends isn't*
> *the same! But I'm still trying to read the unofficial confrence thread!!*
> *So i may be here sometime!*
> *Hope your saturday is better!*
> *Love Lucy XXX*
> Done!!
> Love Lizxxx

Here the section in italics is what TKatcher said earlier and Raisin Cake is able to make it clear that she is addressing her remark straight to TKatcher. In her simple response, 'Done!!' she accepts the hand of friendship and uses her 'real' name too, returning the compliment of intimacy and showing closeness. Further, by embedding TKatcher's words directly into her thread she takes on those words herself and her turn on the board is partly made up of TKatcher's previous words. Bakhtin's notion of 'double voicing' emphasises how words are never purely our own; we inherit and share language with our culture and each articulation imbues the utterance with meanings anew. He explains:

> The word in language is always half someone else's. It becomes one's own only when the speaker populates it with his own intention, his own accent, when he appropriates the word, adapting it to his own semantic and expressive intention....[The word] exists in other people's mouths in other people's concrete contexts, serving other people's intentions; it is from there that one must take the word, and make it one's own. (Bakhtin, 1935/1981, pp 293-4)

In the example of 'double voicing' above, Liz is able to show graphically how she acknowledges TKatcher's contribution and to reflect how closely assimilated their views are – quotations are used in this way to literally speak the views of the others and take them on as their own, in a demonstration of intimacy.

There is a strong sense that AYMERs share a sense of space together – that while they are in fact geographically separated, they work together to create, through their language, a feeling that there is a real place that they inhabit together. People with ME frequently spend hours awake in the night, when the rest of the household is asleep. The discussion below, which takes place at 1.30am, is evocative of the silence of the night:

Lilangel: Is anyone here?????*calls loudly* 😊😊

Sue: I'm here – just about! *eerie echo of footsteps as I arrive*

Jonesy: Me too! *sound of door squeaking open*

Lilangel: here's me thinking I was all alone 😊😊

> Fairygirl: I have noticed it's been really quiet lately!!!!

Through developing the idea of their voices and movements echoing in one space, these AYMERs share an intimacy, an open source of contact that provides them with some comfort that while it may seem that they are alone they share understandings, and this is shown through the metaphor of space that they develop together. Lilangel's use of 'emoticons' undermines the message her words articulate, that she is lonely; the 'smileys' imply that she is not depressed but wanting fun, and she signals through the use of asterisks how she wants her words to be interpreted (as if stage directions). The use of what appear to be paralinguistic features ('calls loudly') draws on the sense of sound for additional meanings – something that the others pick up on and imitate. In adopting this convention they make an alliance and skilfully build up a coherent text where they adopt the nuances and meanings begun by Lilangel. The feeling of the night in their respective geographical locations is opened out as a kind of stage set, a shared arena where they describe themselves almost in the third person for others (and themselves) to envisage, and develop the idea that they are all in the same space. There is a notion in which the discussion board allows AYMERs to look at themselves, as well as at others. The sense of a shared space is articulated in the following example, which took place during daytime:

> Sheena: Ooh goodness they've changed the colour scheme in here. It's very IKEA isn't it – clean and practical!!

Both these examples show how AYMERs envisage themselves inhabiting space together, and how they are creative in the ways in which they develop ideas through a process of collaboration.

It is not always the case that AYMERs discuss their feelings of sadness and isolation; there is a good deal of upbeat play and some of it seems surprisingly energetic. The following example is ludic in the extreme, relying on humour that reflects how cultural values develop over time. Here I represent not just the AYMERS' words but also the full layout of the board, so that it is possible to see ways in which modes other than language are relevant to their meaning-making activities.

This example represents just the start of a conversation that was protracted across a number of days and went on over 12 'pages' of the discussion board. The text is set out in sections and it is possible to see the time lapses between the exchanges, and in this case the

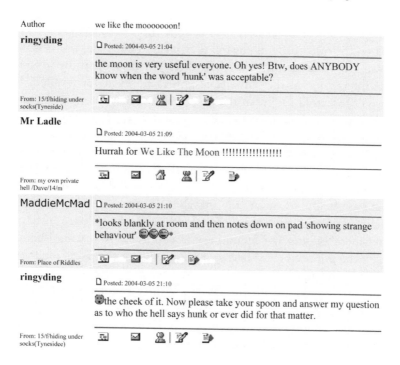

Author	we like the mooooooon!
ringyding	☐ Posted: 2004-03-05 21:04
From: 15/f/hiding under socks(Tyneside)	the moon is very useful everyone. Oh yes! Btw, does ANYBODY know when the word 'hunk' was acceptable?
Mr Ladle	☐ Posted: 2004-03-05 21:09
From: my own private hell /Dave/14/m	Hurrah for We Like The Moon !!!!!!!!!!!!!!!!!
MaddieMcMad	☐ Posted: 2004-03-05 21:10
From: Place of Riddles	*looks blankly at room and then notes down on pad 'showing strange behaviour' 😊😊😊*
ringyding	☐ Posted: 2004-03-05 21:10
From: 15/f/hiding under socks(Tynesidee)	😊the cheek of it. Now please take your spoon and answer my question as to who the hell says hunk or ever did for that matter.

synchronicity of the two final contributions. The first column not only shows 'screennames', or pseudonyms the AYMERs use on the board, but also additional details or notes they may want to add. As can be seen, AYMERs use this feature playfully, and in so doing contribute additional meanings to the posts they make.

In the main section, the first row gives the date and time of the contribution, the next row contains the actual 'speech' and the next line shows hyperlinked icons. Each user can add or delete the hyperlinked icons that allow others to connect with them in different ways – for example to talk with them in another space such as on an instant message board; to email them; to send a private message within the AYME space; to see their personal website. A long row of icons suggests that the AYMER has a broad online repertoire of connectivity, and thus appears quite expert and sociable. In this way the icons act as markers of identity with significations in terms of online popularity. In order to understand this coding, one needs to be an 'insider'; as will be seen, a great deal of information is encoded in this implicit way. There is an assumption that AYMERs will read the board carefully and pick up on the social cues; as I show, there is evidence that this is indeed the case.

The first line on the board is the title of the discussion, invented by the first 'speaker', ringyding. This title will have appeared on the homepage of the discussion board; from this board, AYMERs can click on the title of any discussion they wish to open and join. Clever contributors strategically title their thread as they open discussions, since interactivity is the aim and responses are excitedly awaited. As one AYMER told me in an online interview, 'there are stars on the board. The ones who everyone talks to. No different from school, with popular kids who others listen to and follow their lead'. Good titles are typically intriguing or funny; some users quickly gain reputations for both, and so attract lots of interactivity through reputation over time. It therefore pays off to be articulate and good with language in order to be popular online; invariably this also means the need to be 'well connected' in the sense of having an interesting knowledge of what is 'out there' online. As I mentioned earlier, students in school know exactly the importance of having a knowledge of the latest YouTube craze, or Bebo affair.

The first contribution initially seems incomprehensible, where ringyding continues the intrigue started in the title of the discussion, 'we like the moooooooon'. She says, 'the moon is very useful everyone. Oh yes! Btw, does ANYBODY know when the word 'hunk' was acceptable?'. The term 'useful' in relation to the moon is odd, and the second sentence does not seem to link with the first. Further, conversations traditionally begin with a clearer opening, some help to listeners in understanding. This all seems extremely strange in comparison to what one might expect in a piece of written English. However, Mr Ladle understands and supplies the key to the meaning; his response contains a hyperlink to a website with an animation where strange creatures are singing a nonsensical song called 'we like the moon'. His immediate understanding shows he is an insider, and his use of the hyperlink, embedded in his words, implicitly displays this understanding; he avoids explicitly explaining, for the convention is to simply join in and *show* comprehension rather than clumsily articulate an explanation. Embedded in his words, the hyperlink to the animation represents a kind of 'double voicing'; his words at once echo both ringyding and the animated song. The textual links (the hyperlink and the repetition of ringyding's words) draw him and ringyDing closer, so that affinities are made through textual collaboration.

The next contributor, MaddieMcMad, does not appear to have understood, but nevertheless joins the game: '*looks blankly at room and then notes down on pad 'showing strange behaviour'☺☺☺*'. This move is playful, emphasised in the multiple laughing emoticons, and MaddieMcMad speaks words from a psychology-type script. She plays a psychiatrist here, and the incongruity of the role fits well with previous absurd non-sequiturs and obtuse remarks; here it is her ability and willingness to join in the genre that helps her become part of the group. ringyding's next comment is, to the uninitiated, even stranger. It refers to a joke that has been going on for several weeks in a number of other discussions: '☺the cheek of it. Now please take your spoon and answer my question as to who the hell says hunk or ever did for that matter'. The spoon reference, and Mr Ladle's current screen name, both make an intertextual reference back to a series of other online discussions. Those previous discussions collectively made up an elaborate role-play, where AYMERs developed bizarre characters who behaved strangely; it was set in an imagined kitchen where participants had been running around with different types of cutlery and playing games with them. MaddieMcMad's psychologist character had developed in that space and continued for months afterwards – yet on other occasions all participants did not refer at all to the kitchen scenario. The culture of this online space is highly complex and has jokes with multiple layers and words which develop meanings that do not exist elsewhere. To join this group, one needs to be a careful reader and to adopt the codes and rituals of the group making a specific online culture. In this way, this group of youngsters, often alienated from other aspects of life, collaborate in building a text together, simultaneously creating a context where they feel at home and where newcomers would be confused.

The processes I describe here, where youngsters develop shared understandings through multimodal means, is ubiquitous online. For example, when I researched sites where teenage girls presented themselves as teen-witches, they used specialist spellings such as 'magick', and ritualistic phrases such as 'Blessed Be' or 'Merry Meet' as salutations and greetings. They used pentangle icons, dark colours as backgrounds to their sites, and played eerie background music. Making the texts cohesive in this way endorsed, enacted and comprised the girls' social networking and served to implicitly emphasise the shared understandings that they also explicitly expressed through their conversations in forums and across their site pages. The girls were able to implicitly signal their membership to the group; in using these codes, or as Gee (2005) would say, adopting the 'discourses' of the group, reflected their understandings of the culture and at the same time gave additional significations to the codes each time they were used. I have even seen young people congregate in the chatrooms of eBay, playing similar games and talking about issues that concern them in their lives. It is as if they inhabit corners of the online world as they used to gather on street corners in spaces betwixt spaces, unofficial sites where they can explore different ways of being and connecting with others.

Across the internet, I see constellations of sites that seem to revolve around each other, connecting and moving synchronously, sharing jokes, passing ideas from one to the other, and finding ways of developing cultures that allow individuals to play out different roles at different times.

Conclusions

In this chapter I have shown some of the ways in which young people use textual devices and affordances as a way of marking out affiliations and shared values. As well as aligning myself with the view that literacy, language and education are of great importance in our lives, I also begin from the premise that children have important things to say about themselves and the world they live in. In some instances, these textual practices have been perceived negatively, for example as working against formal education (BBC, 2003a) or encouraging anti-social behaviour (BBC, 2003b). Yet this social interactivity is a crucial part of young people's lives and helps them stay in contact and in the same life rhythms as their peers. Young people's voices are so often dampened in public life and mainstream media remain dominated by adult views and opinions. Competing and popular discourses in the press and television news suggest that young people represent a threat to public life at the same time as being depicted as powerless victims of adult sexuality and violence. Yet it is clear that there are many articulate, creative and responsible voices to be heard – young people who wish to participate in wikis and in providing a service of citizenship journalism or to put across viewpoints of minority or marginalised groups. Just as important, however, are those young people who simply want to 'hang out' together online (Valentine and Holloway, 2002; Leander and McKim, 2003; Beavis et al., 2005) who have a right to socialise in these new ways and to present themselves in ways that are important to their sense of identity and personhood.

I am fully aware of the concerns that many people hold about the welfare of young people when they are online; and it is true that some have unhappily been the prey of undesirable and dangerous people. Part of the way forward with this is to continue to have faith in the role of education and to help young people, as well as their parents, to read online texts skilfully and critically so that they can learn to conduct themselves safely. Further, however, we should remain vigilant to hear what young people tell us about what they have learned from their experiences and allow them to guide us in our adult forays into cyberspace.

References

Bakhtin, M.M. (1935/1981) 'Discourse in the novel', in M.M. Bakhtin, *The Dialogic Imagination: Four Essays*, (ed. M. Holquist, trans. C. Emerson and M. Holquist), Austin, TX: University of Texas Press.

Barton, D. and Hamilton, M. (1998) *Local Literacies: Reading and Writing in One Community*, London: Routledge.

BBC (2003a) *Is Txt Ruining the English Language?*, http://news.bbc. co.uk/1/hi/talking_point/2815461.stm

BBC (2003b) *Experts Debate Text Bullying*, http://news.bbc.co.uk/1/ hi/talking_point/2815461.stm

Beavis, C., Nixon, H. and Atkinson, S. (2005) 'LAN cafes, places of gathering or sites of informal teaching and learning?', *Education, Communication and Information*, 5(1), pp 41-60.

Benkler, Y. (2006) *The Wealth of Learning Networks*, E-book, Chapter 10, www.benkler.org/Benkler_Wealth_Of_Networks.pdf

Bortree, D.S. (2005) 'Presentation of self on the web: an ethnographic study of teenage girls' weblogs', *Education, Communication and Information*, 5(1), pp 25-39.

boyd, D. (2006) 'G/localization: when global information and local interaction collide', O'Reilly Paper presented at the Emerging Technology Conference, 6 March, www.danah.org/papers/Etech2006. html

Buckingham, D. and Willett, R. (2006) *Digital Generations: Children, Young People, and New Media*, London and New York: Lawrence Erlbaum Associates.

Cammack, D. (2005) 'No straight line: wrinkling binaries in literacy and technology research', *E–Learning*, 2(2), pp 153-68.

Carrington, V. (2005) 'New textual landscapes, information and early literacy', in Marsh, J. (ed) *Popular Culture, New Media and Digital Literacy in Early Childhood*, London: Routledge/Falmer.

Carter, R. (2004) *Language and Creativity: The Art of Common Talk*, London: Routledge.

Christensen, P. and James, A. (2000) 'Researching children and childhood: cultures of communication', in P. Christensen and A. James, (eds) *Research with Children*, London: Routledge/Falmer, pp 1-8.

Cope, B. and Kalantzis, H. (eds) (2000) *Multiliteracies: Designs of Social Futures*, London: Routledge.

Davies, J. (2004) 'Negotiating femininities on-line', *Gender and Education*, 16(1), pp 35-49.

Davies, J. (2006) 'Escaping to the borderlands: an exploration of the internet as a cultural space for teenaged Wiccan girls', in K. Pahl and J. Rowsell (eds) *Travel Notes from the New Literacy Studies: Instances of Practice*, Clevedon: Multilingual Matters, pp 57-71.

Davies, J. (2007) 'Display, identity and the everyday: self-presentation through digital image sharing', *Discourse: Studies in the Cultural Politics of Education*, 28(4), pp 549-64.

Davies, J. (2009) 'A space for play: crossing boundaries and learning online', in V. Carrington and M. Robinson (eds) *Contentious Technologies: Digital Literacies, Social Learning and Classroom Practices*, London: Sage Publications.

Dowdall, C. (2006) 'Ben and his army scenes: a consideration of one child's out-of-school text production', *English in Education*, 40(3), pp 39-54.

Dumit, J. (2006) 'Illnesses you have to fight to get: facts as forces in uncertain, emergent illnesses', *Social Science and Medicine*, 62(3), pp 577-90.

Gee, J.P. (2004) *What Video Games Have to Teach Us About Learning and Literacy*, London: Palgrave Macmillan.

Gee, J.P. (2005) *An Introduction to Discourse Analysis: Theory and Method* (2nd edition), London: Routledge.

Greig, A. and Taylor, J. (1999) 'Introduction to research with children: a special relationship', in A.D. Greig and J. Taylor (eds) *Doing Research with Children*, London: Sage Publications, pp 1-14.

Hannon, C. and Green, H. (2007) *Their Space: Education for a Digital Generation*, London: Demos.

Horton-Salway, M. (2007) 'The ME bandwagon and other labels: constructing the genuine case in talk about a controversial illness', *British Journal of Social Psychology*, 46(4), pp 895-914.

James, A. and Prout, A. (1997) 'A new paradigm for the sociology of childhood? Provenance, promise and problems', in A. James and A. Prout (eds) *Constructing and Reconstructing Childhood*, London: Falmer, pp 7-33.

jenny (2006) *The Travelling wig*, Group on Flickr.com, www.flickr.com/groups/travelingwig/discuss/72057594089465715/

Lankshear, C. and Knobel, M. (2006) *New Literacies: Everyday Practices & Classroom Learning*, London and New York: Open University Press/McGraw Hill.

Leander, K. and McKim, K.K. (2003) 'Tracing the everyday "sitings" of adolescents on the internet: a strategic adaptation of ethnography across online and off line spaces', *Education, Communication and Information*, 3(2), pp 211-40.

Lewis, C. and Fabos, B. (2005) 'Instant messaging, literacies and social identities', *Reading Research Quarterly*, 40(4), pp 470-501.

Maybin, J. (2007) *Children's Voices: Talk, Knowledge and Identity*, London: Palgrave.

Riverbend (2003-2007) 'Baghdad burning', Blog by Riverbend, http://riverbendblog.blogspot.com/

Street, B. (2003) 'What's "new" in new literacy studies? Critical approaches to literacy in theory and practice', *Current Issues in Comparative Education*, 5(2), pp 77-91.

tommigodwin (2005) 'Sentinel 47 keeping the gate', Blog by tommigodwin, http://keepingthegate.blogspot.com/

Valentine, G. and Holloway, S. (2002) 'Cyberkids? Exploring children's identities and social networks in on-line and off-line worlds', *Annals of the Association of American Geographers*, 92(2), pp 302-19.

Verdi, D. (2004) 'The Dylan show', Blog by Dylan Verdi, www.dylanverdi.com/

Vincent, D. (2000) *The Rise of Mass Literacy*, Cambridge: Polity Press.

Wikinews (2005) *Coordinated Terrorist Attack Hits London*, Wiki report on Wikinews, http://en.wikinews.org/wiki/Explosions,_'serious_incidents'_occuring_across_London

Wildfyre (1997a) 'The Silvercircle', www.dreamwater.net/silvercircle/

Wildfyre (1997b) Sliver Circle discussion boards, www.dreamwater.net/silvercircle/messageboard/

Website references

Association of Young People with ME: www.AYME.org.uk
Bebo: www.bebo.com
Facebook: www.facebook.com
Myspace: www.myspace.com

Conclusion: autonomy, dialogue and recognition

Nigel Thomas

> We don't need no education;
> We don't need no thought control;
> No dark sarcasm in the classroom;
> Teacher, leave those kids alone.
> Hey! Teacher, leave those kids alone.
> All in all you're just another brick in the wall.[1]

These words by Roger Waters were sung by pupils from Islington Green School on the recording of *Another Brick in the Wall (Part 2)*, the rock band Pink Floyd's biggest hit single. The record reached Number 1 in the British music charts on 15 December 1979, and stayed there for five weeks, the much-desired Christmas Number 1. It was put there by young people, many of them still at school, who one presumes were responding to the words at least as much as to the music. Along with its popularity, the song aroused intense hostility, not only from the tabloid press who launched a venomous attack on the head teacher of the school, but also from luminaries like Clive James in *The Observer*.

In this chapter I will try to draw together some of the themes raised by the contributors to this book, in order to ask some questions about child–adult relationships, about participation and autonomy, about language and communication, and about politics and citizenship. But I want to start by asking about the 'oppositional talk' exemplified in the above quotation.

Why did that song – those words – provoke such strong feelings, for and against? Perhaps it has something to do with the power of that 'We don't need no…'; whether we think what is meant is education as such or a particular kind of education, perhaps one done *to* children rather than *with* them. A strong negative can be positive, especially for a group that experiences itself as being oppressed or 'done down'. Indeed, in 1980 the same song was adopted as a protest anthem by black students in South Africa, and was subsequently banned by the apartheid government. Hearing what children have to say is not always comfortable.[2] They don't always say what adults want to hear; but that is surely part of the point of listening to them. It is easy to talk about 'listening to children' as if it were a straightforward process, simple and good. It is true that the very act of listening carefully to someone else can be affirming and mutually beneficial. However, 'listening' is not the whole story. Not only is non-verbal communication important, but what people do may be as meaningful as what they say, and the action to which communication leads – or fails to lead – can be crucial.

In this book we have seen some of the many ways in which children and young people use language creatively to create space for themselves in an adult-dominated world. This may mean talking to adults, as with Vicky Johnson's young people contributing to evaluations of their social environments and public services (Chapter Two), or Li Wei's British Chinese adolescents using their linguistic resources to negotiate with teachers and parents (Chapter Seven). It may mean *not* talking to adults, as with Ravi Kohli's refugee children (Chapter Six). It may also mean talking to each other, as with Julia Davies' online teenagers offering each other mutual support (Chapter Nine), or Amelia Church's preschoolers managing their disagreements (Chapter Eight).

We have seen that careful attention to *what* and *how* children and young people communicate can tell us a great deal about their lives, and their aspirations. We have also seen how often what they say is disregarded – or interpreted to fit adult preconceptions, as with Heaven Crawley's 'age-disputed' refugees (Chapter Five); and how any engagement by children in areas that might be defined as political is seen as problematic, for example in Palestine (Jason Hart, Chapter Four) or Mexico (Anne-Marie Smith, Chapter Three).

Roger Hart (Chapter One) reminds us that participation is fundamental to social life and to personal development, that there are many kinds of participation, and that it takes place on many levels and in different social locations. Elsewhere (Thomas, 2007, pp 214-5) I have tried to produce an initial list of the different sites at which 'children's participation' may or may not take place:

1. Ordinary family interaction, where from babyhood children may be constantly engaged in a variety of dialogue with other family members....

2. The different situation of children in public care, where everyday relationships may be less familiar or 'natural' but where there may be formal rights to a say in important decisions and formal or informal processes for exercising these.

3. For 'ordinary' families, the processes which come into play when custody or residence is contested following

parental divorce or separation, or in disputes over such matters as educational needs, where again there may be formal arrangements for children's views to be expressed.

4. Schooling – in most schools relationships are hierarchical and more or less authoritarian, and children often experience themselves as having little say or control, but there may also be structures such as school councils which to some degree give some children an opportunity to contribute to decision-making....

5. Public life in neighbourhoods and communities, where children's autonomous activity may meet a variety of reactions from adults and authority figures....

6. Commercial settings where children may be tolerated, excluded or specially catered for according to the organisation's perceived purposes.

7. Community and civil society organisations where children are rarely present except as appendages of adults.

8. 'Traditional' children's and young people's organisations – clubs and societies whose principal purpose is to provide activities for children, where 'participation' may not be an explicit part of the culture but where children in practice may make a substantial contribution to determining what takes place.

9. Children's and young people's organisations established for the purpose of promoting 'participation' – these may be locality-based or centred on a special interest, for instance being disabled....

10. Organisations established for the purpose of consulting children and young people in relation to specific public services....

11. Formal representative institutions for children and young people – local young people's forums, youth councils, assemblies and 'parliaments'.

12. Formal representative institutions based around
    political suffrage, which normally exclude children
    and young people explicitly or implicitly.

This list is almost certainly not exhaustive. It is also based very largely on experience of, and thinking about, children's participation in the context of the UK. It is likely that in other parts of the world, especially in countries with endemic conflict or political instability, other categories would be necessary.

Communication and recognition

The main point of distinguishing sites and locations in this way is to be able to assess differentially the presence or absence, the character and the effectiveness, of children and young people's participation. However, it is also instructive to consider what, if anything, may be common to all these settings. I would argue that, in all of them, what children and young people are looking for is to be taken seriously, to engage in dialogue with adults and each other and to have an appropriate degree of autonomy.[3] Exploring how these things can be achieved, what shapes they may take and what barriers may lie in the way, is extremely complex. It is here that I think social and political theories may be useful to us, even if they do not explicitly concern themselves with children and young people.

One such theory is Iris Marion Young's theory of democratic inclusion, which seeks to establish 'the norms and conditions of inclusive democratic communication under circumstances of structural inequality and cultural difference' (Young, 2000, p 6). Young acknowledges that structural inequalities have a tendency to be reinforced by the operation of formal democratic systems. The challenge, she argues, is to deepen democracy by making it more inclusive. This means both enabling a wider range of social groups to have access to democratic institutions and processes, and also adapting those institutions and processes to meet the needs of a wider range of social groups. She does not mention children as such a group, but the relevance of her arguments to children is very clear — for instance in what she says about modes of communication, as I will explain.

Young argues that inclusion is not just about bringing groups into existing systems, but is also about modifying those systems in order to accommodate new groups with different perspectives and different ways of expressing themselves. In particular, inclusive communication is crucial if 'internal exclusion' (2000, p 55) is to be avoided. In Young's version of deliberative democracy, deliberation is not to be equated solely with 'rational argument'. The discourse also includes other important modes of communication, which Young calls 'greeting', 'rhetoric' and 'narrative'. Greeting, or public acknowledgement, refers to 'communicative political gestures through which those who have conflicts aim to solve problems, recognize others as included in the discussion, especially those with whom they differ in opinion, interest, or social location (2000, p 61). Rhetoric refers to 'the various ways in which something can be said, which colour and condition its substantive content' (2000, pp 64–5). This includes (i) emotional tone, (ii) figures of speech, (iii) non-verbal and symbolic gestures and (iv) in general, 'orientating ones claims and arguments to the particular assumptions, history and idioms' (2000, p 70) of a particular audience. Finally, narrative and 'situated knowledge' are essential in enabling groups to understand the experience of others and develop a shared discourse.

As Young makes clear, logical and rational argument is not the only respectable way in which political discourse takes place, especially between disparate groups. This applies at least as strongly to children as to excluded adult groups; and her analysis is useful, I suggest, as a way of thinking not only about established political institutions and processes, but also when applied to the micropolitics of everyday life. Related to this are Habermas' (1984-87) conceptions of 'communicative reason' and 'communicative action', which underlie his proposal that a community of discourse, in which all voices are equally heard, understood and respected, is fundamental to a civil society.

A pupil of Habermas who has developed his own distinctive understanding of political communication is Axel Honneth (1995), already mentioned in Chapter Four. Honneth argues that a 'struggle for recognition' is fundamental to both personal and societal development. His starting point is Hegel's (1977) theory of recognition, based on his examination of the master–slave relationship. However, Hegel's rather abstract philosophical account is given empirical flesh and blood by drawing on Mead's (1934) analysis of the ways in which we develop our sense of personal identity through internalising our reflection in the eyes of others. Honneth also makes use of political theories, in particular those of Marx and Sorel, and the existential philosophy of Sartre.[4]

Honneth distinguishes three modes of recognition: emotional support, cognitive respect and social esteem. These are achieved at different stages in the struggle of individuals and groups to be recognised and included, and in different social arenas. Emotional support is achieved in primary relationships, expressed as love and friendship; cognitive respect is achieved through legal relations, expressed in the form of rights; and social esteem is achieved through a community of value, expressed as solidarity. It is only in modern society that this differentiation reaches its full extent.[5]

Although Honneth does not talk directly about childhood, his approach is a useful one for thinking about the relationships between children and young people and the 'adult world'.[6] It identifies recognition, respect and esteem as key to the development of humanity and to membership of a community, and it points to the ways in which recognition, respect and esteem are contested, not just in general terms, but quite specifically in different settings and arenas. Children may be recognised and valued in their families, but ignored or devalued in the wider community. They may be granted substantial legal rights, but be ill-treated or rejected by those closest to them. Although Honneth sees love and emotional support as fundamental, in that individuals without these basic resources are incapacitated for engaging in any wider struggle for recognition, I would argue that the three modes must also have some degree of relative independence from each other.

Toby Fattore and Nick Turnbull (2005) start from Habermas' theory of communicative action, but point out that it excludes children by insisting on a communicative competence defined in adult terms and also by enforcing a public–private distinction that by implication confines children to the private sphere. By drawing on Merleau-Ponty's account of intersubjectivity, they 'reconstruct' communicative action to restore a place for children, arriving at a point that they themselves acknowledge is not dissimilar to Honneth's account. Their object is a model of communication between children and adults that includes 'both children actively participating in processes of political will formation and also adults acting with and on behalf of children by adopting child-oriented communicative practices' (Fattore and Turnbull, 2005, p 55).

Honneth's interpretation of social history in terms of a 'struggle for recognition' has wide implications, which cannot be adequately discussed here. The idea that interpersonal recognition is the foundation for identity has been criticised among others by Lois McNay (2008), who argues that it pays insufficient attention to power. Similarly, Chantal Mouffe (2000) has criticised accounts of democracy such as that offered by Habermas for downplaying the importance of conflict and opposition. Fattore and Turnbull's model is, it seems to me, in its present form vulnerable to the same criticism. Incidentally, when Mouffe (2000, p 75), reflecting on Wittgenstein, points out that 'bringing a conversation to a close is always a personal choice, a *decision* which cannot be simply presented as mere application of procedures....', I am reminded of Amelia Church's preschoolers negotiating conflict by opting for different forms of closure (Chapter Eight).

Another theorist who seems particularly useful in thinking about these issues, in part because he faces conflict (especially conflict of interest) head-on, is Pierre Bourdieu. His concepts of *cultural capital* and *habitus* can help us to understand the ways in which layers of acquired dispositions (on the part of children and of adults) can serve to exclude children from many social and political processes. In *The Logic of Practice*, Bourdieu (1992, p 56) describes the *habitus* as 'embodied history, internalized as a second nature and so forgotten as history ... the active presence of the whole past of which it is the product'. Here the term 'embodied' is key – habitus is not merely a feature of the mind or of language, but is inscribed in the bodies through which our lives and interactions are mediated.[7] In *Language and Symbolic Power* (Bourdieu, 1991), Bourdieu explicitly applies the concepts of cultural capital and habitus to language, analysing how relative mastery of linguistic codes distinguishes social actors and maintains an unequal distribution of other resources. His analysis is based on class, but it may easily be applied in a similar way to intergenerational relationships.

This is not merely a question of drawing attention to the many ways in which children and young people are at a disadvantage in all kinds of communicative settings – either because they are completely excluded from participating or because they lack the resources to participate successfully. It is also possible to examine the ways in which children can use their own cultural capital, and their own linguistic habitus, to establish and maintain zones of autonomy for themselves. Our recognition is due, I would argue, both for children's right and capacity to take part in settings that tend to be dominated by adults, and also for the skill with which children and young people create and manage their own settings, sometimes using language that is relatively impenetrable to adults – perhaps deliberately so. There are vivid examples of this in the preceding chapters, particularly those by Li Wei and Davies (Chapters Seven and Nine), and arguably those by Kohli and Church too (Chapters Six and Eight).

Migration, displacement and citizenship

Four chapters in this book focus on refugee and migrant children, reflecting what a critical issue this is for our times. It is noteworthy that at least three of our contributing authors now live and work in a different continent from the one in which they were children (and that in each case they have moved in a westerly direction). Children who migrate, whether they do so with their families or without them, face different challenges from adults who do the same, and face them in different ways. Children and young people who are seeking asylum face very particular challenges, both in their host communities and in dealing with the authorities, as the contributions by Heaven Crawley (Chapter Five) and Ravi Kohli (Chapter Six) have shown. The claim made by a young person to citizenship is an ambiguous one in some ways, because the nature of young people's citizenship is in any case unclear.

The concept of *displacement* is an interesting one in this context. Children's place in contemporary society is circumscribed in many ways, both geographically and functionally. All the children and young people whose stories underpin this book are in particular ways marginal (for example, as refugees or migrants, as people with a stigmatised medical condition, or just by virtue of being small). I would argue that they are also in a general sense marginal, simply by virtue of being children and young people in a society and culture where adulthood is hegemonic, and where adult language and adult practices are normative; hence the subtitle to this collection. James et al. (1998) suggest that one of the defining features of childhood as a social category is that children are often regarded as being out of place, or in the wrong place. Children's proper place is at home with their family, or at school or in other socially prescribed locations. Exceptions to this tend to attract attention, sometimes positive, more often negative. Children at large in the streets may be subject to moral concern and control, as in Western Europe, or to hostility and violence, as, for example, in parts of Latin America. Children and young people who take part in activities that are defined as 'political', and therefore adult, may be the occasion of incredulity or scandal, as several contributions to this book have shown.

Children who left their schools to demonstrate against the invasion of Iraq in 2003 were the subject of criticism and attempts to prevent them – their place was at school being educated, not on the streets expressing their political and moral views. But this is nothing new: in 1911, for example, a wave of school strikes swept across Wales, England and Scotland. Strikers' demands ranged from 'shorter hours and no stick' in Hull to 'less caning, more play, more holiday, and reinstatement of strikers without punishment' in London, according to press reports (Marson, 1973). Marson's account is of a real struggle in which children of all ages were engaged, and of public response that appeared to range from the patronising and dismissive to reactions of shock and alarm. He also describes how '[a]way from their classroom the jubilant children began to express themselves in various ways. To some it would be a "street theatre" and to others the sheer feeling of freedom would exhilarate them enough to address the crowds of boys in the manner of the factory-gate or street-corner agitator' (Marson, 1973, p 34).

However, adults' responses to such juvenile agitation do not have to be negative. When pupils of Pontllanfraith Comprehensive in Caerphilly in Wales staged a protest walkout over teacher redundancies, blocking a road and prompting three arrests, it appears that pupils had the support of their teachers, and also of the local Conservative MP. The proposed redundancies were put on hold by the local authority following the action (BBC News, 2008).

A crucial respect in which children and young people's citizenship is incomplete is in the right to participation in elections. Although support for a reduction in the age at which young people can vote appears to be increasing, there is still opposition, some of it from surprising quarters. For example, Dawkins and Cornwell (2003) use evidence from neuroscience to argue against a proposal to lower the voting age to 16. Their contention is that, because the human brain undergoes major changes between puberty and age 20 or beyond, 'especially the frontal lobes or prefrontal cortex, the very bit that enables us to think in the abstract, weigh moral dilemmas and control our impulses' (2003) young people are likely to make poor decisions and so should not be allowed to take part in electing governments. A counterargument is that decisions as to who is entitled to take part in our political life are themselves a matter of political judgement, dependent on what we think political choices are about and on who we think should count as a citizen. Science may help to inform the answer, but it cannot provide the answer; indeed, those who opposed giving the working class or women the vote also used scientific (or pseudo-scientific) arguments. Deciding which party or candidate to vote for is not an issue that requires uniquely sophisticated thought processes, compared to many other decisions that young people are expected to make in their lives. It is actually much more about social awareness, about following through ethical principles and about making assessments of people's honesty, and there is evidence that young people are good at all of those things. One might ask whether Dawkins would argue that the children in the film *Turtles Can Fly*, with which Jason Hart opens his chapter (Chapter Four), should not defend themselves against military attack until their frontal lobes are fully developed.

A more truly scientific approach to children and young people's understanding of politics was taken by Olive Stevens (1982), who tried to find out how children aged seven, nine and eleven years conceived of political processes, principles and institutions, by talking to them in groups and asking them to complete questionnaires. She found that even the younger children seemed to have an ability to grasp political principles, almost 'an innate capacity for the grammar of politics' (1982, p 94), and that the 11-year-olds had a depth of understanding comparable with that of many adults. In Chapter Three of this book, Anne-Marie Smith refers to the work of Robert Coles, who also has extended our knowledge of the ways in which children engage with politics. He has done this by meeting and talking with, listening to, and studying pictures by, children around the world, often in situations of intense conflict where citizenship is precarious or contested, such as Palestine or Northern Ireland (Coles, 1986). Listening carefully to children and young people, and engaging in real conversation with them, has more to teach us than we can learn by making deductions based on neuroscience, and has the potential to challenge some unquestioned assumptions.

I hope we have done enough in this volume to justify the inclusion of work from such apparently diverse fields and disciplines, and to demonstrate how urgent it is to think about children and young people's participation in society and politics in relation to communication and language. While the earlier chapters in the volume are principally about the spaces for children and young people's autonomy and engagement, and the middle ones about how young people cope with dislocation and displacement, the last three chapters have taken a different tack, by looking in detail at the linguistic practices of children and young people. Similarly, recent research in the field of linguistic ethnography shows how close attention to children and teachers' language use combined with analysis of context and social practice can offer a rich resource for an understanding of social processes, in particular through observation and analysis of the creative and imaginative ways in which children and young people adapt language, switch codes, experiment and subvert expectations (Maybin, 2009). Greater engagement between experts in this type of empirical research and those of us who theorise about children and young people's participation can only be helpful.

Of course, communication and language do not make the whole story. Jason Hart's work with young Palestinians has elsewhere drawn attention to how their political engagement is substantially founded on collective action, rather than the talk on which 'participatory' work is often based (Hart, 2006). Honneth has elsewhere reminded us of Dewey's account of democracy, which, in contrast to the deliberative and procedural stories told by Habermas and others, founds the democratic process on joint action and on the interdependence embodied in the societal division of labour (Honneth, 1998). But that is another part of the story, for another book perhaps. For now it is enough to think carefully about how we communicate with each other and how we understand and respect each other's communicative competence, adults and children, and through this enable children to claim their rightful place as social and political actors.

Implications for research and practice

In the end, this is surely what children and young people have the right to expect: that adults will respect what they have to say and the ways in which they express their views; that adults will engage in dialogue with them on a basis of mutual respect and recognition; and that their contribution to society will be valued. Research has a real contribution to make, as I hope we have shown in this volume – by working to understand the perspectives of children and young people in different situations and the social contexts in which they communicate and take action together, and by studying with care and rigour the language and other devices they use to express themselves.

Practitioners working with children and young people have an enormous contribution to make, and I hope that this volume can help in some way with their work. Each chapter has something to offer in helping to understand children and young people's engagement with political and social issues, and their use of language to exercise control over their lives and to enhance their relationships with others. What the book as a whole points to is the importance of listening carefully, skilfully and respectfully to children and young people's communications, of seeking to understand them from the young people's own perspective rather than assuming that adults know best, and of recognising and respecting children as relatively autonomous social actors, with a contribution to make to all areas of social life, and not simply as objects of adult concern and intervention.

Notes
[1] Quoted by kind permission of Roger Waters and Warner-Chappell Music.

[2] There is of course an ambiguity in the case of *Another Brick in the Wall (Part 2)*. The words the young people sang were not their own, but were written for them by Roger Waters. At first they sang like a school choir, but when encouraged to sing in their London voices as though they were in

the playground, they made the words their own, giving the song some of its force.

[3] When Claire O'Kane and I asked children in care about their experiences of decision making, we identified from interviews the main reasons children gave for why they ought to be involved, and then asked the children in small groups to rank these reasons in order of importance to them. The results showed consistently that the process of dialogue, and recognition of their contribution, was more important to children than any specific outcome. However, it was suggested to us (by Walter Lorenz) that this might be an indication that children's expectations of their influence had been suppressed as a consequence of adult hegemony.

[4] Honneth is not the only political or social theorist to employ the concept of recognition. Both Charles Taylor and Nancy Fraser also use the concept, although in different ways. For a clear explanation of the different conceptions and their implications, see Thompson (2006).

[5] There is perhaps an analogy to be drawn here with Marshall's (1950) three dimensions of citizenship, which are also achieved in succession. Therborn (1993) notes that children appear to be achieving the different components of citizenship in the reverse order to that which Marshall identified, in that the social rights have come before the political ones.

[6] In fact, in a more recent work, Honneth (2007) does begin to address issues of recognition and respect as they relate to children, particularly in the context of family relationships.

[7] See Thomas (2007) for further discussion.

References

BBC News (2008) 'Cuts "on hold" at protest school', http://news.bbc. co.uk/go/pr/fr/-/1/hi/wales/south_east/7358662.stm

Bourdieu, P. (1991) *Language and Symbolic Power*, Cambridge: Polity Press.

Coles, R. (1986) *The Political Life of Children*, New York, NY: Atlantic Monthly Press.

Dawkins, R. and Cornwell, E. (2003) 'Dodgy frontal lobes, y'dig? The brain just isn't ready to vote at 16', *The Guardian*, 13 December.

Fattore, T. and Turnbull, N. (2005) 'Theorizing representation of and engagement with children: the political dimension of child-oriented communication', in J. Mason and T. Fattore (eds) *Children Taken Seriously in Theory, Policy and Practice*, London: Jessica Kingsley Publishers.

Habermas, J. (1984-87) *The Theory of Communicative Action* (trans. T. McCarthy), Cambridge: Polity Press.

Hart, J. (2006) Contribution in the seminar 'Theorising children's participation: international and interdisciplinary perspectives', University of Edinburgh, 4-6 September.

Hegel, G. (1977) *Phenomenology of Spirit* (trans. A.V. Miller), Oxford: Clarendon Press.

Honneth, A. (1995) *The Struggle for Recognition: The Moral Grammar of Social Conflicts*, Cambridge: Polity Press.

Honneth, A. (1998) 'Democracy as reflexive co-operation: John Dewey and the theory of democracy today', *Political Theory*, 26(6), pp 763-83; reprinted with revisions in Honneth (2007).

Honneth, A. (2007) *Disrespect: The Normative Foundations of Critical Theory*, Cambridge: Polity Press.

James, A., Jenks, C. and Prout, A. (1998) *Theorizing Childhood*, Cambridge: Polity Press.

Marshall, T. (1950) *Citizenship and Social Class and Other Essays*, Cambridge: Cambridge University Press.

Marson, D. (1973) *Children's Strikes in 1911* (History Workshop Pamphlet No 9), London: Routledge & Kegan Paul.

Maybin, J. (2009) 'A broader view of language in school: research from linguistic ethnography', *Children & Society*, 23(1), pp 70-8.

McNay, L. (2008) *Against Recognition*, Cambridge: Polity Press.

Mead, G.H. (1934) *Mind, Self and Society*, Chicago, IL: University of Chicago Press.

Mouffe, C. (2000) *The Democratic Paradox*, London: Verso.

Stevens, O. (1982) *Children Talking Politics: Political Learning in Childhood*, Oxford: Martin Robertson.

Therborn, G. (1993) 'The politics of childhood: the rights of children in modern times', in F. Castles (ed) *Families of Nations: Patterns of Public Policy in Western Democracies*, Aldershot: Dartmouth.

Thomas, N. (2007) 'Towards a theory of children's participation', *International Journal of Children's Rights*, 15(2), pp 199-218.

Thompson, S. (2006) *The Political Theory of Recognition*, Cambridge: Polity Press.

Young, I.M. (2000) *Inclusion and Democracy*, New York, NY: Oxford University Press.

Index